SOUTHWEST BC ROAD MAP

LEGEND

Rivers ————————

Primary highways — — — — —

Secondary gravel
logging roads · · · · · · · · · · · · · ·

Stein Watershed
Boundary · — · — · — · —

Cache Creek

Lillooet

Texas Creek

Duffey Lake Road

99

West Side Road

12

Blowdown Creek

Van Horlick Creek

Pemberton

Stein Valley NLAKA'PAMUX Heritage Park

Stein River

Lizzie Creek

Mt Currie

Whistler

Lytton

5

Kwoiek Creek

Merritt

1

Boston Bar

99

Garibaldi Provincial Park

Lillooet River

Fraser River

Squamish

Harrison Lake

Golden Ears Provincial Park

5

Yale

N

Vancouver

Hope

3

Fraser River

1

Kamloops

Stein Valley
Wilderness Guidebook

Gordon White

Selcouth Publishing, North Vancouver, BC
selcouth.ca

Library and Archives Canada Cataloguing in Publication

White, Gordon
    Stein Valley Wilderness Guidebook—2nd edition

Includes bibliographical references. ISBN 978-0-9694618-1-4

1. Stein River Valley (BC)—Guide-books. 2. Trails—British Columbia—Stein River Valley—Guide-books. 3. Outdoor recreation—British Columbia—Stein River Valley—Guide-books. 4. Natural history—British Columbia—Stein River Valley. I. Title.

FC3845.S73W55 2007   917.11'72   C2007-900996-4

Selcouth Publishing, North Vancouver, BC. selcouth.ca

Front cover photo: Andy Mons.
Title page photo: Jane McRae.

Rear cover photos, clockwise from top left: Leo deGroot, Jane McRae, Jane McRae, Gordon White.

Cover design: Pat Walker and Michael McInulty.
Fold-out map and book production: Pat Walker.
One-page maps: Mark McMillan
Vignette illustrations: Chris Tunnoch
Before You Go illustrations: Tami Knight

This book was printed and bound in Canada by Friesens in Altona, Manitoba and the fold-out map was printed by Hemlock Printers in Burnaby, BC.

This book is printed on Rolland Enviro 100 paper made from 100% poost-consumer waste, which saved 10 trees, 7 million BTUs of energy, 863 pounds of greenhouse gases, 3583 gallons of water, and 460 pounds of solid waste. Forest Stewardship Council, Ecologo and Biogas certified. And, this paper is Ancient Forest Friendly.

This book is dedicated to the people of Kumsheen and to my parents, Carman and Diane White.

"In saving wilderness, every victory could be temporary, every defeat is permanent."

–Bristol Foster

Disclaimer:

This guidebook is intended to serve as a resource for recreational opportunities within and adjacent to the Stein River Valley; it should be used as a general guide only. Persons using this book do so with the understanding that the roads, trails, and routes described in this book are constantly changing. While every effort has been made to note the real and potential hazards found in the book's trails, routes, and roads, readers should be prepared for conditions other than those described. Neither the author nor the publisher is liable or responsible to any person or entity for any loss or damage caused or alleged to be caused directly or indirectly by the information contained in this guidebook.

TABLE OF CONTENTS

Table of Contents 6
Acknowledgements 8
Preface: Chief Emeritus Ruby Dunstan and Chief Byron Spinks 11
Introduction 12
How to use this Guidebook 13

PART I: **ROAD ACCESS** **21**

PART II: **CULTURAL HISTORY** **29**

PART III: **NATURAL HISTORY** **39**
                 Ecology 40
                 Geology and Landforms 47
                 Vegetation 52
                 Fish 57
                 Birds 62
                 Mammals 68

PART IV: **BEFORE YOU GO** **75**

PART V: **RECREATIONAL INFORMATION** **85**

                 HIKING TRAILS AND ROUTES **86**

                 Lower Stein **86**
                 1. Stein–Fraser Confluence 86
                 2. North Shore Trail 88
                 3. Bluff Trail 88
                 4. Stein–Stryen Divide (Route) 89
                 5. Trailhead to "The Forks" 90
                 6. Stryen Creek, East Fork 92
                 7. Stryen Creek, West Fork 93

                 Trailhead to Stein Lake **96**
                 8. Trailhead to Lower Crossing 96
                 9. Lower Crossing to Ponderosa Creek 101
                 10. Ponderosa Creek to Cottonwood Creek 105
                 11. Cottonwood Creek to "Logjam Camp" 107
                 12. "Logjam Camp" to "Lookout Camp" 110
                 13. "Lookout Camp" to "Avalanche Creek" 112
                 14. "Avalanche Creek" to Upper Cable Crossing 114
                 15. Upper Cable Crossing to Stein Lake 115

                 Lizzie Lake to Stein Lake **120**
                 16. Lizzie Lake to Lizzie Cabin 120
                 17. Lizzie Cabin to Caltha Lake (Route) 121
                 18. Caltha Lake to Tundra Lake via Figure Eight Lake (Route) 124
                 19. Caltha Lake to Tundra Lake via North Shore of
                     Tundra Lake (Route) 126
                 20. Tundra Lake to Stein Lake (Route) 127

Stein Lake Area **130**
21. Elton Lake (Route) 130
22. "5000 Foot Meadows" (Route) 131

Siwhe Creek–Cattle Valley **134**
23. East Fork Texas Creek to "Brimful Lake" 134
24. East Fork Texas Creek to Stein Divide 136
25. Siwhe Creek to Stein Divide 137
26. Stein Divide to "Brimful Lake" via "Rainbow Ridge" (Route).. .. 139
27. Stein Divide to "Brimful Lake" via Cattle Valley
      Headwaters (Route) 140
28. Stein Divide to Upper Ponderosa Creek (Route) 142
29. Upper Ponderosa Creek to Cottonwood Creek (Route) 144
30. "Victoria Ridge" (Route) 145

Blowdown Pass–Cottonwood Basin **148**
31. "Kidney Lakes" (Route) 148
32. North Fork of Scudamore Creek (Route) 149
33. Silver Queen Mine Ridge Walk (Route) 150
34. Summit South of Blowdown Pass (Route) 151
35. Gott Peak (Route) 152
36. "Three Summits" (Route) 153
37. "Marmot Gardens" (Route) 154
38. Blowdown Pass to Cottonwood Creek Junction 155
39. South Cottonwood Creek to Silver Queen Mine 156
40. Silver Queen Mine to Stein River (Route) 157
41. Cottonwood Creek Junction to Stein River 159

North Stein **164**
42. Van Horlick Road to Van Horlick Pass (Route) 164
43. North Stein Viewpoint (Route) 165
44. North Stein Meadows (Route) 165
45. North Stein Ridge from Van Horlick Pass (Route) 166
46. Van Horlick/Scudamore Divide (Route) 167

KAYAKING THE STEIN **170**

WINTER RECREATION **172**

Backcountry Skiing **172**
Texas Creek 172
Blowdown Pass–Cottonwood Creek 173
Van Horlick Creek–Scudamore Creek 174
Lizzie Lake 175
Winter Hiking **178**

PART VI: **THE POLITICS OF WILDERNESS PROTECTION** **179**
             The Politics of Wilderness Protection 180

PART VII: **REFERENCES** **187**
             Bibliography 188
             Index 189

Many people assisted with the first and second editions of this book, including: Mitch Anderson, Mark Bayntun, Alistair Blachford, Jack & Louise Christie, Larry Emrick, Roger Freeman, Jackie Garnett, Jean Hamilton, Cecile Helton, Rick Hewat, Michael M'Gonigle, Leo and Hilary McGrady, Deanna McLeod, Jennifer Nener, Devon Page, Tony Ross, David Thompson, Ruth Tubbesing, and Wendy Wickwire. I am indebted to Neil Baker, Chris Bradley and Leo deGroot for their help with for the skiing section and to the International Centre for Sustainable Cities for allowing me the use of their facilities.

All the contributors to the natural history chapters of this book—Murray Lashmar, Jennifer Nener, June Ryder and Clinton Webb—are deserving of special recognition. Also assisting were Alistair Blachford, Dick Cannings, Ralph Cartar, Trevor Goward, and Don McPhail. Providing much needed feedback and assistance with the cultural history information were Chris Arnett, Nancy Turner and Wendy Wickwire.

This book's pictures and illustrations were provided by numerous individuals and organizations, including BC Parks (North Vancouver), Louise Christie, Leo deGroot, Michael McInulty, Jane McRae, Andy Mons, Ruth Tubbesing, Royal BC Museum, and Wilderness Committee. Tami Knight's always entertaining cartoons are most appreciated.

Finally, a few individuals warrant extra recognition. Mark McMillan provided invaluable work on the one-page maps, Michael McInulty assisted with so many aspects of the book's graphics and layout and Chris Tunnoch provided wonderful vignette illustrations. A big thank you goes to Pat Walker for helping guide me into the digital age of publishing and her work on the cover design, maps and layout, Andy Mons for his photography, Louise Christie for assistance with several aspects of the book, and the sponsors of this book.

PREFACE

Respecting The Teachings of Our Ancestors

Welcome to the Stein River Valley

Stein Valley Nlaka'pamux Heritage Park is a Class A provincial park co-managed by the Nlaka'pamux people of TLequmstin and the Provincial Ministry of Environment.

The responsibility of protecting the Stein Valley and maintaining its pristine state has been handed down to the leadership of the Lytton First Nation. As respected leaders of our community, we are striving to maintain high management standards to preserve the beauty and spiritual significance that our ancestors have nurtured through countless generations.

Our ancestors and elders have also taught us that sharing is a part of our life. However, along with this comes a responsibility to become knowledgeable of the core values of the Nlaka'pamux, which some of our elders have interpreted to be the Laws of Our Life. In order to sustain the web of life and to live life to its fullest, we must uphold these laws. There are nine laws that our ancestors have followed in good faith: Health, Happiness, Generations, Generosity, Humbleness, Forgiveness, Patience, Understanding, and Respect. These same laws apply to the Stein River Valley because the valley has been designated as a sacred land for developing the inner strength and visioning of our people.

As caretakers and leaders of the Stein Valley, we welcome your presence in our traditional territory. We ask that you use the information in this book in a good way to…

"Respect the spirit that is this land."

–Chief Emeritus Ruby Dunstan
Stein Valley Nlaka'pamux Heritage Park

–Chief Byron Spinks
Lytton First Nation

INTRODUCTION

Many British Columbians have heard the more common descriptions of the Stein River Valley: An ecologically diverse wilderness area only three hours drive from the lower mainland; the traditional lands of the Nlaka'pamux; a great place to play, whether you're a hiker, kayaker, mountaineer, or backcountry skier; one of the last unlogged watersheds in southwest BC; a refuge for an amazing array of wildlife; and one of the province's showcase parks. Certainly, the Stein is all of the above, and a whole lot more.

In my work on this second edition, I have been pondering what does the Stein mean to individuals who have explored this amazing wilderness. And, given that we were able to secure its protection as a provincial tribal heritage park, should we not also ask what lessons can be learned from the successful 20+ year campaign?

Like many people who have visited the Stein regularly, I have come to think of it as a classroom, a place to heal, a life-long friend, and a retreat for regaining perspective. And, talk about value. Every one of my dozens of trips in the Stein over the past 25 years has made my life richer and more meaningful. Even on shorter journeys, one can gain so much. Such was the case on a solo trip in July 2002 that left me with a smile on my face and a bounce in my step for weeks after the trip, thanks to a magical encounter with a grizzly bear. Years later, I still smile when I think of that remarkable occasion.

Undoubtedly, it is the power of the Stein—so wonderfully articulated by Nlaka'pamux elders—that so many individuals have felt in their first visit to the valley, which led to their becoming involved in the campaign to protect the Stein. As is discussed in the Politics of Wilderness Protection chapter, there is an important lesson to be learned from the campaign to protect this area: Democracy works when people take action. The Stein would be just another logged-out valley if citizens hadn't rallied together and forced our elected representatives to do what was necessary to protect this amazing wilderness area and respect the concerns of First Nations in Lytton and Mt. Currie.

One of the more common questions I receive concerning the Stein is how long a particular trip will take. I urge everyone to resist being one of the "Been-There, Done-That" crowd. Slow down and take the time to feel the rhythm of the Stein and increase your chances of seeing the locals. For some, a visit to the Stein may be the first step in establishing a strong bond with the natural world, which so many of us are in need of given how increasingly disconnected from the web of life we are becoming in our technology-driven urban lifestyles. For others, a wilderness experience is an integral part of a lifelong search for the truth, which Barry Lopez astutely observed, "…cannot easily be stated explicitly. It is something alive and unpronounceable." Since a significant part of Canada's self identity and history is strongly aligned with wilderness, perhaps the Stein will help many of us better understand this important aspect of our culture, especially in light of how we are at risk of losing much of our wild places, and our connection to them. Please tread lightly, for our greatest challenge now is loving the Stein to death through too much visitation and high impact usage.

Gordon White
April 2008

How To Use
This Guidebook

HOW TO USE THIS GUIDEBOOK

In order to protect areas of special ecological value and allow for individual exploration, some regions of the Stein have not been described in this book. Similarly, mountaineering routes and access are not described. See Bruce Fairley's *Climbing and Hiking in Southwestern BC* and Matt Gunn's *Scrambles in Southwest BC* for information on the peaks within and adjacent to the Stein watershed. Those wanting a quick summary of the trips described in this book should consult the trip summary component of this section.

Given the Lytton and Mt. Currie Indian Bands' concerns, information on only a few of the more accessible cultural heritage sites throughout the valley has been included. The observant hiker should be able to recognize and locate other sites.

Please keep in mind that this book is only a guide and is by no means a substitute for common sense, sound judgement and preparedness. Please inform me of any errors or omisssions so that corrections can be made in subsequent editions. Constantly changing conditions due to fire, windfall, landslides, avalanches, erosion, etc., can quickly change the trail and routes described in this book—be prepared for the unexpected. Take the time to read this section so that you are familiar with the format and terms used in this book.

Book Structure

This book is divided into seven parts:

Part I: Road Access—provides information on the various road access points into the Stein Valley. This section is intended to be used with the inside front cover map. Be sure to read this section for precautions such as active logging and potential wash-outs.

Part II: Cultural History—is a brief account of the Stein Valley's human history.

Part III: Natural History—describes the ecology, geology, vegetation, birds, fish, and mammals of the valley.

Part IV: Before You Go—provides an overview of the ethics, precautions, preparations, and equipment involved in wilderness travel.

Part V: Recreational Information—provides information on backpacking, ski-touring, and kayaking.

Part VI: The Politics of Wilderness Protection—looks at the story behind how the Stein was protected from logging.

Part VII: References—contains an index and selected bibliography.

Trail And Route Legends

A legend at the beginning of each hiking trail and route description summarizes the essential information for that particular trip. These points are not necessarily repeated in the text of the description, so ensure that you read the summary carefully. Most hikes will encompass more than one trail and/or route description. Given the considerable variation in cautions, water availability, etc., among individual trails and routes, it is recommended that you read the summaries of all the trails and/or routes you plan to travel. The terms used in the legends are as follows:

Attractions refer to any distinguishing characteristics including scenery, wildlife, good campsites, best siesta sites, and other specific highlights.

Cautions list possible dangers or concerns that you should be aware of before setting out on the trip such as dangerous terrain, unpredictable weather conditions, water availability, wildlife habitat, and devious rodents. These cautions are not repeated in the main text of the trip description and should be noted, particularly by less experienced hikers.

Access is the starting point for the trail or route. Refer to the enclosed fold-out map of the Stein and the inside front cover map of southwest BC to locate the various trails, routes and access roads described in this book.

Season is usually the best time of year for the trip. The months are given in approximate ranges and can vary depending on the weather and snowpack in any given year. Remember, in the alpine, weather can change quickly. At lower elevations, especially in the eastern part of the valley, it may be possible to hike from February to November without encountering snow. Some parts of the Stein's alpine receive heavy snowfall, especially on the western half of the watershed; the melting of the winter snowpack will depend on the depth of snow and spring weather conditions. North and east-facing slopes are usually the last to be snow-free, so take this into account when planning your trip.

Rating refers to the approximate difficulty of the trail or route. These ratings are based on an adult in reasonable shape (exercises at least three times a week and is comfortable carrying a multi-day pack). The ratings give the ease of travel over the terrain, but they do not convey specific hazards and problems for that trail or route. Read the **Cautions** in the legend for this information. Remember that changing conditions can alter these estimates. The following is a general guide to the three ratings:

Easy — even terrain; minimal elevation change (less than 30 m gain per km); clearly marked trails; half-day or day trips. Suitable for novice hikers in average or lower than average physical condition.

Moderate — some rough terrain; moderate elevation change (30 m–150 m gain per km); route-finding may be required; day trips or overnight backpacking. For intermediate or advanced hikers in average physical condition.

Difficult—Rough, sometimes exposed, terrain; substantial elevation gain and/or change (more than 150 m gain per km) may be required; may involve bush-whacking for part of trip; route finding with a compass and altimeter is a possibility; often an overnight trip with a heavier pack (the traverse is rated as difficult since one must carry at least a 17–22 kg (35–50 lb) pack for six to twelve days, often over rough terrain). Best left to experienced hikers in good physical condition with some degree of masochistic inclination.

Distances are stated in Metric with Imperial equivalents in parentheses. Trail and route distances were derived either by direct measurement using a measuring wheel or from large-scale (1:50,000) topographical maps.

Time is given in a range to provide a useful guide for hikers of varying abilities and conditioning. **Unless otherwise indicated, the time is ONE-WAY only.** Record your time along the trail and be prepared to alter your plans if you are taking longer than the high end of the range or if conditions are different than expected. Remember that large groups generally are slower than small ones, river or creek crossings may consume extra time for the inexperienced and hikers unaccustomed to hot weather should not expect to move at their normal speed in summer.

Elevation gain is noted for any appreciable gain in elevation along the trail or route. This number is the total vertical distance the trail or route climbs one-way and is derived from 1:50,000 topographic maps with 30 m (100 ft) contour intervals.

Accumulative elevation change is included where the accumulative vertical ascents and descents on the trail or route are enough to merit mention. This figure refers to the total vertical change over the trail or route, including downhill as well as uphill travel. For example, if a route gains 900 m (3000 ft) and then descends 450 m (1500 ft), the accumulative elevation change is 1350 m (4500 ft). This term has been included to give the reader a better understanding of the terrain one will encounter when travelling that particular trail or route. The majority of backpackers find large successive vertical gains and drops to be the most tiring, especially for those with arthritic joints.

Map refers to the number of the Energy, Mines and Resources Canada topographical map (1:50,000 series) covering the area of the trail or route. A distinction is drawn in this guide between trails and routes. Trails are cleared and marked while routes require topo map reading and, less frequently, compass assisted travel. All route descriptions should be used with the 1:50,000 maps, and where applicable, the one page maps. The fold-out map included with this guide is intended to give an overview of the Stein Valley and its access points; it should not be considered a replacement for a topo map.

In the lower mainland, topo maps can be reliably obtained from the Geological Survey of Canada (625 Robson Street, Vancouver V6B 5J3, (604) 666-1147), Mountain Equipment Co-op (130 West Broadway, Vancouver V5Y 1P3, (604) 872-7858 MEC.ca) and International Travel Books & Maps (530 West Broadway, Vancouver V5Z 1E9, (604) 879-3621, ITBM.com. In Victoria, try MEC (1450 Government Street, Victoria

V8W 1Z2, (250) 386-2667). In places other than southwest BC, try local bookstores or ordering from the above outlets.

Place names Official and unofficial place names are differentiated in this book differently than in the fold-out map. In the book, those names which have been accepted by the Canadian Permanent Committee on Geographic Names are printed in regular typeface. Unofficial names are put in quotations in the table of contents and in the trail and route headings. Unofficial place names identified within the text, but not listed in the trail or route headings, are also put in quotations. The fold-out map differentiates official and unofficial names by typestyle: Unofficial names are in calligraphy while official names are in type.

Trips Summary

To assist you in choosing a trip, many of the more popular trails and routes described in this guide are organized below according to trip time. Use the fold-out map and the trail and route legends to determine the location of the trip and its access. You will want to account for travel time to and from the Stein, especially when using the less accessible roads.

1. DAY TRIPS

The Stein's lower canyon sees the vast majority of hikers because of its easy access, accommodating terrain and cultural richness. Other parts of the watershed offer day trips, notably the Blowdown Pass area, but they are not as easily accessed and have more demanding terrain. If you want a day or weekend of easy hiking, the lower canyon is your best bet, particularly for groups with children.

Less than half-day (round trip):

- Lower Stein
  Trips 1, 2, 4, and 8 (Trailhead to Devil's Staircase).

- Siwhe Creek–Cattle Valley
  Trip 24.

- Blowdown Pass–Cottonwood Basin
  Trips 31, 34 and 35.

- Lizzie Lake to Lizzie Cabin
  Trip 16.

Half-day to full day (round trip):

- Lower Stein
  Trips 5,6,7, and 8 (long day trip).

- Siwhe Creek–Cattle Valley
  Trip 23.

- Blowdown Pass–Cottonwood Basin
  Trips 32 and 36.

- North Stein
  Trips 42 and 43.

2. WEEKEND TRIPS (2–3 DAYS ROUND TRIP):

- Lower Stein
  Trips 8, 9—Trailhead to Ponderosa Creek. For faster hikers or long week ends, Cottonwood Creek, trip 10, is possible.

- Siwhe Creek–Cattle Valley
  Trips 23, 24, 25, and 28 (to Earlobe Lake).

- Blowdown Pass–Cottonwood Basin
  Trips 31–39. One moderately difficult loop trip of 3 days encompasses trips 31, 33, 39, and part of 38 (see fold-out map).

- North Stein
  Trips 42–45.

Recommended Ridge Walks

- Trip 20, Tundra Lake to Stein Lake (must be done in conjunction with other trips as it is in the middle of the traverse).

- Trip 29, Upper Ponderosa Creek to Cottonwood Creek.

- Trips 33 & 39, which includes the Silver Queen Mine ridge and Angel's Walk.

- Trip 45 & 46, North Stein.

3. EXTENDED BACKPACKING (MORE THAN 3 DAYS):

Longer trips inevitably pose a problem for hikers. A round-trip may involve travelling over the same terrain twice but it does permit you to avoid transportation logistics. One-way trips are logistically more complicated since you must arrange for transportation at both ends—the price you pay to see new country during the entire trip. Be sure to read the Road Access section of this book for information and ideas on how to arrange for transportation at one or both ends of a one-way trip. A few phone calls to local taxi operators in the towns closest to your entry and exit points may prove to be very useful.

For those wanting to experience the Stein's unique diversity, two different one-way trips are recommended. The six to twelve day traverse of the watershed from its headwaters to its confluence with the Fraser (or vice-versa) is the obvious choice for experiencing the Stein's alpine, subalpine, mid-valley forests, and lower canyon.

Stein Traverse

Overview

The complete traverse description has been split in two for the benefit of the majority of hikers who enter the Stein from the east or west ends but do not actually hike the entire traverse. The eastern half, Stein Trailhead to Stein Lake, is described from east to west. Lizzie Lake to Stein Lake, the western half, is described from west to east. This means that those hiking the entire traverse will have to read part of the descriptions in reverse.

It is possible to hike from the Trailhead near Lytton to Stein Lake along a cleared and well-marked trail. The alpine route from Lizzie Lake to Stein Lake requires route-finding in some sections. Those seeking a more lengthy and demanding trip that allows one to experience the different climatic zones, landscape and vegetation within the valley will find the 90 km traverse to be the answer. In fact, the traverse is now considered a must-do classic in backpacking circles. It may be a matter of time before we see the Stein traverse gaining an international flavour similar to the West Coast Trail and Canadian Rockies.

Requirements

The demands of hiking the full length of the valley should not be underestimated. Unpredictable weather, steep ascents and descents, and rough terrain are part of the experience, especially in the western half. You should be in good shape and properly equipped; if you find the West Coast Trail to be demanding, do not even think about this trip. Solid route-finding skills are an absolute necessity, as the weather can change quickly, sometimes resulting in a whiteout, which will require travel by compass and altimeter. Remember, once at Stein Lake, the halfway point, you are at least two long days of travel from any assistance.

Logistics

While it is possible to hike the traverse from the east or west, transportation is most easily arranged by starting at Lizzie Creek. You can reduce your carbon count significantly by leaving your vehicle at home and taking the bus to Pemberton, which will save you significant time as you won't have to retrieve your vehicle or have to arrange for someone to take you to the trailhead. Greyhound Bus Lines (greyhound.ca, 1-800-661-8747) serves Pemberton, which is located north of Whistler, several times a day. At Pemberton, local taxi service is available from Pemberton Taxi (604 894-1111) to take you the 30 km from downtown Pemberton to the Lizzie Creek trailhead.

At the east end, Greyhound serves Lytton twice a day (an eight km hike or drive from the Trailhead to town may be necessary if you can't catch a ride). Travelling west to east allows you to get a "warm-up day" hiking up Lizzie Creek (it's actually quite a pleasant jaunt alongside the creek and the elevation gain is gradual), follow the Stein from its headwaters to its confluence with the Fraser River and avoid hiking up the trail from Stein Lake to Puppet Lake and

Tundra Lake (not recommended but certainly possible, just be sure to carry lots of water). Conversely, starting at Lytton allows you to lighten your pack and strengthen your legs before tackling the much rougher western section. Just be aware that there isn't much traffic along the Lillooet Lake road, meaning that hitchhiking into Pemberton can be a time-consuming affair.

Time and season

While it is possible to do the entire traverse in two very long days (I met an Ironman athlete doing just that a few years ago, although he did start from Lizzie Lake, which is no longer possible now that the road is no longer driveable), plan on at least six days; ten to twelve days is ideal. This allows you to experience rather than just visit the valley. The high snowfall on the western half of the watershed limits the traverse season from mid-July to mid-October. September and early October are recommended as the bugs are gone, most hikers are back at work and the temperatures are cooler. Just keep in mind that the weather systems aren't as predictable at this time and the west coast monsoon season often starts in October, which can result in rather wet conditions.

The "Mini Traverse"

Hikers with less time, energy, experience, or pain tolerance but still intent on visiting the various ecological zones should consider what I call the "Mini Traverse." This three to six day trip takes you from Blowdown Pass to Cottonwood Creek and then out via the mid-valley and lower canyon to the Trailhead near Lytton (trips 38, 41, 10, 9, and 8). See the fold-out map for an overview.

Other trips

To fully experience what, in large part, makes the Stein different from most of BC's parks (an unlogged valley bottom!), an eight-day round trip from the Trailhead to Stein Lake and back is recommended. Variations on the "Mini Traverse" are possible, as there are numerous routes—including some amazing ridge walks that take you into the mid-valley—on the Stein's northern alpine boundaries. Once again, the fold-out map will give you a good overview.

Updates and Corrections

Please contact me regarding omissions, errors or updates that subsequent editions and others would benefit from. My website—selcouth.ca—will provide updates on conditions in the Stein.

PART I

Road Access

Stein Trailhead parking lot.

ROAD ACCESS

Access to the trails and routes described in this book is gained through the roads described below. Special care is necessary when travelling the logging roads that give access to the Stein. Road construction, washouts, and logging affect distances and access points, so be prepared for variations in road conditions.

Areas currently being logged or scheduled for further cutting have been indicated. When in doubt, you may want to check with the Ministry of Forests (see individual road description for specific numbers) before driving on certain roads. During the warmer months there may be restrictions on travel due to fire closures. The distances given are accurate, but allow for 0.25 km error, as there is often a notable variation in the odometer readings of different vehicles. If in doubt as to the location of these roads, refer to the inside front cover map, which is intended to show the proximity of pertinent roads relative to the Stein.

Of considerable concern to every weekend backcountry explorer is the prospect of encountering a logging truck on a tight bend of road. These trucks have limited maneuverability and often operate dawn to dusk seven days a week. Be sure to give them the right of way and exercise caution when approaching blind curves, switchbacks and narrow sections. Park your vehicle well to the side of any road that is travelled by logging trucks. Given the toll that gravel and dirt roads take on your automobile, be prepared by making sure it is well maintained and have as close to a full tank of fuel as possible given that gas consumption is much higher on these roads. A spare tire and jack are essential, and basic hand tools, a shovel and jumper cables are also recommended.

Lower Stein via Lytton

Situated on the Fraser River 260 km (160 mi) from Vancouver, 76 km (48 mi) from Cache Creek, and 164 km (102 mi) from Kamloops, the Town of Lytton gives you access to the Stein's lower canyon, Highway #12 between Lillooet and Lytton, and the West Side Road. Downtown Lytton is accessed via exits from the Trans-Canada Highway both north and south of town. If approaching the town from the south, look for the turnoff at the junction with an ESSO service station (you should see highway signs indicating this turnoff as the road to Highway #12). Similarly, from the north look for signs indicating access to Highway #12 and Lytton. Both these turnoffs bring you onto a road that runs through Lytton, becoming Main Street.

Your starting point once in downtown Lytton is the junction of Main Street and the Highway #12 turnoff. At this junction you will find a sign indicating the route to Highway #12, with the the post office, the RCMP station and Lytton Hotel (and pub) close at hand. Lytton also has several stores, cafes and hotels, which can provide most of your basic needs except for specialized camping supplies. Please support the local businesses. The only public transportation to and from Lytton is Greyhound Bus, which ATP stops at the ESSO station on Highway #1. Taxi service to the Trailhead may be available — enquire at the Lytton Hotel.

Downtown Lytton to Ferry

Starting from the junction of Main Street and 6th Avenue, proceed one block west towards the river to the junction of 6th Avenue and Fraser (follow the signs indicating Highway #12).

	km	mi
Junction of Main Street and Highway #12 turnoff	0.0	0.0
Bridge over Thompson River	0.4	0.3
Botanie Valley road on right	0.9	0.6
Turn left onto Lytton Ferry access road, leaving Highway #12	1.1	0.7
Lytton Ferry	2.0	1.3

This reaction ferry—powered by the force of the river—accommodates two vehicles and is free. As of the time of printing the ferry's year-round operating schedule was: 6:30 a.m. to 10:15 p.m. with half-hour breaks at 10:30 a.m. and 6:30 p.m. The ferry serves vehicles on a first come basis with waits of more than 5 minutes being rare. Note: The ferry may not operate during high water in spring, sometimes for weeks at a time. Contact VSA Highway Maintenance Inc. at 1-888-315-0025 for a status report when in doubt.

Lytton Ferry   ANDY MONS

Lytton Ferry to Stein Trailhead

	km	mi
Start on the west side of the Fraser	0.0	0.0
Road intersecting from left	0.6	0.4
Earlscourt Farm on left	1.4	0.9
Sharp bend in road	4.0	2.5
Turnoff to Stein Trailhead	4.8	3.0

Stein Trailhead

Access to the main Stein trail is possible by driving the 0.9 km road from the West Side Road to the parking lot at the Trailhead. This access crosses reserve property and should be respected as private property. At the Trailhead, which is not on reserve property, you will find ample parking. Ensure that your vehicle is locked and all valuables are removed.

The Trailhead access road is indistinguishable from the numerous other roads intersecting the West Side Road. Be sure to follow the above distances from the ferry.

	km	mi
Trailhead road leaves West Side Road	0.0	0.0
Descend down side of hill	0.2	0.1
Road on left; pass under hydro lines	0.5	0.3
Trailhead parking lot	0.9	0.6

West Side Road

A rough, winding gravel road that runs along the west side of the Fraser River from south of Boston Bar north to Lillooet, the West Side Road may be used if you desire an alternate route to Lillooet or if the ferry is not working (you must drive north to Lillooet via Highway #12 and then return south on the West Side Road). The 68 km (42 mi) of Highway #12 to Lillooet, on the east side of the Fraser, is faster, more scenic and safer, however. Also, the West Side Road is muddy until mid to late June. Do not even think about travelling on the section south of the Lytton Ferry towards Boston Bar unless you have a high clearance four-wheel drive vehicle.

	km	mi
Lytton Ferry, west side of Fraser	0.0	0.0
Road intersecting from left	0.6	0.4
Earlscourt Farm on left	1.4	0.9
Sharp bend in road	4.0	2.5
Turnoff to Stein Trailhead	4.8	3.0
Stein Bridge	5.6	3.5

	km	mi
Junction in road, stay left	6.7	4.2
Bridge over creek	18.0	11.3
Sharp switchback in road	24.1	15.0
Access Siwhe Creek trail here		
Bridge over Siwhe Creek	25.4	16.0
McPhee Creek	40.0	25.0
Texas Creek Road on left	46.8	29.3
Junction of Duffey Lake road and West Side	64.3	40.2
Road (marked as Texas Creek Road)		
Lillooet townsite approximately 1.5 km north		

Texas Creek Road

Located 19.8 km (12.5 mi) south of Lillooet, the Texas Creek logging road provides access to the Siwhe Creek–Cattle Valley and "Brimful Lake" alpine areas. Unfortunately, as of the fall of 2006 one can only drive—with considerable caution in a 4WD vehicle— approximately 10 km up this 22 km long road as it is no longer being maintained and is falling into disrepair. ATVs and bikes can reportedly negotiate the remaining 12 km. In all likelihood, the road won't be opened unless there is more logging in the upper Texas Creek drainage. Contact BC Parks in Kamloops through Enquiry BC (604 660-2421) for current road status or check Selcouth Publishing's website (selcouth.ca).

The start of the Texas Creek road is clearly marked with a Ministry of Forests sign, rest area and bridge.

	km	mi
Leave West Side Road and follow the road into	0.0	0.0
into the steep-sided lower canyon of Texas Creek		
Cross Texas Creek	0.1	0.1
Cross Texas Creek again	2.2	1.4
Molybdenite Creek Road on right	7.8	4.9
Cross Molybdenite Creek	8.7	5.5
Skimath Creek branch road on left; stay right	12.7	8.0
Junction. Take left road to East Fork		
(right hand road is West Fork)	17.4	11.0
Junction. Follow road to right for 0.2–0.3 km	22.3	14.0
if going to Brimful Lake area		

Left hand road extends 0.3 km, ending in a wide turnaround. Access to hikes in the Siwhe Creek–Stein Divide are gained here.

Duffey Lake Road

Originally a forest access road, this 95 km paved road connects Pemberton and Lillooet and must be travelled when using the Blowdown and Van Horlick access points. Also, if travelling from areas east and north of the Stein, you may want to use this shortcut to gain entrance to the Lizzie Creek access on the west side of the Stein. Despite fairly high avalanche dangers, the Highways Ministry is now maintaining this road year-round.

Several BC Forest Service campsites are located on the Duffey Lake Road. These sites offer little more than cleared campsites and are often crowded on summer weekends, but can offer a quiet break in spring and fall. No other services are found on the Duffey Lake Road, so be sure to top up the gas tank before leaving Pemberton/Mt. Currie or Lillooet.

	km	mi
Junction at terminus of Highway #99 (1.0 km west is Pemberton townsite)	0.0	0.0
Mount Currie; junction with road north to D'arcy	6.7	4.2
Junction of Duffey Lake Road and road down the east side of Lillooet Lake to Lizzie Creek	16.5	6.7
Joffre Alpine Recreation Site	28.9	18.2
Casper Creek Logging Road on south	40.9	25.5
Van Horlick Road on south (2 entrances)	41.7	26.1
Duffey Lake Recreation Site	47.7	29.8
Junction with Blowdown Logging Road on right	51.1	32.0
Roger Creek Recreation Site	63.6	39.7
Bridge across Cayoosh Creek	64.5	40.3
Cottonwood Recreation Site	72.9	45.6
Cinnamon Recreation Site	76.2	47.7
Junction with road to Seton Lake	91.1	57.0
Junction with West Side Road (marked as Texas Creek Road)	94.6	59.1

Lillooet townsite is approximately 1.5 km further north.

Located on the eastern end of the Duffey Lake Road, near the Fraser River, the town of Lillooet offers most essential goods and services. Pemberton and Mt. Currie, at the western end, offer similar services, while Whistler, 30 minutes to the south on Highway #99, offers a greater variety of goods and services, especially last minute backcountry gear. Pemberton is serviced by Greyhound Bus (greyhound.ca).

Blowdown Logging Road to Blowdown Pass

The Blowdown Creek logging road provides access to the most accommodating alpine area in the Stein watershed. Normally fine for two-wheel drive vehicles up to the recommended parking area, this well-travelled road is currently being used for new logging operations on the east side of the Blowdown Creek drainage, so watch out for logging trucks and heavy equipment. For current road status, contact BC Parks in Kamloops through Enquiry BC at (604) 660-2421 or check Selcouth Publishing's website (selcouth.ca).

A retractable road barrier lies approximately 60 m west of the intersection of the Duffey Lake and Blowdown roads. Look for a "No-Thru Road" sign at the beginning of the road. A series of gentle switchbacks quickly bring you within sight of the Blowdown Creek basin. The road continues at a lesser grade on the east side of the creek for the remainder of the distance. This main road is clearly discernable from the numerous haul lines and branch roads that intersect it.

	km	mi
Intersection of Duffey Lake and Blowdown Roads	0.0	0.0
Road on right	2.4	1.5
Road on right	4.9	3.1
Road on right	8.3	5.2
Blowdown Creek		
Junction and large level area	9.1	5.7
Take left branch and begin to climb		
Road on right (access to "Cirque Lake" trailhead	9.6	6.0
To access Cirque Lake trailhead, follow road across		
Blowdown Creek and up hill for 0.2 km to large		
clearing. Trail is on south side of clearing)		
Road on right. Park here and take right hand road	9.9	5.9

Blowdown Pass is now 2.9 km (1.8 mi) further and 525 m (1750 ft) higher. Several streams cross the road, providing a welcome respite on hot days. The route is straighforward as you travel the road towards the pass. At 2045 m (6800 ft) and 1 hour–1 hour 30 minutes from the parking area, the access to Blowdown Lake is met. Descend 45 m (150 ft) through the meadows to the lake, which is only 0.3 km (0.2 mi) from the road. Numerous tent sites are found here. The pass is now only 0.7 km (0.4 mi) distant, offering access to many fine alpine rambles and great views.

Van Horlick Logging Road

This road, which is also accessed from the Duffey Lake Road, gives access to the North Stein via Van Horlick Pass. Two-wheel drive vehicles should not have any problems with this road except in the wetter months of spring and the steep ascent starting at the east fork turnoff at the 8.9 km (5.5 mi) point.

	km	mi
Junction with Duffey Lake Road	0.0	0.0
Avalanche path on left	3.5	2.2
Road on left	5.9	3.8
Junction; keep right	6.3	3.9
Junction; keep left	7.6	4.9
Major fork; go left, uphill	8.4	5.2
Major fork, go left. You may want to park here	10.2	6.4
Road on right	11.5	7.2
Small clearing, park here	14.0	8.6
The end of the road is a 5 minute walk from here.		

Lizzie Creek to Lizzie Lake

A popular recreation destination for over 30 years, the Lizzie Lake area is being visited by significantly fewer people after the road was closed by the October 2003 monsoon, which impacted many roads and rivers in southwest BC. The road won't likely be re-opened in the foreseeable future. For most people, the closure of the road means at least a half day of hiking, one way. On the plus side, the road is now a pleasant hike and an enjoyable start to a visit to the Stein's westernmost alpine and, of course, the Stein traverse. The following begins at the intersection of the Duffey Lake and Lillooet Lake roads and proceeds south along the east side of Lillooet Lake.

	km	mi
Duffey Lake–Lillooet L./In-SHUCK-ch roads junction	0.0	0.0
Twin Creek Forest Recreation Site	9.4	5.9
Twin One Creek crossing	9.8	6.1
Lizzie Bay Recreation Site	14.8	9.3
Bridge over Lizzie Creek	15.2	9.5
Lizzie Creek Road on left; turn here	15.4	9.6
End of road, park here	16.3	10.2

Lizzie Lake is approximately 12 km and 1050 m (3500 ft) above your current position. To gain the intact roadbed above the washed-out section, which lies roughly 50 m upstream, go uphill on the road to the left for appoximately 100 m, at which point the road flattens out and a trailhead is marked. Follow this trail—with caution as there is some loose footing—for roughly 10–15 minutes, and it will take you back on the old roadbed, which you will then hike to Lizzie Lake.

Bus & Taxi Transporation

Pemberton and Lytton are served by Greyhound Bus Lines (greyhound.ca, 1-800-661-8747). Lytton is within walking distance of the Stein Trailhead, but has limited service so be sure to get an updated schedule. Pemberton has more frequent bus service and an excellent local taxi company (Pemberton Taxi, 604-894-1111) who will—with adequate advance notice—transport you from the Pemberton bus station to the Lizzie and Blowdown trailheads. I have used this service regularly over the years and highly recommend it as it makes the logistics of one-way trips through the Stein much easier.

PART II

Cultural History

LEO DEGROOT

CULTURAL HISTORY

Native History

In the Beginning

Modern anthropological explanations of the origins of North America's native peoples contrast sharply with the natives' own beliefs and mythology. The most accepted scientific explanation remains the migration of early ancestors from Asia to North America via a Bering Sea land bridge before the end of the last ice age, 10,000 years ago. Native people offer a different history which is consistent with their perception of life as an endless series of cycles. Since the Nlaka'pamux and other native people kept oral but not written records of their history, several explanations are given for the origin of the earth and its inhabitants. A great being figures prominently in these stories.

LEO DEGROOT

This is one of the more recognizable and accessible pictographs found on the Stein's trails.

In one account, Old One created the earth from the soil of the upper world in which he lived. In other accounts, Old One, also referred to as Chief, Great Chief, or Big Mystery, created the earth from a woman. As recorded by James Teit, the ethnographer who lived with the Thompson People in the late 19th and early 20th centuries, the woman and her husband, the Sun, had an argument. As a result, the husband moved away from the woman to live with his relatives, the Moon and the Stars. Old One punished the husband and his relatives by transforming them into the heavenly bodies we know today and created the Earth from the woman.

Archeologists have reconstructed a rough sketch of the Nlaka'pamux pre-history. The earliest evidence of human habitation in south central B.C. indicates the presence of man approximately 9000 years ago. Close to the Stein, sites have been dated as far back as 6500 years. Establishing winter homes on the shores of the Fraser near its confluence with the Stein was a logical step for the Nlaka'pamux. A dependable salmon stream and accessible hunting and gathering areas in the nearby Stein and Botanie Valleys provided a dependable food supply. Besides offering food sources and an agreeable climate, the area surrounding the Stein was important in their mythology. The Nlaka'pamux attached considerable importance to the confluence of the Fraser and Thompson rivers just south of the Stein. This junction, called Lkamtci'n (today spelled Kumsheen), meaning "the forks" or "confluence," was central to native mythology as it was known as the center of the world.

Growth and Bonding

In the Nlaka'pamux world the individual was intrinsically linked to the larger group, the natural environment, and the spiritual world. These nurturing forces provided for the spiritual enrichment and development of the physical and psychological being of an individual. Conversely, western society's focus on individualism tends to isolate the individual from the community and the natural world.

Central to the individual's growth was a life-long process of traditional rituals. Children bathed in cold creeks or streams to develop discipline and a strong cardio-vascular system. During puberty, considered the most formative time for a Nlaka'pamux boy or girl, physical skills and spiritual values were refined. The individual became a fully-functioning member of his or her tribe's ancestral and spiritual worlds only at the end of puberty. Not only did the individual grow through these processes, but more importantly he or she acquired a strong sense and awareness of cultural identity.

A key element in this maturing and learning process was the development of a strong understanding of, and bond with, nature. This was achieved through isolation in remote parts of the mountains for periods of four months to a year or longer.

One important aspect of a youth's development was the quest for a guardian spirit. This search would begin when the youth travelled to a prominent peak or ledge above the river at dusk. After lighting a fire, and then singing and dancing until dawn, he or she eventually collapsed from physical exhaustion. In the dreams which followed, the spirits, which would give the youth life-long strength and protection, were revealed. The guardian spirit, a bird, animal, or other natural being, entered the youth's dream and spoke and sang. This song was of considerable importance at later times in the boy's or girl's life as it was used to summon his or her nature partner. By allying oneself with a "shna-am," one could then enter into a powerful, altered state known as "hah-hah," attaining special attributes such as great endurance and strength, immunity to danger, and the ability to change into other forms. Having gained special power through the spirit, the youth had completed his or her puberty experience and rituals.

Today, the most visible evidence of these rituals in the Stein are the pictograph panels distributed throughout the lower valley. These paintings, drawn in a red paint made from a mixture of powdered rock and water, are found primarily in places known

BC PARKS

Kinnikinnick
(Arctostaphylos uva-ursi)

The most common trailing evergreen in the Stein. Its bright red berries, which are in season from August to late winter, were used by native people for pemmican, and are a favorite of grouse and bear. The flowers are small, bell-shaped, and pink. Kinnikinnick means smoking mixture in Algonquin.

as power spots, where spirits resided. The caves, peaks (Mt. Roach, or "k'ek'azik," was one place of highly regarded power), high ledges, waterfalls, and lakes of the Stein were favoured for their special ambience, and also because they were secluded from the area of Kumsheen. Interpretation of these drawings is difficult since they were normally painted by a lone individual and reflected that person's dreams or experiences not necessarily known to others.

Cycle of the Seasons

While a good portion of their time was spent hunting and gathering, tribal societies also spent time enjoying recreational and artistic activities. Nlaka'pamux soapstone sculptures

Pictographs of the Stein

The mythological and spiritual importance of the Stein River Valley is evident in the valley's concentration of native rock paintings. Indeed, over the years, archeologists and Lytton Band members have rediscovered no less than 13 rock painting sites along a 32 km (20 m) stretch of the river. They range in size from a single painting on a rock boulder to one of the largest rock paintings in Canada with almost 200 paintings rendered in red along the base of a cliff close to the river's edge.

Ethnographer James Teit was intrigued by the rock paintings and made numerous inquiries into their origin and function. Teit was told that the paintings:

"...were largely in the nature of records of the most important of the novice's experiences whilst training, such as things obtained or partially obtained as guardian spirits, things wished for or desired to be obtained, things actually seen during training or during vigils which were considered good omens [and/or] actual experiences or adventures of the novice, especially those in connection with animals."

"By making paintings of these things on rocks the novices believed they would make such powers as they had attained or obtained stronger or more permanent and what they desired to attain (for instance, to be a shaman, warrior, proficient hunter, etc.) or to obtain (as for instance a certain guardian spirit, or certain powers or benefits) more easily and quickly obtainable."

Charles Hill-Tout, another early student of Nlaka'pamux culture, visited the Stein in the 1890s and was shown "certain spots and localities where celebrated shamans underwent their fasts and training to gain their powers." He was told that the paintings at these sites had been "made in the past by native shamans."

The paintings of owl, two-headed snake, grizzly bear, mountain top, and mystery lake that we see today on the banks of the Stein River are just some of the powerful guardian spirits witnessed in the dreams and visions of those shamans of long ago.

Not all rock paintings were made in the context of the guardian spirit quest. Some, and ornate basketry and clothing designs suggest an artistically rich society. Storytelling, games, and gymnastics were regular activities.

To the Upper Nlaka'pamux, the year was divided into five seasons. The counting of the moons began when the marmots of the high country entered their dens, usually in November. During the first three moons (December–February) hunting and fishing became sporadic as the people moved into their winter pit houses at the mouth of the Stein and consumed preserved foods prepared the previous spring, summer and fall.

From this site, the people of Kumsheen had easy access to hunting and fishing in the Stein, sometimes venturing as far as Nesbitt Creek in search of deer and goat, rainbow

according to information recorded by Teit:

"were made by both novices and adults of any age for what seems to have been chiefly protective purposes such as after a very striking dream or an event believed to portend evil, for the purpose of warding off the disaster or evil happenings."

These paintings, often representing guardian spirits, were painted on rock surfaces overlooking the route or trail "by which enemies or evil might approach. These pictographs by reason of their connection with the guardian spirits of the people who made them were believed to help in the protection of the latter." Other rock paintings were said to represent historical events and it is believed that some of the paintings in the Stein Valley are associated with incidents in the conflict between the Lil'wat (Mount Currie) and Nlaka'pamux (Lytton) peoples. And, as James Teit noted, still other paintings were believed to have been made not by humans but "are pictures made and shown by the mysteries, or powers, or spirits of the places where they are to be seen."

Teit's Nlaka'pamux informants told him that rock paintings had been made "from time immemorial." When he conducted his research at the turn of the century there were a number of elderly natives still living who had made the pictographs. Teit concluded that the practice of rock painting began to decline around 1860 because of the increasing influence of non-native culture. He estimated that the majority of rock paintings "now to be seen" were created between 1800 and 1860. "But in some places," he added, "where the rock or their situations are favourable to the preservation of the paint, [the pictographs] no doubt are very much older."

The rock paintings of the Stein, preserved in the wilderness environment which inspired their creation, are important to the preservation of native history and culture. They also serve as reminders to us all of our shared primordial past when humanity lived in close proximity to nature, dependent upon it for sustenance and spiritual well-being.

–Chris Arnett

Hidden Place

This watershed's name apparently comes from white man's misinterpretation of the Nlaka'pamux word "Stagyn," which means hidden place. Given how the Stein, especially in light of its size, is not apparent from the Lytton area because of the steep, narrow terrain of the lower canyon, this term is most appropriate.

trout, Dolly Varden char, and Rocky Mountain whitefish. In addition to accessible food sources, this winter site was close to water, fuel, and construction materials.

As the first edible shoots and spring salmon began to appear in March, the people moved out of the pit houses and recommenced hunting and gathering. If the salmon failed to come upriver, game was scarce, and winter food stores were depleted, famine became a possibility and the importance of root harvesting increased greatly. Avalanche lily, cow parsnip, Indian carrot, and thistle provided staple foods until the more readily obtainable summer food sources became available.

By the beginning of May, people began to gather food once again. Roots, corms, bulbs, and tubers were harvested primarily by the women, while the men hunted game and fished. The berry season would usually begin around the eighth month. The early berries such as wild strawberries, squaw currants, and some varieties of Saskatoon berries were followed by red huckleberries, soapberries, blueberries, wild gooseberries, and wild blackberries. The inner bark of Ponderosa and lodgepole pine, balsamroot seeds, hazelnuts, and Douglas fir sugar were harvested in the Stein's lower canyon and mid-valley.

The Role of Plants

The importance of plant foods in the traditional diet of the Thompson people is attested to by the fact that no less than 120 species of plants were utilized in some way as sources of foods, flavourings or beverages…. The total of these various types is higher than 120, because many species yielded more than one type of food. Balsamroot, for example, provided edible roots, shoots, and seeds. Thimbleberry, blackcap, and salmonberry were used for their edible shoots as well as for their fruits. In addition to these various species, at least 7 species were used for smoking, and at least 10 were specifically used in the preparation of foods, for lining and covering food containers or to surround food in cooking pits.

– Turner, Nancy, et al,
Thompson Ethnobotany,
Royal British Columbia
Museum, 1990, p.19.

In early fall, August and September, the Nlaka'pamux moved to harvest the salmon runs. Even today, many of the same catching, preparing, and drying techniques and equipment are used. In addition to salmon, a main winter staple, the Nlaka'pamux also harvested, dried and stored many plants. According to ethnobotanist Nancy Turner, each family may have picked more than 150 litres of berries and over 50 litres of roots. Despite this rate of harvest, the Nlaka'pamux were able to maintain bountiful plant populations. The continual cultivation of the soil that accompanied root harvesting, selective harvesting of larger roots, and periodic burning, enhanced the productivity of the land. Late blooming berries, autumn choke cherries, mountain-ash fruits, blue elderberries, black tree lichen, seeds of the whitebark pine, and many mushrooms were also harvested at this time. Oyster and pine mushrooms were two favorites found throughout the lower valley, while cedar bark and root were harvested in the fall.

Hunting, primarily of deer and goat, took many of the people to higher elevations in October and November. Grouse, hare or rabbit, squirrel, marmot, black and grizzly bear, beaver, duck, goose, and less frequently, lynx or coyote were also hunted. Between this hunting and the harvesting of alpine roots, such as avalanche lily and spring beauty, much of the group spent the summer and fall at higher elevations, returning only for short stays before settling in for the winter.

As the snow began to fall, the final kills were dried or smoked and transported back to the winter village. Once again, they returned to the main group and to their winter homes. The Nlaka'pamux aptly referred to this time as "going in time" (N'ulxtin). With the cold and snow making travel more diffi-cult, this was the time for making clothing, baskets, and tools, playing games, and telling stories.

Ethnographic accounts suggest that this cycle of five seasons served the Nlaka'pamux well for thousands of years. Early explorers' journals like Simon Fraser's confirm that the Thompson People were healthy, rarely subject to disease, and lived long lives. The bond between the indigenous people and the land which had sustained them for so long was to be broken, however, as European settlers moved into the interior.

ROYAL BC MUSEUM

Cow parsnip
(Heracleum lanatum)

The leafstalks and bud-stocks of this plant were an important spring time food source for native people. Commonly found in stream banks and moist slopes from sea level to subalpine, this large perennial has a single, leafy, hollow, 1–3 m tall stem, large leaves and numerous white flowers that are in a large, flat-topped umbrella-like cluster.

LEO DEGROOT

Western red cedar
(Thuja plicata)

Many of the cedar groves in the lower Stein contain culturally modified trees (CMTs). These trees were used by Indians for shelter, clothing and utensils; especially note-worthy were their water-tight baskets.

Contact

Contact with white people in 1808 changed life for the Nlaka'pamux forever. In less than 70 years the landscape was transformed from its natural state into a major transportation corridor. The traditional hunting and gathering areas which had sustained the native people were disrupted by the influx of white settlers who pre-empted large tracts of land for agriculture.

In 1812 a fur-trading post was established in Kamloops by the North West Company of Montreal. For the first time, Indians no longer acquired resources solely for their own use. Rather, the market forces of consumers far removed from the impact of over-trapping presented an endless demand for furs, which the natives exchanged for consumer goods such as blankets, guns, and jewelry. This fur trade was short-lived, however, because by the mid 1800s the once-plentiful fur-bearing animal populations were greatly depleted.

Another resource extraction boom of unprecedented magnitude began in 1858. Over 25,000 American prospectors descended upon Kumsheen and the surrounding area in search of gold. While the native people had managed to cope with the new people until then, they had no way of preparing for the onslaught of the miners. With no law enforcement agency in place, the impact of the miners was devastating. Families were disrupted as many native women and girls were abducted from their homes. Poor transportation systems made delivery of food supplies from the lower mainland difficult. The lack of food led to the plundering of native winter villages and food caches. Fights between Indians and whites inevitably ensued.

Settlement and Development

In its efforts to settle the interior, the colonial government gave priority to the construction of feasible transportation routes. The Harrison Trail, a route to Lillooet via the Fraser River to Port Douglas at the north end of Harrison Lake, and then to Anderson Lake and Lillooet, was established in the late 1850s. The Cariboo Wagon Road replaced the Harrison Trail upon its completion in 1864. Steamers began to ply the lower Fraser in the late 1850s.

Native people contributed to the building of these roads. But the breakup of families, neglect of their traditional hunting and gathering activities and loss of food stores resulted in upheaval and starvation for many. Their plight was further compounded by a smallpox epidemic in 1862.

In 1860 Constable John Hill undertook the first official survey of the Stein. In search of a new mule trail, Hill travelled from Lytton to the Stein's western divide before turning back, concluding that the trail was unsuitable for mule travel. As the gold rush moved northward, settlement of the land became a priority for the colonial government. By the late 1870s small reserves were being surveyed for native people while white settlers obtained much larger tracts of the best land for farming. From this land allocation emerged a vibrant agriculture-based economy that was well established by the early 1870s. Native people became an integral part of the farms, taking work as farm labourers on local white farms to supplement their own small, subsistence farms. Unlike the previous short-term resource extraction booms, this renewable and community-based economy showed considerable promise. The diversity of crops included beets, barley, potatoes, hay, and cattle and dairy farming. This new agrarian way permitted some self-sufficiency within the community.

In 1882 the construction of the Canadian Pacific Railway began. While the railway was to bring increased prosperity to BC, it provided few benefits to the Lytton area other than the short construction boom in 1884. The greater access to goods from distant markets that the railway provided was of greater concern to small interior communities such as Lytton. No longer did communities or regions need to be self-sufficient. Instead, specialization and large-scale production became essential in an increasingly international market. For smaller towns such as Lytton, achieving the scale of production necessary to compete was not always possible.

The most renowned farm of the Lytton area was Earlscourt Farm, a multi-crop farm from the 1850s through to the late 1910s. Under the direction of owner Thomas Earl, the BC interior's first fruit inspector, Earlscourt produced world class apples which were shipped as far away as London, England. In 1905, production reached a peak of 25 railcars of apples for export.

Post World War One

This changed after World War I as the labour intensive crops of grapes, apples and beans could no longer compete with the large-scale farms of California and Washington. Less labour intensive alfalfa crops and livestock became the primary commodities, resulting in lower employment. This hurt the local native people who depended on the farms for work. In 1920 Earlscourt was sold to Colonel Spencer, who made Earlscourt famous for its purebred Herefords and prize bulls. The farm remained a strong economic force in the Lytton area until Spencer's death in 1960.

The construction of the Canadian National Railway from 1911 to 1914 had similar affects as the CPR 30 years earlier. For a short period, industry thrived and the population swelled. Upon completion, however, the workers moved on and supporting industries such as saw mills shut down. Agriculture again became the mainstay. Mining was a key player in the local economy throughout the late 1800s and early 1900s. From 1892 to 1911 gold was dredged on the Van Winkle Bar area on the Fraser by the Van Winkle Bar Hydraulic Company of Vancouver and the Fraser River Gold Dredging Company.

Tourists began to travel along the Cariboo Road to Barkerville with the completion of the Alexandra Bridge in 1927. Being a necessary mid-way stopover, Lytton benefitted.

The upgrading of the Fraser Canyon Highway in 1964 greatly reduced Lytton's tourism industry, however. Commercial trapping returned to the Stein in the 1920s and 1930s, providing a livelihood for many native people until the crash of the fur market in 1938.

Post World War Two

With the decline of tourism and agriculture, and mining and trapping exhausted, the economy of the Lytton area suffered. Forestry was at the forefront of the post-war industrial expansion. By the early 1960s, mills were operating throughout the area as roads were pushed into virtually every valley. The Lytton mill was a welcome reprieve for what was now an economically depressed area. For the native people the local mill was an economic blessing as it provided badly needed jobs. Unfortunately, the timber companies opted for mass production in order to take advantage of the accessible forests in the surrounding area.

By the late 1960s, the Stein River Valley was also assessed for logging. By the early 1980s it was apparent that the companies were overcutting. As valley after valley was roaded and logged, the Stein stood untouched because of the natural barriers its lower canyon presented to road building (see The Politics of Wilderness Protection, p.180 for the history of the successful Stein protection campaign).

In addition to forestry, transportation became another economic force in the Fraser Canyon. The two railways and the Trans-Canada Highway made this area a major transportation corridor. Agriculture, while not as strong as before, was still a key component of the Lytton area's economy. The recent increase in Lytton's tourism may be an indication of Lytton's future given the area's accessible rivers and mountains.

Lytton Today

Despite limited land holdings and the cultural strife they have endured, the native people of Kumsheen retain many of their traditional ways. They continue to fish for salmon, gather mushrooms, pick berries, gather wild vegetables and traditional medicines, and hunt. The Lytton Band's efforts to protect the Stein and pursue its land claims has brought them into a new age. Recent political developments have seen both federal and provincial governments begin to slowly start settling the many native land claims in BC.

PART III

Natural History

RUTH TUBBESING

ECOLOGY

Clinton Webb

Ecology, by definition, refers to the branch of science that studies the inter-relationships between living things and their physical environment. To many people, the word ecology also symbolizes the wisdom, beauty, and mystery underlying the workings of undisturbed nature. From the blossoming flowers in a sunny alpine meadow to the infinitely complex nutrient cycling system of an old growth forest, natural ecosystems embody a perfection and balance far beyond the design of human minds.

Ecology Basics

The patterns and structures of the Stein ecosystem, as with ecosystems everywhere else on the planet, grow out of the relationships between the plants and animals to their physical environment, specifically water, earth and air:

water
- precipitation (rainfall and snow)
- downslope surface water movement
- seepage through soil
- rivers, creeks, and lakes

earth
- geological parent materials
- terrain
- soil types

air
- temperature
- wind

Of these, water is the major underlying force in both connecting the different parts of the ecosystems together as well as shaping the land. The sun's energy drives the endless water cycle in which the Stein watershed receives and releases moisture. In a sense, the Stein is a temporary holding area between falling precipitation and the Fraser River, which then transports the water back to the ocean. The rivers and streams transporting water through the watershed have carved V-shaped valleys out of millions of years old bedrock. Today, the flow of water continues to erode and transport soil particles and gravel from mountain tops to valley bottoms.

Seasonal freezing and thawing processes combine with chemical interactions involving water in what is perhaps the most fundamental ecological process of all: The weathering of the bedrock to form soil particles and the release of dissolved nutrients into the soil. These nutrients are in turn absorbed by the roots of plants whose growth, death, and decay provide the basis of all the food chains and nutrient cycles of an ecosystem.

While the process of physical and chemical weathering of bedrock is known to be very slow, the actual weathering rates of different bedrock types under different conditions is largely unknown. It has been determined, however, that an inch of topsoil can take over a thousand years to form, and a fully developed forest soil, many thousands of years.

In addition to helping shape the land and form the soil, moisture received by the Stein watershed interacts chemically and physically with everything it comes in contact with. Falling precipitation exchanges nutrients and material with alpine rock and scrub, tree leaves and stems, shrubs, herbs, and, finally but most importantly, decomposing organic matter and soil of the forest floor. Watercourses of all sizes collect this surface water flow and underground water seepage, and in so doing respond to varying amounts of rainfall and snowmelt with fluctuating levels of flooding, erosion, and siltation.

At every point of its path through a watershed, the amount, nutrient composition, and purity of the water is the end product of the processes taking place all the way upstream to the mountain tops. In essence, water is the thread which connects a watershed, both functionally and symbolically.

Climatic Diversity Equals Ecological Diversity

The Stein's remarkably diverse array of terrain and vegetation is a product of the different climatic conditions found throughout the watershed.

Glaciation

The large ice sheets that once covered much of the Stein were the most formative form of moisture the valley has been exposed to (see Geology and Landforms, p.47). Since the glaciers receded about 10,000 years ago, downward erosion by water and gravity has kept the soils on the steep glaciated valley sides relatively thin and coarse. As a result, the vegetation here is sparse and scrubby, but nevertheless, it plays an important role in providing shelter and root systems, which slow further erosion.

In comparison, the flatter valley bottoms have been less exposed to the effects of erosion. Here, the soils have accumulated to greater depths and retained fertile fine soil particles. In addition, the milder valley-bottom climate allows for more biological activity and decomposition in the soil, enhancing soil fertility. Thus, the valley-bottom soils have produced plant communities that have greater biomass and more complex structures, which in turn support more plentiful and diverse animal populations.

J.M. RYDER

One example of the impact of different geological processes on the vegetation cover is found in talus and avalanche slopes such as those shown here near the head of Nesbitt Creek. An examination of these areas shows that these processes produce different rates of soil development, which in turn influence the plants that are able to colonize these slopes.

Pileated woodpecker
(Pyrocopus pileatus)

This bird's large size (length: 40 cm) and distinct red crest (males) on the top of its head make it easy to identify. It can be found on dead or dying trees, logs, and stumps in search of carpenter ants. This old growth forest dependent woodpecker is commonly seen between the lower crossing and Scudamore Creek.

Geography

As described in Vegetation, p.52, the Stein's geographic location and mountainous terrain also contribute to its ecological diversity. The cool, moist Coast Mountains climate, which extends into the western end of the valley, has been most favourable for cedar, hemlock, and balsam forests with a dense undergrowth of blueberry and other shrubs. Conversely, the dry, warm climate of the eastern half of the Stein has resulted in sparse Douglas fir and pine forests with an open ground cover of grass and shrubs.

Similarly, from the Engelmann spruce–subalpine fir forests of the lower subalpine to the open heather meadows, herbs, and lichens of the alpine, a dramatic change in vegetation takes place as one moves up the mountain slopes. This transition reflects the increasingly longer winters and colder, moister weather associated with gains in elevation.

The River

The middle portion of the river is flat not only in cross-section due to the effects of past glaciation, but also in stream gradient, resulting in the river's meandering path. This in turn causes the river to sometimes change course during high water. The flooding river often cuts through sharp bends, leaving behind old unused sections of riverbed, and covers surrounding lowlands.

The resulting conditions have allowed a lush, predominantly deciduous forest ecosystem to develop in the otherwise dry conditions of the mid-Stein. A common vegetation cover here is black cottonwood trees with a thick undergrowth of willow, both of which thrive in the moist conditions and rich silty soil laid down by countless floodwaters.

South facing slopes

Another climatic factor that greatly enhances ecological diversity in the Stein is the relative dryness of south and southwest facing slopes. These slopes' exposure to scorching summer sun results in summer drought conditions, which restricts plant growth and triggers frequent forest fires. As a result, the vegetation is often sparser on south and southwest facing slopes than on the north and northeast facing slopes. This pattern is common throughout the Stein, especially in the drier central and eastern portions of the valley.

Fires, Insects, and Disease

The Stein watershed has a long history of natural forest fires, insects, and disease, probably dating back to the first forests after the ice ages. These natural processes are absolutely essential for the overall health of the ecosystem.

Individual occurrences of fire, insects, and disease in the Stein have been limited in size, and uneven in shape and impact. These characteristics have encouraged healthy natural regeneration following the "disturbance," with the end result being a great enrichment of the natural patchwork of different aged forests, structures, and species throughout the Stein. Each kind of forest disturbance cannot spread very far before coming up against a different type of forest. Hence, this mosaic of different forest types is inherently resistant to large scale disturbances of any single kind—except logging, of course! A major ecological principle illustrated here is that "ecological diversity creates ecological resiliency and stability."

Animals

Each of the countless variants of terrain and vegetation described previously provide food and habitat requirements for a variety of animals during all or part of the year. Many of the interactions of these animals with their habitat environment and

The Stein's diverse forest cover has helped to stop the numerous disturbances that regularly occur such as fire.

WILDERNESS COMMITTEE

GORDON WHITE

The cavities created by pileated woodpeckers in search of wood-boring insects are unmistakable. Eventually these cavities will be used by numerous other birds and mammals for nesting.

with each other have been studied under such scientific topics as "population dynamics," "food chains" and "trophic levels."

A few aspects of animal ecology are especially applicable here in the context of the watershed ecology of the Stein. These include some of the ways in which animals themselves sustain the health of the habitat they live in, and the dependence of many species on the Stein's well-being.

Detritus feeders

The wheel of life in the Stein's ecosystems can be said to begin with the many tiny animals and insects known as "detritus feeders" that work to decompose dead plant and animal matter. Thousands of species of microscopic mites and larger centipedes, worms, ants, beetles, fly larvae, and other insects chew up and excrete everything from dead leaves and needles to fallen logs and dead animals. Along with the action of bacteria, fungus and chemical leaching by water, this decomposition releases nutrients for another cycle of absorption by plant communities, which in turn provides food and habitat for animals.

This is by far the most active level of the nutrient cycling pathways of an ecosystem. As much as 90–95% of the plant matter produced by perennial terrestrial plants is eventually consumed by detritus feeders, compared to only 5–10% by herbivores (plant-eating mammals). Despite this, much remains unknown about detritus feeders and nutrient cycling.

Rodents and forest regeneration

Recent research on the predominantly Douglas fir forests in Oregon and Washington has shown that small rodents such as the northern flying squirrel, deer mouse, and red-backed vole play a crucial role in the maintenance and regeneration of a forest ecosystem. It was discovered that rodents that feed on the fruiting bodies of underground fungus unknowingly distribute the fungus spores around the forest floor in their droppings (see The Deer Mouse, p.111, for more on the role of rodents in the forest ecosystem). These spores eventually germinate and extend fungal strands down to the root tips of coniferous trees.

The strands are important to the trees' health, supply nutrients, nitrogen-fixing bacteria, and water (see No Tree Should Be Without, p.109). The above rodent species all have BC equivalents in the Stein, so it is very likely that these animals serve an equally crucial role in the Stein's forests' maintenance and regeneration.

Wildlife Distribution

Both the detritus feeders and the small rodents described above stay within relatively defined areas throughout their lives. The detritus feeders are preyed upon by animals that are similarly confined in their movements such as spiders, salamanders and shrews. The small rodents, however, are preyed upon by weasel, marten, lynx, coyote, owl, and other larger carnivores and birds of prey that are broader ranging but whose numbers and distribution are not well known.

Larger animals in the Stein are known to follow migration routes to match their food and habitat requirements with the changing seasons. Their wide-ranging movements make them especially vulnerable to habitat disturbance. Again, their exact numbers or distribution patterns have not been determined.

Mule deer, black bear and mountain goat spend winters in or near the valley bottoms and move to higher elevations in the summer. The mid and lower Stein contain the relatively warm and dry lower levels of south facing slopes that are preferred winter habitat for all of the above species. If the Stein had been logged, road building and clearcutting would likely have eliminated the forests that intercept snow, provide visual and thermal cover, and give escape routes from predators. Similarly, the forested North Stein valley is known grizzly habitat and yet the logging that was proposed for this and the other valley bottom areas would almost undoubtedly have eliminated this magnificent creature from the watershed.

Other wilderness-dependant wildlife species living in the Stein include human-avoiding species such as wolverine, lynx, cougar, and wolf. A large proportion of other wildlife species in the Stein are highly dependant on old-growth forests for their habitat needs, and include marten, pileated woodpecker, salamanders, and the endangered spotted owl (see Mammals, p.68 and Birds, p.62 for more information).

Streams

The Stein River itself supports both migratory and resident fish populations, important food sources for numerous carnivores including black and grizzly bear. The flat meandering middle portion of the Stein provides especially important spawning and rearing habitat for numerous species (see Fish, p.57, for a complete listing). This part of the Stein is extremely sensitive to damage by sedimentation and flash flooding.

BC PARKS

Heart-leaf arnica
(Arnica cordifolia)

Found from valley bottom to subalpine, this 25–45 cm tall plant has yellow flowers and large, heart-shaped leaves.

Watershed Ecology

A new branch of ecology applicable to the Stein is watershed ecology. The word watershed refers to an area of the earth's surface where all the precipitation drains into a single watercourse. In this view, the Stein Valley is both a watershed comprised of smaller tributary watersheds, such as the Cottonwood and Scudamore valleys, and itself a tributary of the larger Fraser River watershed.

The key fact is that many of the connecting processes that weave the Stein together as a single ecological unit cross the boundaries of even the largest tributary watersheds. For example, the seeds of trees and other plants are transported throughout the Stein by wind and birds, connecting all areas in a single genetic mixing pool. Similarly, the seasonal movements of large wildlife species such as deer, bear, mountain goat, and cougar across the length and breadth of the Stein make these animals vulnerable to disturbances in any part of the watershed. The purity and stability of the mid and lower Stein River as spawning and rearing habitat for migratory and resident fish is dependant on the pristine intactness of the entire area drained by all the upstream tributaries.

Leaving the Stein in its natural state goes beyond simple wilderness preservation goals. As an intact watershed, it will also serve as a valuable classroom of nature's wonders. Its value as an intact wilderness watershed cannot be measured or even fully imagined, since we have barely even scratched the surface of understanding it.

GEOLOGY AND LANDFORMS

J.M. Ryder

The landforms of the Stein Valley reflect the erosion and deposition that have created the present-day landscape out of the bedrock of the Coast Mountains. The effects of rock-forming processes, molten rock, glaciation, gravity, streams, and climate can be recognized and interpreted by any observant visitor.

Earth Materials

The bedrock of the Stein is typical of BC's Coast Mountains. The widespread granitic rocks were formed by the cooling and crystallization of molten rock deep within the Earth's crust, about 50 million years ago. Since then, uplift and erosion have exposed these materials at the land surface. Granitic rocks are sufficiently coarse-grained that large, irregularly shaped crystals of quartz (glassy), feldspar (white), mica (shiny black or silver), hornblende (black), and chlorite (green) are clearly visible.

Granitic rock's great strength enables it to support very steep mountainsides. Criss-crossing these rocks are joints (cracks) that tend to be farther apart than in other rocks. Consequently, blocks of granite that break free are very large, and their internal strength allows them to survive subsequent movement by ice and water. The bouldery nature of the terraces of the lower canyon is one result of this effect. Some major joints have been etched out by weathering or stream erosion to form deep clefts and gullies. Glacial erosion

The boulder-strewn terraces of the lower canyon.   J.M. RYDER

The toe of a rock glacier in a north-facing cirque at the head of Cottonwood Creek.

of granitic rock has produced rounded rock knobs and smooth cliffs with conspicuous sheeting joints (pseudo-layering).

Small areas of the Stein basin are underlain by metamorphic, sedimentary and volcanic rocks. Metamorphic (altered) rocks such as schist (a shiny, micaceous rock with a fine, sheet-like structure) occur throughout the basin. They were formed by the effects of heat and pressure on the original sedimentary rock into which the molten granite was intruded. Schist that contains crystals of garnet and staurolite (as well as mica) can be found on the ridges south of Scudamore Creek.

Sedimentary rocks, chiefly argillite and conglomerate (cemented mud and gravel respectively), underlie the most easterly 3 km of the Stein Valley. These sediments accumulated in a marine environment, and were then displaced by faulting into their present position adjoining the granitic rocks. The north-south trending fault plane crosses the lower canyon.

Older schists and dark coloured ultramafic (iron and magnesium rich) rocks, which have been squeezed up from great depths, extend along the ridges and cirques between Doss Peak and Antimony, Skihist, and Petlushkwohap mountains. These rocks can be easily recognized from a distance by their dark and rusty red (when weathered) colours, and their tendency to disintegrate into very small fragments. Relatively young volcanic rocks are present in the western part of the Stein basin on some ridges, such as between Stein River and Rutledge Creek and between Cottonwood and Scudamore Creeks. They date from eruptions about 16 million years ago and can be distinguished by their columnar jointing (clearly-defined vertical cracks).

Shaping the Landscape

The most striking features of the Stein landscape are the landforms that were created by glacial erosion during the ice ages of the Pleistocene Epoch, 12,000 to 2 million years ago. The final cold period, known as Fraser Glaciation in BC, started about 30,000 years ago when the climate began to deteriorate. Small snowfields in cirques gradually grew into long valley glaciers that eventually expanded out of the mountains and covered adjacent lowlands. At the height of the glaciation, about 14,500 years ago, the Stein basin was almost completely ice-covered. Only peaks higher than about 2600 m (8500 ft) protruded, forming barren, rocky islands in a vast, featureless snowfield. The ice sheet was short lived, however. Climatic warming resulted in rapid melting and glacier recession, so

The well-defined, U-shaped north Stein River valley is an
excellent example of a glacially eroded trough.

that by 11,000 years ago the valley was largely ice free and at least partly colonized by forest.

Most of the glacial landforms of the Stein basin remain relatively unscathed because they were chiselled into hard bedrock that has resisted the effects of subsequent weathering (rock disintegration and decomposition) and erosion. Today, all of the main valleys except the lower canyon have the characteristic U-shape of glacially eroded troughs. The floor of the main Stein River valley is now lower than the floors of its tributary valleys because the main valley was severely eroded by a large, fast-flowing glacier. Rapids and waterfalls mark the sites where these hanging tributaries join the main river. Steep-sided, bowl-shaped valley heads and shelf-like features on mountain walls are the cirques where the glaciers originated. Many of the alpine lakes occupy cirques: "Earlobe," Tundra and Blowdown lakes are but a few of these. Stein Lake, in contrast, occupies a depression in a glacial trough.

The Finishing Touches

Today's small glaciers are not simply the shrunken remnants of Fraser Glaciation ice sheet. In fact, glaciers may not have existed here at all between 10,000 and 6000 years ago because the climate was warmer and drier then. Glaciers reappeared at the end of this period, and since then they have expanded and contracted several times in accordance with minor changes in the climate. Most recently, they began to expand about 1000 years ago, and continued to grow until the nineteenth century. At

Little Ice Age moraines of a receding glacier at the head of Kent Creek.

this time, they were larger than they had been at any time since Fraser Glaciation. This recent period of cool climate, known as "Little Ice Age," was a world wide phenomenon.

In the Stein basin, the extent of the Little Ice Age glaciers can be easily deduced from the position of the still incompletely vegetated end moraines (ridges of glacial debris) that lie beyond the modern shrunken glaciers. A few of the larger glaciers, such as the Rutledge, have extensive forefields of bare glacial soil that have been uncovered by recent glacier recession. In some forefields, closely spaced morainal ridges about a metre high mark the yearly positions of the receding glacier. Fine silt particles (rock flour) are formed by the glacial grinding of rocks and carried downstream in meltwater. These microscopic rock fragments remain suspended in the waters of alpine lakes where they refract blue light from the sky, giving the lakes their distinct colours.

Even though most of the rocks of the Stein basin are relatively resistant to weathering and the pull of gravity, downslope movement of rocky debris has occurred frequently during the past 11,000 years and still continues. Rockfalls occur when loose rock is released by ice melting in cracks and joints, resulting in talus slopes such as the "Devil's Staircase." Some loosened rocks lodge temporarily in steep gullies, only to be washed out during heavy rains as debris flows, which contribute to the build up of debris fans on the valley floor. These fans are most easily identified in the lower canyon.

Major catastrophic rockslides have also shaped the landscape. For example Kent Lake and "Devils Lake" are dammed by rockslides. The "Devils Lake" slide was so large that it travelled for several kilometres down the Siwhe Creek valley. Similarly, the huge granitic blocks that extend for more than a kilometre below "The Forks" of Stryen Creek are a rockslide. A comparatively small but recent rockslide has affected a steep slope on the south side of the Stein River, approximately two kilometres east of Ponderosa Creek.

Snow avalanches are frequent during winter and early spring in all but the lowest and most easterly parts of the basin. Active avalanche slopes below tree line are clearly marked by avalanche tracks of low, shrubby vegetation that appear as paler green stripes between darker swaths of mature forest. In the more snow-laden western areas, such as the North Stein, some avalanche tracks are so broad that they encompass entire mountainsides.

Not all gravitational processes result in the rapid falling or sliding of rocks. In areas above timberline, solifluction (slow downhill flow of soil) results in the formation of steep-fronted lobes and terraces of gravelly soil, a metre or two high. Rock glaciers (glacier-shaped masses of angular rock fragments which contain buried ice) are a much larger but equally slow-moving landform. Good examples exist on the north sides of Stein and Siwhe Mountains and smaller features can be found high on north-facing slopes.

Glacier meltwater, debris flows and slope wash provide silt, sand, gravel and boulders to the river and its tributaries. The sand and coarser materials are then transported downstream sporadically. Where stream gradients decrease or are gentle, these sediments are temporarily deposited, resulting in the formation of gravel bars, floodplains, and alluvial fans. During floods, sediment is remobilized by erosion and conveyed on the next leg of its journey. The mid-section of the Stein has a well-developed floodplain across which the river meanders irregularly. The channel constantly shifts its position because erosion occurs rapidly during high water on the outside banks of the meanders. The beaver pond between the lower crossing and Ponderosa Creek is one such meander that has been cut off from the main channel. Alluvial fans and debris flow fans are located where steep tributaries flow out onto the floodplain. The fans of Cottonwood and Ponderosa Creeks are two of the more obvious alluvial fans encountered when hiking in the valley.

The Valley Today and Tomorrow

Millions of years of Earth history are represented in the physical landscape of the Stein. Its rocks and landforms are the result of an interweaving of processes generated by both the Earth and the atmosphere. Glaciers etched out the major features of the valley, and when the ice melted, glacial soils were rapidly colonized by vegetation. Now, the forest and the alpine tundra are ruptured only occasionally by falling rocks and floods of debris, while ice is confined to remote heights. Within the span of geological time, however, evolution of the landscape will continue inevitably. Will warm, Ponderosa-pine covered slopes predominate, or do the glaciers on the valley's rim have another major role in the future?

J.M. RYDER

The large alluvial fan of Ponderosa Creek is apparent from many vantage points.

VEGETATION

Introduction

The Stein Valley's diverse vegetation reflects the pronounced differences in precipitation that occur throughout the watershed. The cool, wet Coast Mountain peaks on the western boundaries of the Stein collect much of the moisture from passing Pacific storms, forming a strong rain shadow effect eastwards towards the Fraser River. Whereas annual precipitation in the headwaters west of Stein Lake is roughly 200 cm, the lower Stein receives only 45 cm of precipitation per year, on average.

In classifying the different ecosystems of BC, ecologists have identified 12 climatically distinct zones. These biogeoclimatic or ecological zones are differentiated by distinct patterns of vegetation and soil, and are usually named after the climax tree species which dominate the ecosystem. Under this system, the Stein's diversity is apparent; no less than six different zones are found within the Stein. For ease of use, the following section is broken into more easily identified areas within the Stein watershed.

The River Mouth

The rain shadow's effect is most evident at the eastern end of the valley, especially near the mouth of the river. Ponderosa pine, a species typical of hot, arid areas, dominates the forested benches surrounding the river mouth. Douglas fir is also present, but it is not as common as further west in the valley. This generally open forest has abundant shrubs and grasses growing on rocky soil between sparse trees. This is the Ponderosa Pine–Bunchgrass (PPBG) zone, the hottest and driest zone in BC. Unfortunately, the lower Stein is one of the few relatively undisturbed dry belt areas left in BC.

The pine tree-dominated alluvial fan of the Stein-Fraser rivers confluence.   ADELBERT BEEKMANS

Some of the more common shrubs found here include Saskatoon berry, rabbitbrush, ceanothus (two species), sagebrush, and Oregon grape. Clumps of blue-bunch wheatgrass, one of the original grasses now rare due to overgrazing, roadbuilding, and cultivation, are found on some steep enbankments. Cheatgrass and knapweed are much more common.

The Lower Canyon

Ponderosa Pine/Fir Forest

The first few kilometres of the main trail pass through mixed forests of Ponderosa and lodgepole pine, and Douglas fir. Ponderosa pine is predominant on steep, rocky areas, especially on south facing slopes.These trees, in fact, occur in dry sites as far west as Stein Lake. Douglas fir is more prevalent on north-facing slopes and on areas that are shaded and moister. As one moves further west, Douglas fir becomes the dominant tree cover in this, the largest and most diverse ecological zone in the Stein, the Interior Douglas Fir (IDF) zone.

Shrubbery and flowers

Shrubs found in the lower canyon include Oregon grape, kinnikinnik, soopalalie (soapberry), Douglas maple, ceanothus, Saskatoon berry, and birch-leaved spirea. Wildflowers blossom in the lower canyon from late April to early June. Sage buttercup, yellow bell, larkspur, and shrubby penstemon appear first. Later there are chocolate lily, death camas, silky lupine, balsamroot, paintbrush, alum root, gromwell, three-flowered avens, and both rosy and dwarf pussytoes. From late June through July you may find mariposa lily, heart-leaved arnica, yarrow, salsify, brown-eyed Susan, slender hawk's beard, hawkweed, sand goldenrod, white thistle, and dogbane. Rabbitbrush flowers latest, from September into October.

Covering the tree trunks, branches, and boulders of the lower canyon are lichens of numerous textures and colours. From the Trailhead to "Devil's Staircase," the colourful yellowish-green wolf lichen (*Letharia vulpina*) is strikingly evident. (See Divorce is out of the Question, p.160, for more information on lichens.)

Cedar Groves

The diversity of the Stein's forests is evident in the eastern reaches of the valley. Situated along the creeks that cross the dry, hot benches next to the Stein are the cool, moist cedar groves of Stryen, Teaspoon, and Earl Creeks. Such cedar stands are rare in the rain shadow east of the Coast divide. These pockets of

ANDY MONS

Oregon grape
(Berberis repens)

This low-lying shrub's distinctive, evergreen, holly-like leaves distinguish it from other plants also found in open forests.

Aspen
(Populus tremuloides)

One bear's signature on the trunk of an aspen.

western red cedar are important to the valley's diverse wildlife, and become more common as one travels westward into the watershed. Cedar was used extensively by the native peoples, as evidenced by the number of culturally modified trees (CMTs). See Making Use of the Parts, p.100 for more information on the Indian uses of cedar roots and bark.

The Mid-Valley

The Interior Douglas-fir zone extends throughout the mid-valley of the Stein, where the forest composition varies greatly. Douglas fir, the dominant species, is found on much of the lower elevation slopes and benches alongside the river. It is also predominant along the lower and middle reaches of tributary valleys. Lodgepole pine is common in the mid-valley, especially on the dry ridges of the main valley's slopes.

Occurring less frequently are aspen, which tends to be scattered amongst tall conifers, and western yew, a deciduous tree that grows slowly under the Douglas fir canopy. The occasional birch may be found in mixed groves. On moister sites, western white pine and western red cedar appear, becoming more common as one travels farther up the Stein. Engelmann spruce also occurs fairly frequently, especially upriver, on major upper Stein tributaries and on northern exposures.

These mixed forests serve as travel corridors for wildlife, and are important winter habitat for animals as only small amounts of snow ever carpet their floors. Unfortunately, this forest is vastly under-represented in our parks system, as it is one of the forest industry's principal timber supplies.

Many different shrubs and herbs grow in the rich central valley forests. Shrubs found here include common juniper, Oregon grape, Douglas maple, Sitka mountain-ash, soopalalie, Saskatoon berry, huckleberry, thimbleberry, snowberry, chokecherry, redstem ceanothus, kinnikinnik, falsebox, ocean spray, and western trumpet honeysuckle. In the drier eastern valley forests pinegrass dominates the ground cover, often accompanied by yarrow, aster, wild strawberry, pussytoe, and twinflower. Further west, moister conditions promote mosses and herbs such as twisted stalk and foamflower. Also present are rattlesnake plantain, star-flowered Solomon's seal, false sarsaparilla, vanilla leaf, bunchberry, and wintergreen.

Floodplain Cottonwood Forests

From the lower crossing to Nesbitt Creek, floodplain forests have developed where flooding regularly occurs. Deciduous trees such as northern black cottonwood (see The Cottonwood, p.105 for more information), birch, western red cedar, and mountain alder dominate these vegetation communities, which contrast sharply with their neighbouring conifers. On less frequently flooded terraces, a mixed forest of Douglas fir, cottonwood, aspen, western white pine, and Engelmann spruce appears. Shrubs tend to be dense and tall in these forests, as best exemplified by willow thickets. In addition to several species of willow, red osier dogwood, beaked hazelnut, thimbleberry, wild rose, black twinberry, snowberry, Saskatoon berry, and birch leafed spirea are also present.

The Upper Valley

In the western regions of the valley where moisture is abundant, forests become more "coastal" in character. Here, the dense canopy and moss carpeted forest floor of the Coastal Western Hemlock (CWH) zone is apparent. This zone is characterized by mixed stands of hemlock, cedar, spruce, and fir. In the North Stein and Rutledge systems and along the upper Stein River below Stein Lake, pockets of Pacific silver fir, western hemlock, and amabilis fir appear in moist areas. Such stands of original forest are now becoming rare in BC.

Subalpine Forests

The subalpine is a transition zone between the denser, lower elevation forests and the barren, higher elevation alpine. Here, elevation has a major effect on factors such as average temperature, moisture availability, and wind exposure, all of which change significantly as you move from the valley floor to the mountain peaks.

Above the valley bottom forests, more sparsely forested Engelmann spruce and subalpine fir forests predominate. These are the Montane Spruce (MS) and Engelmann Spruce–Subalpine fir (ESSF) zones. Lodgepole pine, amabilis fir, the occasional Douglas fir, and even western hemlock may also be found here. On drier and warmer slopes to the north and east, lodgepole pine and whitebark pine are quite common, while amabilis fir, Douglas fir and even western hemlock occur in the western regions of the Stein.

Subalpine Parkland

As you climb higher, the subalpine forest thins out into subalpine parkland—an attractive mosaic of tree clumps and

ROYAL BC MUSEUM

Bracken fern
(*Pteridium aquilinum pubescens*)

The most common fern in BC, the bracken fern is found in lower elevation coniferous forests.

open heath or herb meadows. In the upper western Stein where the climate is moister, subalpine fir is the most common parkland tree. Engelmann spruce is a fairly frequent associate and mountain hemlock is occasional. In the drier mountains towards the east there is no mountain hemlock. Subalpine fir, though still frequent, decreases and Engelmann spruce and whitebark pine predominate. Shrubs tend to cluster around tree clumps. Open meadowland is primarily heath in the west, herb meadows in the east.

Alpine

The Alpine Tundra (AT) zone begins at treeline, which occurs between 1620 m (5400 ft) and 1890 m (6300 ft) in the Stein. The severe environmental conditions of this zone limit the vegetation types to a few specialized species. Trees are limited in their growth and size, resulting in stunted—less than a metre in height and twisted shrubs known as krummholz (German for "bent wood"). Krummholz tree species include Engelmann spruce, subalpine fir, and whitebark pine. Mountain hemlock is found in higher snowfall areas. Step carefully around these trees; one branch may take up to 50 years to grow, with some trees growing for hundreds of years.

Several types of vegetation cover exist in the subalpine and alpine. Heather meadows (heaths) are the most common in the higher snowfall reaches of the Stein. A soft carpet of evergreen dwarf shrubs, especially the white, red, and yellow heathers, rowberry, and low blueberries predominate in these meadows.

At the edge of tarns, along the banks of alpine streams, and in deep snowbed areas in depressions, sedge marsh vegetation is prevalent. In snow patch areas, sedges are well established. Alongside streams, blackheaded sedge, willow thickets, and numerous flowers occur. On slopes that are more moderate, moister and that have deeper soils, alpine flowers such as avalanche lilies, western anemone and spring beauty appear.

Low-lying plants and colourful lichens are most common in the true alpine areas, which are dry, relatively snow-free exposed ridges. On boulder-strewn slopes with relatively barren, gravelly soiled slopes, only crevices and moist, textured soil are inhabited by plants. Rock surfaces that do not receive large snow accumulations are covered by lichens such as the green map lichen *(rhizocarpon geographicum),* the distinctly orange xanthoria lichen, umbilicaria genus lichens, and crustose lichens.

FISH
Murray Lashmar

Introduction

Six fish species, all members of the salmonid family, live in the Stein River Valley: Rainbow or Steelhead trout, Dolly Varden char, mountain whitefish, and pink, coho, and chinook salmon. Other species may be present. The same quality that makes the Stein attractive as a wilderness area—its remoteness—also limits what is known about its fish populations.

The spawning season is probably the best time for fish watching. To observe fish, you may want to wear polarizing sunglasses, which reduce the glare off the water. Also, be sure to move slowly near the water to avoid disturbing the fish.

History

Salmonids re-entered the Stein River after the glaciers of the last ice age receded 10,000 years ago. From ice-free areas in the lower Columbia River, they followed the retreating ice northward into BC. Reaching the headwaters of the Columbia, the salmonids crossed into the Fraser River drainage through a series of glacial meltwater lakes lying between Golden and Valemount. From the upper Fraser, they moved downstream to the Stein. In contrast, pink salmon reached the Stein from the west coast after the ice which was blocking the lower Fraser melted.

Life History

Trout, salmon, char, and whitefish begin their life cycle as fertilized eggs deposited on or under the surface of the streambed. Oxygen-rich waters flow through the gravel, supplying the eggs with nutrients necessary for growth. The eggs hatch, producing alevins, young fish with an attached yolk sac or food supply. After the alevins have consumed the yolk, they emerge as free-swimming fry from the shelter of the stream bottom to feed on insect larvae such as mayflies, stoneflies and caddisflies, and crustaceans such as amphipods and freshwater shrimp.

Developing salmonids, eggs and alevins, in particular, are very vulnerable to changes in streamflow, water quality, temperature, and siltation. Fry also have a tough time of it—fewer than ten percent survive past the first few months, the victims of predation and competition.

The surviving fry either remain in freshwater permanently (rainbow, mountain whitefish, and Dolly Varden char), or spend up to two years in freshwater before migrating downstream to the ocean for one to five years (steelhead and salmon) and then returning to their freshwater spawning grounds. Those species which mature in saltwater before returning to freshwater to spawn are termed anadromous. Biologists believe that salmonids evolved in freshwater and later adapted to saltwater after being in the ocean during the ice ages.

In the ocean, salmon and steelhead grow rapidly, feeding initially on small prey such as shrimp, and later on, larger fish such as sandlance and herring. Before returning to freshwater, they may travel up to 3000 kilometres across the Pacific Ocean.

While all salmonids migrate to their spawning grounds, anadromous fish undertake the most dramatic journey. Guided in the open ocean by the position of the sun, they swim towards the mouth of the Fraser River until they are able to detect the unique chemical smell of their home stream. Entering the Fraser, they continue upriver, ignoring streams lacking this "fingerprint" until they finally reach the Stein. Salmon spawning in other rivers such as in the upper Fraser may migrate upriver 1000 km further. Amazingly, spawning fish complete their entire journey without eating. They rely totally on energy reserves of protein and fat stored during their last months at sea.

After finding the stream where they were born, members of the salmonid family search for well-aerated, even-sized stream gravel. Males and females pair up, quiver and simultaneously release eggs and sperm directly onto the stream bottom or into redds (depressions) excavated by the female. They continue spawning until all eggs and sperm are released.

Eggs are fertilized immediately and settle into crevices in the gravel or are covered over again in the redd by the female. The redds can sometimes be seen as lighter areas in the stream bottom where the overlying rocks have been removed. Spawning completed and their energy spent, anadromous spawners usually die within one or two days after spawning, although coho salmon may live for several more weeks. Freshwater species, on the other hand, may survive to spawn several years in a row. And so the cycle begins again.

Fish Habitat and Distribution

The main Stein can be divided into three sections: The lower canyon, the mid-Stein, and the upper Stein. Each area differs from the others in the fish species present and opportunities for watching fish.

Between the mouth and the lower canyon, where the river cuts through the terraces of the Fraser River, look for pink salmon spawning. At the mouth itself, non-salmonids such as peamonth chub, northern squawfish, longnose and leopard dace may be

BC PARKS

Stonefly nymph
(Order Plecoptera)

Found on the bottom of streams and well-aerated lakes, this yellowish or brown 40 mm long larvae has two distinct sensory organs projecting from its rear end. It feeds on vegetation, but is sometimes omnivorous, and may live up to three years before leaving the water to begin the adult part of its cycle.

seen. Above the terraces, the river squeezes through the steep-sided lower canyon. There, large boulders and steep gradients make spawning highly unlikely. Deep pools and still water behind boulders enable adults and young fish to rest during their travels.

In the mid-Stein between Earl and Nesbitt Creeks, the river meanders through the wide valley. Excellent spawning grounds of well-aerated, uniform gravel for all species except pinks (which are probably stopped by the lower canyon) are found here. Each year, small runs (less than 100 fish each) of steelhead, coho and chinook migrate to this part of the river to spawn.

The mid-Stein also contains high quality nursery areas for young fish. Riffles of rocks and gravel provide a source of aquatic insect larvae, the most common fish food. The larvae graze over the rocks, eating algae and small prey. When tired, young fish rest in the numerous side channels, pools and quiet waters behind boulders.

Look for coho fry under well-vegetated streambanks or in pools. Steelhead, on the other hand, prefer riffles and boulder areas. Dolly Varden are the only fish seen in Scudamore Creek, a tributary of the Stein. The presence of Longnose and largescale suckers there has not been confirmed, but the habitat is suitable for these species.

Above Nesbitt Creek, the river straightens and steepens, and the riverbed gravel becomes larger, producing conditions more conducive to rearing fry. Roughly 42 km from the Fraser River, a five metre high waterfall blocks upstream movement to all but flying fish.

Between the waterfall and Stein Lake, only rainbow trout live. No one knows for sure how they got there. Perhaps an early pioneer carried them over the falls to ensure a food source. Or perhaps the rainbow become isolated when an earthquake raised the barrier. Fish—likely trout—are found in Stein Lake and apparently are the result of stocking.

BC PARKS

In September–October, look for pink salmon (Thuja plicata) *spawning in the lower canyon, especially upstream of the "Asking Rock" and as far as the lower crossing.*

Fish of the Stein

ANADROMOUS

Pink Salmon (*Oncorhynchus gorbuscha*)

Pink salmon, the smallest of the Pacific salmon, spawn in late summer or early fall, their fertilized eggs developing and hatching under the cover of winter. The fry emerge from the gravel in the spring and migrate immediately to the sea. They spend two to three months in estuaries and nearshore waters, feeding and adapting to the saltwater environment before migrating farther offshore. In the autumn of the following year, at two years of age, they return to spawn.

Pinks spawn each year in the Stein, but because of the two-year cycle, heavy runs in odd-numbered years (e.g., 1991) alternate with light runs in even-numbered years. In the 1980s, approximately 2000 pink salmon per odd year spawned compared to about 200 per year in the 1960s.

Coho Salmon (*Oncorhynchus kisutch*)

Rivers swollen by autumn rains provide coho salmon with the water volume needed to migrate upstream to their spawning grounds. Several weeks later they spawn, leaving their fertilized eggs to mature over the winter. Fry emerge from the gravel the following spring to feed on larval and adult insects. Coho are very territorial, defending their feeding areas aggressively. They stay in fresh water one to two years, then migrate seaward to grow for two more years, feeding on the abundant microscopic animals. Coho mature sexually after three to four years.

Chinook Salmon (*Oncorhynchus tshawytscha*)

The largest of the Pacific salmon, chinook spawn between September and November. Where spawning grounds are far from the ocean, they begin migrating as early as May. Chinook fry emerge in the spring, and spend two to twelve months in fresh water. Not as aggressive as coho, chinook gather in schools briefly before dispersing to form territories. They mature after three to five years in salt water.

Steelhead Trout (*Salmo gairdneri*)

Steelhead trout, the anadromous form of rainbow trout, migrate in late summer to early fall. Unlike salmon, but like freshwater salmonids, steelhead feed during migration. Steelheads spawn

ROYAL BC MUSEUM

Barred owl
(Strix varia)

An occasional consumer of fish, the barred owl is more likely to pursue rodents, birds and insects. This commonly heard but less frequently seen owl can be identified by its hornless head, large barred ruff below its bill and a streaked front.

in late winter or early spring as water temperatures rise. Eggs incubate during the spring and fry emerge into the streams in June or July. Juvenile steelhead remain in fresh water for two to three years before moving to saltwater for a further two to three years of growth. They are ready to spawn at four to six years of age. A small number, usually females, migrate downstream again to the ocean and then return the following year to spawn a second time.

RESIDENT

Rainbow Trout (*Salmo gairdneri*)

Rising spring or summer water temperatures stimulate rainbow trout to spawn in fine gravel riffles (shallow, fast moving areas with rocky or gravelly bottoms) above a pool. Four to eight weeks later, the fry emerge to feed on larval and adult insects, leeches, molluscs (e.g., freshwater snails), and small fish. Adults add larger insects and crustaceans to their diet, and mature in three to four years. Rainbow normally spawn once in their lifetime, but have been known to spawn up to five times.

Mountain Whitefish (*Prosopium williamsoni*)

On late fall or early winter nights, mountain whitefish lay their eggs and sperm (or milt) directly on the stream bottom rather than in a redd or nest. The fertilized eggs hatch in March or April. Fry emerge to feed along the stream bottom on aquatic insect larvae, fish eggs, and as they mature, occasional adult insects. Mountain whitefish fry may protect themselves by forming large schools instead of hiding under rocks. They mature at three years of age.

Dolly Varden char (*Salvelinus malma*)

September brings spawning Dolly Varden char to stream sections with medium to large sized gravel beds and moderate currents. Males are extremely aggressive, driving off competing males. Females may be accompanied by several males, but only one will dominate. Eggs and alevins develop during the winter and fry leave the gravel by late April to mid-May. Feeding on larval and adult insects, snails, and leeches, the young fish grow rapidly. As adults, Dolly Varden feed on bottom-dwelling organisms, salmonid eggs, fry, and small trout. By late summer, Dollies move into headwater and tributaries. At five years of age, they are ready to spawn.

BIRDS
Jennifer Nener

The Stein's diverse landscape supports a tremendous variety of birds. The following focuses on the appearance, habitat and behaviour of 16 birds commonly seen in the Stein.

Raptorial Birds

Raptors can be loosely defined as "birds of prey." These flesh-eating birds have a strong, hooked beak, and four well-developed toes, each endowed with a sharp claw or talon for seizing prey.

Sharp shinned hawk (*Accipiter striatus velox*)

The 35 cm long sharp shinned hawk has a 60 cm wingspan and is identified by its horizontally barred, reddish breast, blue-grey back and upper wing feathers, black crown, and red eyes. It is also distinguished by its short, rounded wings and square-tipped tail, which has a slight notch when folded. The similar but larger Cooper's hawk, which is occasionally sighted in the Stein, has a long, rounded tail. In mid-mountain country look for the sharp shinned hawk gracefully threading its way through the trees at low levels, in pursuit of small birds such as kinglets, sparrows and towhees. Its diet is supplemented by lizards, insects and small mammals.

Merlin (*Falco columbarius*)

Previously known as the Pigeon hawk, the merlin is one of the smallest falcons (length 30 cm, wingspan 58 cm). It is endowed with grey-blue plumage above and brown below. Black bands on the tail help one to avoid confusing this bird with the similar but larger peregrine falcon; pointed wings distinguish it from the sharp shinned hawk. The merlin can be found over open fields, moorlands, and short grass benches near the mouth of the Stein River. Unlike other raptors it does not swoop or soar. Instead it hunts at tree-top level, capturing small birds in mid-air. Insects, bats and other small mammals are also consumed.

Barred owl (*Strix varia*)

This large (length 43 cm, wingspan 112 cm) hornless owl is identified by its grey-brown colour and vertically streaked front. Like the northern spotted owl, this species prefers to live in old growth forest near rivers. Small rodents such as mice and voles, and less often birds, insects, frogs, and fish, are its primary food sources. The barred owl's only known predator is the great horned owl.

Ground-dwelling Birds

These are typically well camouflaged chicken-like birds which feed on insects, seeds, berries, and whatever else they can peck from the ground and low shrubs.

Ruffed grouse (*Bonasa umbellus sabini*)

The forest floor dwelling ruffed grouse is easily distinguished from other species by its crested head and broad, barred tail. This species occurs in two colour phases: Red birds with rufous tails and grey-brown birds with grey tails. Males have a red spot above the eye. From March until May, the slow "thump, thump, thump" mating call can be heard for a half a kilometre but is not easily located.

Blue grouse (Sooty Grouse)
(*Dendragapus obscurus fuliginosus*)

At a length of 43 cm, this is the largest species of grouse to inhabit the Stein. Males have dark breasts, instead of the mottled brown and white breasts characteristic of other species, and also feature a yellow spot above the eye. Females are grey-brown, barred with black. Both sexes sport a black tail with a grey band at the end. The blue grouse is common in subalpine-fir forest close to timberline. Blue grouse will freeze upon approach, relying on their camouflage to keep them safe. Like other grouse, they take wing under a loud flurry of noise if approached too closely. Inflated throat sacs are the source of the ventriloquist voice of the blue grouse, which can be heard for several kilometres.

White-tailed ptarmigan (*Lagopus leucurus*)

Ptarmigan plumage changes with the seasons in order to provide year-round camouflage. In the summer this species is mottled brown and white, with white breast, wings, and tail. In the winter, individuals are pure white except for a black beak and eyes. With a length of only 25 cm, ptarmigan are substantially smaller than grouse and have feathers on their feet, which grouse lack. The white-tailed ptarmigan has been described as fearless, and perhaps more accurately as somewhat daft, as it may march right over the front of your hiking boots if you keep still enough!

Warblers

Numerous species of warblers are commonly found in the Stein. They are generally active little birds, usually smaller than sparrows. Warblers often have some yellow pigmentation, and characteristically have narrow, pointed beaks. They are about 12 cm in length.

ROYAL BC MUSEUM

Pygmy owl
(*Glaucidium gnoma*)

The smallest of the owls in BC, measuring only 15 cm in length with a wingspan of 40 cm. This tiny owl is mostly active at dawn and dusk in pursuit of rodents, small birds and insects.

Yellow-rumped warbler *(Dendroica coronata auduboni)*

Previously known as Audubon's Warbler, this bird is one of the most common warblers in the Stein. It is one of the few warblers seen throughout the year. The bright yellow rump, crown, and side patches together with a white tail patch are the primary markings of this species. Both the Audubon's race, which has a yellow throat, and the Myrtle race, which has a white throat, occur in the Stein. These were originally considered to be two separate species.

The agile yellow-rumped warbler is often seen bursting from tree tops in pursuit of insects, zig-zagging as skillfully as a flycatcher. Look for it hunting among firs, pines, and, less frequently, willows. During breeding season it is found at higher elevations.

Townsend's warbler *(Dendroica townsendi)*

Identified by its dark crown, yellow breast, and dark ear patch bordered by yellow, the Townsend's warbler is a difficult bird to detect since it spends most of its time near the tops of tall fir and spruce trees. Exhibiting typical warbler behavior, it flies nervously out from a high perch in pursuit of insects, less frequently supplementing its diet with fruits and nectar.

Wilson's warbler *(Wilsonia pusilla chryseola)*

Undoubtedly one of the prettiest warblers in the west, with its olive upper, bright yellow lower body, and distinctive small black cap (male). Wilson's warbler is found in willow marshes or similar thickets near streams, on avalanche slopes, and amidst scrubby coniferous growth. This brightly coloured bird can be observed moving about the shrubbery, gleaning insects off the branches and out of the air. When perching, the Wilson's warbler may twitch its tail up and down intermittently while emitting its fluctuating thin and rapid chatter.

ROYAL BC MUSEUM

Pine siskin
(Carduelis pinus)

This small (12 cm long) finch is very common in forests, normally travelling in flocks above the forest canopy. The upper body is greyish-brown with darker streaking while the wings and tail are edged in white or pale yellow.

Chickadees (Parus species)

Chickadees are rotund little birds (length 11 cm) with long tails and no neck. They have disproportionately large heads and small beaks. The unmistakable bib and black cap, white cheek patches, and characteristic "chick-a-dee-dee-dee" call distinguishes the small black-capped chickadee from others. It also lacks rufous on the back and flanks, allowing one to distinguish this species from the chestnut-backed chickadee.

The mountain chickadee sports a white eyebrow stripe, and

has a white breast with grey sides. The somewhat rare boreal chickadee has a brown cap and a white breast with cinnamon coloured sides, in contrast to the plain grey breast of the black-capped chickadee. Insects and insect eggs and larvae are primary components of their diet, although they also feed on seeds and fruit. Chickadees are often observed hanging upside down as they forage amongst the conifers and mixed woods, or flying through the trees in small, irrepressibly cheerful groups.

Nuthatches (Sitta species)

Nuthatches are small, stubby birds. They are distinguished from the chickadees by their lack of a black bib and relatively large beaks, which are similar in form to the beak of a woodpecker. The white-breasted nuthatch is the largest species of nuthatch found in the Stein (length 13–15 cm). The back is slate-blue, while the crown, hindneck, and shoulders are shiny black. As you might guess from the name, its breast is pure white, as are its cheeks.

The red-breasted nuthatch is about 11 cm long. This black-capped, white throated, rusty bellied resident of semi-open Ponderosa pine forest near mid-mountain range is easily identified. Like other nuthatches the back is slate-blue. However, it is the only species of nuthatch having a broad black line through the eye and a white line above it. The pygmy nuthatch is the smallest of the nuthatches in the Stein (length 10 cm). Like the other species it is slate-blue on the back; however, the crown is greyish-brown to olive-grey instead of black and it has a white spot on the nape. Below, it is creamy white with grey flanks. Its cheeks are white, and a dark bar runs through the eye, blending into the crown without any light eyebrow streak in between.

Nuthatches are the only tree-climbers which habitually go down trees head first. They also travel upwards, forwards, backwards, and sometimes even creep along the underside of branches, in search of beetles and other creepy-crawlies. This contrasts with their frequent companion, the brown creeper, which gleans up a tree trunk and then flies to the low end of another trunk to start the process again. Nuthatches use their long, narrow bills to probe out protein-rich tree-dwelling insects, an important supplement to their primarily coniferous seed diet. The name nuthatch comes from nut-hack, which refers

ROYAL BC MUSEUM

Black-capped chickadee
(Parus atricapillus)

This common chickadee is often found in conifers and mixed woods searching for insects, larvae and seeds.

ROYAL BC MUSEUM

Golden-crowned kinglet and **ruby-crowned kinglet**
(Regulus satrapa and *Regulus calendula)*

Frequently seen in trees and shrubbery, these active little birds can be confused with other small birds. Their colourful crowns are key to proper identification. The 5-gram GCK is a miracle of winter adaptation, as it negotiates a very fine line between survival and death each cold winter night. Scientists have recently learned that this species' ingenious winter survival strategies include non-stop foraging for insects in the forest canopy (apparently there are enough in the winter to sustain them) and huddling together at night. Extreme weather and/or lack of food may result in 100% mortality rates, however.

to their habit of placing a conifer cone in the furrows of a tree and hammering it apart with their bill.

Kinglets

Golden-crowned kinglet *(Regulus satrapa olivaceus)*

Regulus means "little king," a reference to its bright yellow head crown, bordered with black. Kinglets are olive-grey, and smaller than most warblers (about 9–10 cm in length). The male has a red stripe down the middle of the crown; the female is yellow only. Also useful in identification are the tiny, plump build, and long white stripe above the eye, which distinguish it from the golden crowned sparrow. Flocks are common in spruce and fir forest below 1350 m (4500 ft). These insectivorous birds can be seen moving quickly through the middle and upper conifer branches, gleaning and twittering merrily as they go. During the winter and into spring, one may find kinglets in a mixed flock of chickadees, brown creepers, nuthatches, and small woodpeckers.

Ruby-crowned kinglet *(Regulus calendula)*

This busy little bird is similar in appearance and habit to the golden-crowned kinglet, however it lacks both the eye-stripe and the bright yellow cap. Males have a scarlet crown, visible only when the bird is excited, while the females lack any conspicuous crown patch. The ruby-crowned kinglet flits through the lower boughs of coniferous trees in search of insects, usually hunting singly or in pairs.

Other Birds

Pine grosbeak *(Pinicola enucleator)*

A large (length 20 cm), plump, long-tailed bird with a dark bill. The male has a red back, breast, and head, interspersed with patches of grey. The female is grey, brown, and variable yellow. This bird may be identified in the air by its undulating flight, and can be distinguished from the evening grosbeak by its long tail. The pine grosbeak is commonly observed in small flocks in coniferous forests at subalpine elevations in the warmer months, moving to lower elevations for the winter. An opportunistic feeder, the pine grosbeak consumes buds, fruit, and seeds of coniferous and deciduous trees.

Pileated woodpecker *(Dryocopus pileatus)*

North America's largest woodpecker (length 38 cm) is identified by its solid black back, white chin, red cap, and white under-wing pattern (seen only in flight). The presence of a large crest, red on the male and black on the female, is a further identifying feature. Like all woodpeckers, it has a long, stiff tail which it uses to brace itself while climbing. You will hear the familiar loud hammering of this bird as it chisels away at dead trees in the mixed forest of the mid valley region in search of bugs, which are extracted with its long and sticky tongue. Hammering also serves as a mode of communication and territorial defence. The pileated's rectangular-shaped nest and holes are easily differentiated from those of other woodpeckers, which tend be more square. Insects, fruits, acorns, and sap are its major food sources.

Rufous hummingbird (*Selasphorous rufus*)

This tiny species (7.5 cm length) is actually a relative of the woodpeckers. The adult male has a reddish-brown back, green crown, brilliant iridescent orange-red throat, and a white breast. Females are predominately green on the dorsal side, with some rufous at the base of the tail. The rufous hummingbird is normally found in coniferous forests, amidst flowering shrubs which yield red or yellow blossoms. Nectar, which it laps from flowers with its long tongue, and tree sap, which is obtained from woodpecker holes, provide sugar—the most important component of a hummer's diet. Protein is obtained from spiders and small insects.

Listen for the humming sound of the rufous' wings as it swoops by at speeds of up to 80 km/hour! Watch for the spectacular courtship display of the males in spring and early summer as they dive-bomb from a height of 15 m or more, and swerve upwards again at the last possible second, with the hope of impressing a nearby female.

ROYAL BC MUSEUM

Common nighthawk
(*Chordeiles minor hesperis*)

Look for this dark-coloured bird at dusk in pursuit of flying insects. The best spot for viewing them in the Stein is near the Trailhead parking lot in the warmer summer and fall months, where you may see them flying high above. More likely, you will hear their loud, piercing call, which is difficult to describe but quite distinct at dusk as few birds are active at that time. They winter in southern Mexico or South America.

MAMMALS

A significant part of what makes the Stein special is its inhabitants. Only three hours from a major metropolitan area, this intact ecosystem is home to over 50 mammalian species including wolf, cougar, grizzly bear, and wolverine. The presence of these large carnivores, which are also called indicator species, is significant because they depend on healthy populations of other mammals, birds, insects, reptiles, amphibians, and fish. The following is an overview of some of the more common mammals in the Stein.

Shrews

What appears to be a mouse with a long pointed nose and thin tail is probably a shrew. Most species are about 10 cm long, including a 4 cm tail. This active little creature is actually an insectivore, which eats at least its own weight in food each day. The four different species of shrews found in the Stein's forests and meadows are often heard at night as you lie in your tent. The rustling of leaves and grass suggests a shrew is close by, seeking out insects, slugs, snails, spiders, fungi, and seeds. In winter, the shrews continue to seek food using tunnels built in air pockets of snow.

Bats

At least seven different members of the bat family live in the Stein. From the valley bottom (Stein Lake logjam and the mouth of many of the major creeks such as Ponderosa, Cottonwood, and Scudamore are active places in the early hours of the evening) to timberline, these nocturnal, airborne mammals are perpetually hunting flying insects, especially mosquitoes. Living in colonies, bats roost during the daytime in caves, rock overhangs and tree hollows. Some hibernate during the winter, living off accumulated fat layers, while others migrate south (see Winging It, p.118).

Snowshoe hare

Found primarily in wooded areas, the nocturnal snowshoe hare—the name comes from its large feet—feeds on wildflowers, grasses, and leaves in summer, and buds, twigs, bark, and leaves of perennial plants in winter. In summer, it is brown or grey with a white belly and turns white with black tipped ears in winter. Snowshoe hare average 50 cm in length, including a 5 cm tail. A high reproductive rate allows the snowshoe hare to maintain its population, which is important since it is continually pursued by weasels, coyote, wolf, lynx, bobcat, and cougar and many birds of prey. Given its yearly survival rate of 10–50%, a snowshoe hare's life is not for those who seek longevity.

Pika

Heard, but not often seen as they lay perfectly still or hide between the rocks of their home, pikas are a fixture of boulder-strewn alpine slopes. Stacks of grasses, alpine wildflowers, sedges, and other vegetation laid out on boulders to dry indicate the presence of these "rock rabbits." Pikas are grey-brown in colour, 20 cm long, have no visible tail, and have unmistakably large round ears. Come the first snowfall, pikas have a store-house of dried veggies to help them through the long alpine winter (see The Pika, p.155).

Squirrels

The two most commonly seen animals in the Stein's forests are the northwestern chipmunk and the red squirrel. A chipmunk is easily identified by its striped head and back and upright tail when moving. Seeds, fruit, roots, and flowers are the primary food sources of this solitary ground-dwelling squirrel. Noticeably larger than the chipmunk (31 cm long vs 22 cm for the chipmunk), the vocal red squirrel actually has two coats, the summer one being a darker reddish-grey turning to a paler rusty grey in winter. Its food consists of conifer seeds supplemented by bark, fruits, buds, mushrooms, insects, bird eggs and baby rodents.

Unlike the diurnal northwestern chipmunk and red squirrel, the nocturnal northern flying squirrel is rarely seen. It is similar in size to the red squirrel and is a consumer of lichens, buds, fruits, mushrooms, and seeds. If located in flight, the flying squirrel is easily identified by its gliding motion as it extends its feet and uses the folds of skin attached from the front to rear feet for flight control.

Rodents

Mice and pack-rats

Rodents are the most numerous mammals, occuring in a variety of shapes, sizes, and forms. The Stein is inhabited by at least 11 species of rodents, the most common of which are the deer mouse, Cascade deer mouse, and bushy-tailed woodrat. Common in dry country from valley bottom to timberline, the reddish-brown deer mouse is a nocturnal creature perpetually seeking out tree buds and fruits, seeds, berries, centipedes, insects, and backpacker's granola. Given they are a primary food source for owls and weasels, deer mice have a high reproductive rate in order sustain their populations. The much larger bushy-tailed wood rat (about 40 cm long, half of which is tail, whereas the deer mouse is only 20 cm long, including a 10 cm tail) is much more assertive (some would say obnoxious), brownish-grey in colour, and found primarily in coniferous forests. The foliage of deciduous and coniferous trees and shrubs, fruits, and seeds are this nocturnal rat's main food sources.

NORTHWEST WILDLIFE PRESERVATION SOCIETY

Meadow vole
(*Microtuspennsylvanicus*)

A common resident of meadows, fields, and marshes, the meadow vole is one of the more commonly seen rodents given it is active in the morning and later afternoon in much of the same habitat that humans use. To the casual observer it may appear to be a mouse, but their smaller eyes and ears distinguish them.

LEO DEGROOT

Porcupine
(Erethizon dorsatum)

Few animals are as unique as this denizen of coniferous forests and subalpine. An adult porcupine has over 30,000 quills, which are sharp, stiff, hollow and barbed, so be sure to stop children and Fido from exercising their natural curiosity. Only the face, belly and legs of the porcupine are free of quills, posing an interesting challenge for a hungry predator, whose only option is try to reach under the porcupine, flip it over and then quickly bit its underside, all the while avoiding the quills, just one of which can cause serious harm and lead to death. The only know successful predators are lynx, fisher, wolverine, and wolf. Porcupines are quite the characters and can be fun to watch as they seek food and salt, which sometime leads to them chewing on a wide array of items, including outhouse seats.

Also called "pack rat" because of its attraction to unusual objects, the wood rat can be a rather obnoxious visitor to one's campsite as experienced by the author on several occasions. One night stands out: Camped at "Avalanche Creek" camp, I was awakened by a strange chewing noise outside. Soon it was apparent that a bushy-tailed woodrat was removing the shiny sliders on the tent fly lines, obviously fine additions to his collection. This was just the beginning, however. For reasons unknown to me, the rat proceeded to chew on the material of the tent fly, which I soon retrieved into the tent for fear of it being entirely consumed, and then the tent itself! Despite strong language and numerous attempts to scare it off, the rat kept returning for more. The highlight of the evening for the rat, undoubtedly, was the tent's enraged occupant hiding by a rock at 4:00 a.m. in nothing more than his underwear, armed with a large stick. Fortunately, these rodents are constantly pursued by numerous predators, including owls, weasels and bobcats.

Voles and lemmings

Rarely seen but equally important to predator populations, voles and lemmings are mouse-like rodents found primarily in meadows, fields, and forests. Consumers of all varieties of vegetable matter, these primarily nocturnal mammals can be distinguished from other rodents by their short ears, smaller eyes, blunter heads, and shorter tails. Size depends on the species, but most voles and lemmings are approximately 15 cm long including a 4 cm long tail.

Porcupine

Readily identified by its long yellow and black quills, the porcupine is the Stein's second largest rodent at a length of 75 cm, including a 20 cm tail. Their primary food sources are leaves, twigs, green plants, and clover, and come winter they chew the bark off trees when their normal foliage food is gone. Contrary to popular belief, porcupines do not actually eat the bark. Rather, they strip it—often killing the tree in the process—so that they can eat the sweet cambium layer just beneath the bark.

Muskrat and beaver

Two aquatic rodents found in the Stein are the relatively small muskrat (length 55 cm, tail 25 cm) and the beaver, the largest rodent at a length of 105 cm, which includes a 45 cm tail. They are similar in build and colour, but are differentiated by their size and tail—the beaver's is large and flat while the muskrat's is narrow and long. Beaver and muskrat are found in slower moving streams and ponds. The area west of Stein Lake is prime beaver habitat. Muskrat prefer aquatic vegetation and, when available, crayfish, frogs and fish. Beavers, like porcupines, eat the cambium layer of deciduous trees as well as leaves and twigs. Both beaver and muskrat build homes given suitable conditions or else dig burrows in muddy banks. Both species are primarily nocturnal.

Marmot

The most commonly seen mammal in the Stein's alpine, the hoary marmot is an oversized, ground-dwelling squirrel. It is silvery grey with a black and white head and shoulders, has a bushy tail, and is about 70 cm long, 21 cm of which is tail. Marmots are often seen sunning themselves on boulders close to their underground dens. This close relative of the groundhog (woodchuck) fattens up for its long winter hibernation by eating grasses and almost any other green plant, especially towards the end of summer. Marmots are nicknamed "Whistler" because of their unmistakable shrill alarm whistle.

Weasels

Weasels are amongst the fiercest and most skilled predators. Eight species of these primarily nocturnal mammals are found in the Stein. In or near streams and lakeshore, look for mink (55 cm long, including a 18 cm tail) and river otter (110 cm long with a 42 cm tail) as they pursue small fish, muskrat, rodents, and amphibians. Distinguishing between these dark brown weasels is easy: The river otter is considerably larger. Both will venture into meadows in search of voles.

Marten and skunk are found at lower elevations. The marten prefers forested areas, while the skunk normally stays in grassy and shrubby places. The reddish-brown marten, which often has a pale orange chest and light brown underside, consumes grouse, rodents, bugs, berries, and carrion. Marten are roughly 60 cm long and have an 18 cm long tail. The easily identified striped skunk (60 cm long, tail 23 cm) is more omnivorous in its diet, eating grasses, berries, leaves and buds, insects, rodents, fish, amphibians, bird eggs, and snakes.

The solitary fisher, which despite its name rarely ever catches fish, is found primarily in the subalpine. Next to the wolverine, the chocolate brown or black coloured fisher is the second largest land-based weasel at a length of almost one metre (35 cm tail). It pursues voles, deer mice and other small rodents, snowshoe hare,

Grizzly bear
(*Urus arctos*)

Grizzlies' reputation as a blood thirsty carnivore is yet another myth that needs to be dispelled. True, they are at the top of the food chain alongside the wolf and cougar, they have the capacity to be quite formidable, and when the opportunity arises they can turn into a fierce predator, but consider this: In interior regions such as the Stein, their diet is 90% vegetable matter. Grizzlies once occupied most of North America, but today they are found in less than 10% of their original territory.

grouse, tree squirrels, and the occasional porcupine. Blueberries and grouseberries are other favourites when in season. Sharing the subalpine with the fisher is the short-tailed weasel, a much smaller (28 cm long, including an 8 cm tail) but equally skilled hunter of essentially the same diet. Unlike the fisher, which is active day and night, the short-tailed weasel hunts only at night. The most common of the weasels, the short-tailed weasel has a summer coat which is brown on top and white underneath, changing to all white for winter.

Throughout the watershed, the long-tailed weasel and the wolverine hunt smaller mammals. The one metre long, primarily dark brown wolverine, while rarely seen, is sometimes mistaken for a small bear, but its disproportionately small head and bushy tail distinguishes it (see The Opportunist on the Move, p.173). Unmistakably "weasel like" with its 40 cm long body, longish tail (14 cm), and short legs and ears, the long-tailed weasel may occasionally be seen in meadows and on rock slopes. Its colour changes from a cinnamon brown top and white bottom in summer to an all white winter coat.

Dogs

Both the gray wolf and the coyote inhabit the Stein. These skilled hunters contrast in their adaptability. The coyote is increasing in number, while the wolf, like the grizzly, is becoming scarce since it too has lost most of its former range due to habitat destruction. Wolves are rarely seen (although sometimes heard), whereas coyotes may be seen from dawn to dusk, primarily in forested and grassy areas. The much maligned wolf hunts big game—deer, goat and moose—but it also depends on a healthy population of hare, marmots, mice, and voles. In the early 2000s, evidence of wolves in the Stein became much more common than in the past and is likely due to a sizeable wolf pack making the Stein their primary home. From the lower canyon to the ridge above Stein Lake you can find wolf tracks and scat. And, consider yourself lucky if you hear their midnight seranade.

Coyotes, like wolves, may hunt in groups, especially in winter. In summer, coyotes can be found in meadows pouncing on voles. Carrion and snowshoe hare are also consumed. The omnivorous coyote also ingests vegetable matter. Differentiate between these two by size. The wolf is 175 cm long and 1 metre tall at the shoulder. Coyotes are 120 cm and 60 cm respectively. Also compare tail shape: A coyote tail is proportionately longer, bushier, and is carried low, whereas the wolf's tail is carried straight. The coyote's fox-like look is distinguishable from the wolf's more square face.

Cats

Three wild felids are found in Canada: Cougar, lynx and bobcat. The presence of these large solitary carnivores is indicative of the Stein's wilderness character. These shy, elusive cats prefer dense forest and brush, becoming active primarily from dusk to dawn. Both the lynx and bobcat are small compared to the cougar (the cougar is 230 cm long whereas bobcat and lynx are about 85 cm long). The cougar is also distinguished by its long (75 cm) tail; bobcat and lynx have short tails, no longer than 10 cm for the lynx and 20 cm for the bobcat.

Lynx and bobcat differ in colour. Bobcat are tawny and spotted in black while lynx are grizzled grey and buffy underneath. The cougar's diet includes mule deer, snowshoe hare, porcupine, and beaver (see In Search of a Real Male, p.110, for more information on the cougar). Lynx and bobcat hunt smaller mammals and birds, including snowshoe hare, grouse, duck, perching birds, and rodents.

Bears

Healthy populations of black and grizzly bear are found within the Stein. The black bear is smaller than the grizzly, its only natural predator. Apart from size, grizzlies can be distinguished by their patchy and streaky colouring. Colour variance is significant, from black to light brown, often with white tipped hairs. Black bears are sometimes cinnamon-brown. The grizzly, which resides primarily above timberline has a pronounced shoulder hump that black bears do not have and is larger (grizzlies are about 190 cm long and 130 cm at the shoulder whereas black bear are 170 cm and 95 cm respectively).

Black bears tend to be below treeline, presumably to avoid grizzly. Both bears are omnivores, with vegetable matter being the primary component of their diet; in interior habitat such as the Stein, a grizzly's diet is roughly 90% vegetable matter. A grizzly's long claws allow it to easily dig roots and tubers, which it harvests regularly in avalanche paths once the snow has left. Berries, whitebark pine seeds, fish, and the occasional mammal rounds out a grizz's diet. A black bear depends more on sprouting plants, insects, and the buds or inner bark of shrubs and trees in spring and summer. In the fall, fruit, berries, and salmon are its main food sources.

BC PARKS

Bushy-tailed wood rat/pack rat
(Neotoma cinerea)

The folk-name "pack rat" apparently comes from this nocturnal marader's propensity for dropping whatever objects it is carrying in order to carry away more desirable items, which tend to be colourful items such as coloured rocks, crystals, feathers, and, if mankind is at hand, just about anthing shiny. In the Stein, this rodent is found primarily in the upper canyon, and seems to be on a perpetual quest to chew anything and everything with salt on it. To safeguard your possessions, be sure to take your boots inside your tent and hang your pack, hiking poles, etc. high in a tree.

Ungulates

Healthy populations of mule deer and mountain goat are found within the Stein, whereas moose don't apear to inhabit the valley as there has been no sign of them in any of the areas where they would normally reside. Mule deer are the most commonly seen larger mammal throughout the valley bottoms, although they are not nearly as common in recent years due to the wolf pack's predation on them. Only the bucks move to higher elevations for summer and early fall. Most easily identified by a large white rump patch and a black-tipped white tail, mule deer eat grasses and wildflowers in spring and summer and twigs and tree buds in winter.

For much of the year mountain goat live at higher elevations. Two of the more distinguishing features of mountain goats are their long white coats and black pointed horns. They stand about 100 cm at the shoulder and 175 cm in length. Grass and occasional subalpine fir needles and twigs are their primary food sources.

PART IV

Before You Go

ILLUSTRATIONS BY TAMI KNIGHT

This section is mandatory reading!

BEFORE YOU GO

For your own safety and enjoyment and out of respect for the environment, a basic knowledge of backcountry travel skills, equipment, and ethics is essential. Take the time to read the following, especially the sections concerning ethics, and, if possible, the recommended readings. And, be sure to review the regulations for Stein Valley Nlaka'pamux Heritage Park (bcparks.ca).

PLANNING

Expectations

Prior to any backcountry trip, regardless of how long it is, each member of your group should have a clear picture of where he or she is going, how difficult and time-consuming the trip will be, and what attractions and problems can be expected. Choosing a trip that the entire group is capable of is one of the most important decisions, as the limitations of the weakest member of your party should be your guide. Many accidents in the mountains result from people going beyond the ability or comfort zones of one or more persons in the group. Know each member's limitations and plan accordingly.

Notice of plans

To plan correctly, obtain the necessary maps and read the relevant section of this book for its cautions and the trail and/or route information. Before departing, you may want to cross reference several weather forecasts and gain the latest information on current conditions such as snowpack levels so that you can assess whether the time is right for your desired trip. Leave a detailed description of your trip with a reliable person who will give the authorities the necessary information if you are not back by a specified time. Be sure to indicate when and where you expect to begin and finish the trip and account for bad weather delays in your return time, especially if going into the Stein's western alpine.

Group size and leadership

There is safety in numbers. A group of at least four is recommended when going for more than a day trip. Every member of your party should be familiar with basic backcountry travel skills in map reading and compass work; take a course in backcountry navigation when in doubt. If the group has novices, it is a good idea to have a leader in order to make them feel comfortable.

PHYSICAL FITNESS

If you are not regularly active and grimace at the thought of putting a pack on your back, you had best not go any further than a day trip. The Stein's diverse terrain allows for everything from easy walks in the lower canyon to masochistic bushwhacks and alpine climbs for those with such inclinations. Choose your trip, start slowly and increase the pace if you feel comfortable. Remember, backcountry travel is about having fun and relaxing, not competing.

ETHICS

With the Stein no longer under threat of clearcutting, the greatest danger facing this valley is the "death-by-a-thousand-cuts" impact of individuals not practicing leave-no-trace backcountry travel. While only a general guideline, the following should be your modus operandi in the backcountry. Also, educate yourself and others on the continually evolving code of ethics for wilderness travel.

Pets

Like many people I love dogs, but while Bowser may provide companionship and amusement, he is a disruptive force in the backcountry. Not only do dogs distract from other people's wilderness experiences, they also affect the wildlife. Fact: Ground-dwelling animals will often abandon their home if they detect a dog's scent. Plus, man's best friend is a well-known carrier of Giardiasis (see Water, below). Furthermore, your beloved pet could possibly endanger you and your party by aggravating a bear. In short, leave your dog at home. If you do insist on bringing your dog, BC Parks requires that all dogs be kept on a leash at all times in the park.

Sanitation

The clear, unpolluted water of the Stein is one of its attractions. Water purity is jeopardized, however, by people disposing of their waste too close to rivers and streams, as giardia and other microbes are introduced into the water system. In disposing of solid body waste there are three main concerns: minimizing the chance of water pollution, minimizing the chance anything or anyone finding the waste, and maximizing the rate of decomposition. All means of disposal have their drawbacks, but the cathole method is still the best bet.

While there are now some outhouses in the Stein, be prepared to choose a site at least 50 m from any water, dig a hole approximately 10–15 centimetres deep and cover it with soil and other organic material. You may want to consider packing a lightweight, compact trowel as they can be a big help in digging through roots. Used toilet paper, tampons and sanitary napkins should be wrapped in several plastic bags and packed out.

Tread lightly

How and where you travel is important. Trails have been constructed, in part, to help limit erosion. Resist the temptation to walk around muddy sections or else you will break down the trail edge and widen the path. In the alpine, stay on the trail, if there is one. Otherwise, spread out so as to avoid stepping repeatedly on the same area, especially in the sensitive alpine meadows; alpine vegetation is particularly susceptible to erosion and takes a long time to recover. Avoid the temptation to cut the corners on the switchbacks of trails, so as to not further erosion. In general, look before you step.

The Stein has a wealth of historical cultural sites that should be treated with the same care as any museum. Especially sensitive are pictographs; do not touch the native people's lasting legacy. Similarly, respect private property both adjacent to and within the valley (you must cross private property when accessing the Stein from Lytton and Siwhe Creek).

Vegetation

Most appropriate to this topic is the old adage, "leave nothing but footprints, take nothing but pictures." In other words, leave everything as you found it. As is the case with most of man's destructive habits, it is not the act of one person that is damaging, but rather the cumulative effect of many doing the same thing.

Making Camp

A clean, appropriately placed camp is an important part of leave-no-trace travel. Pitch your tent in designated areas or in places where you will not ruin the vegetation; in sensitive areas, camp on a durable surface such as gravel or rock if possible. Be sure to pack out all your garbage, including uneaten food. Always keep your camp meticulously clean of food scraps so as to not attract unwanted visitors. The recent increase in mice and rat populations in the Stein is directly attributable to people's carelessness. Until you have had your pack

chewed, your chocolate bars eaten, and your tent attacked, you have no idea what a problem these creatures can be.

Garbage

One of the most distressing thing to see in the backcountry is the garbage of others. Be courteous: If you can pack it in, you can pack it out. Similarly, if you come across someone else's garbage, pack it out.

Fires

Now that the Stein Valley is a provincial park, fires are prohibited everywhere in the watershed.

EQUIPMENT

Many of us grapple with our inner gearhead, but there are certain items that should be in your pack at all times. Also, proper equipment can make a real difference in your comfort and safety. Seek out the advice of a reputable outdoor equipment store's staff, search the internet and seek out the many great outdoor books and magazine available, especially if you are seeking to reduce you load by adopting the "ultra" lightweight gear now available, which is mostly made by smaller, lesser known companies.

For any trip including day trips you should have the following:

- compass
- first aid kit
- water bottle
- moleskin
- headlamp
- matches

- map
- extra clothing
- extra food
- fire starter
- bug dope
- batteries

- sunblock
- sunglasses
- hat
- knife
- whistle

I also strongly recommend carrying a pack cover and gaiters for all overnight trips. These two items can make the difference between being miserable with wet footwear and gear, and having a comfortable outing. In the western half of the Stein, precipitation can be of biblical proportions, pushing packcovers and supposedly waterproof stuff sacks beyond their limits. You may want to consider taking lighweight drysacks normally used for watersports for some of your clothing, food and gear, as they provide a high level of protection.

Footwear

Proper footwear and foot care can make or break your trip. If you are hiking the lower canyon for a day or overnight trip, lightweight hiking boots may be adequate. Trips involving a heavier pack and wetter, more difficult conditions require waterproof, full leather boots. Be sure to break in your footwear before going. Applying moleskin on sensitive spots, changing socks during the day, and keeping your feet dry and clean will help minimize blister formation. Two layers of socks are needed for heavier boots: A thin inner sock—preferably synthetic—to keep your feet dry (cotton socks are not as desirable since they tend to abrade the skin when wet, but do aid in cooling the feet and therefore should be used in summer only), and a heavier wool outer sock to absorb the abrading of the boot. Carry extra socks, even for day trips, and use your pack's compresssion straps to hold wet socks while hiking so that they can air dry.

For Overnight Trips

1) **Clothing:** The layering principle, adding or removing layers of clothing depending on the weather and your activity level, is your rough rule of thumb for dressing appropriately for the outdoors. For the skin layer use lightweight synthetic or wool tops and bottoms if the weather is anything other than hot. Cotton can be justified for its cooling properties in hot weather, but beware of using it in wet and cold conditions because it offers no insulative value when wet, unlike synthetics and wool. The insulative or middle layer should consist of a fleece or synthetic fill jacket,

lighweight down jacket or wool sweater, and the outer layer, which stops wind, rain, and snow, is best achieved with one of the proven "waterproof/breathable" fabrics such as eVent®, Entrant® or Gore-Tex®.

2) **Sleeping bag and pad:** If you can afford it, buy a lightweight down bag, learn how to take care of it and you will be rewarded with many years of excellent peformance. Synthetic bags, while heavier and bulkier than down, are getting better and offer good value for those on a limited budget. For most people, at least a -5 to -10° C temperature rating is needed if travelling in the alpine from June to September. For insulation between the ground and comfort for your aching bones and muscles use a close-celled foam pad or a lightweight inflatable air mattress.

3) **A properly fitting pack:** Internal frames are your best bet. Avoid the temptation to buy all the bells and whistles that go with a 3 kg (6.6 lb) pack, as there are now many lightweight packs that offer good carrying comfort for loads under 22 kg (50 lb).

4) **Shelter:** Modern technology has blessed us with many good tents, and the manufac-turers keep improving them each year. Those on a budget or going ultra lightweight may consider a tarp or bivy sack. If heading into the more bug-infested areas, you will definitely want no-see-um netting.

5) **Cooking stove:** Central to leave-no-trace camping is the use of a gas stove rather than a campfire for cooking. A dependable, field-maintainable single burner unit is all you need. Be sure to take extra fuel and spare parts, and learn how to maintain and fix your stove.

6) **Odds and ends:** Extra fuel, rope (at least 12 m), plenty of stuff sacks and plastic bags to pack your items in, and additional insulated clothing. Recommended extras: Repair kit including sewing materials, extra buckles, webbing, Freesole® (the fix everything wonder product), boot laces and an emergency signal device such as flares, or, better yet, a satellite phone.

BEAR COUNTRY TRAVEL

The Stein is home to a healthy population of grizzly and black bears. While they reside primarily within the remote parts of the watershed, they do wander down as far as the lower canyon in their perpetual quest for food. Fortunately, they are still wild—they fear you and want nothing to do with you. That changes, however, if the bear begins to associate humans with easily obtainable food. Read Stephen Herrero's *Bear Attacks: Their Causes and Avoidance.*

At the very least, you should:

- **Leave the rifle at home:** You should be practicing bear avoidance techniques, not crisis management. Herrero sums it best: "Your best weapon to minimize the risk of a bear attack is your brain."

- **Make your presence known** by making loud noise as you travel the trails and routes. Most bear attacks result from:

  1) Surprising a bear and thereby aggravating it.
  2) Disturbing a mother with cubs.
  3) Interrupting a bear with food. You can reduce the chances of encountering a bear by letting it know you are in the area; if given the opportunity, bears will quickly vacate the scene. This is especially important in places where the bear cannot hear or smell you, such as next to a river and in dense vegetation.

- **In camp,** cook at least 100 m downwind of your tent; suspend your food from trees at least 5 m above the ground and at least 100 m downwind from your tent (above treeline, seal all edible and fragrant items in several layers of plastic to minimize the smell and store well away from camp, ideally buried in a boulder field); leave your pack and cooking and eating clothes outside your tent; put all edible and fragrant items—including garbage, sunscreen, and soap—in your tree stash; pack out all garbage and uneaten food; and don't camp where fresh bear signs (tracks, diggings, droppings) are present.

MEDICAL PROVISIONS AND INSECTS

A course in wilderness first aid is highly recommended. For longer trips, ensure that at least two people in your party are competent in first aid. Include in your first aid kit an Epi Pen (and know how to use it) plus antihistamine, as wasps are found in several parts of the valley.

Ticks may be encountered in the spring. These annoying little bugs are found primarily in grassy areas, where they wait for mammals to latch onto. Check your clothing regularly and if you find one embedded into your skin do not touch it with your hands—people have contracted diseases from ticks by handling them. Use tweezers (tissue or gauze otherwise) to grab the tick as close to the head as possible and pull it gently out. Do not twist while pulling and ensure that all tick parts are removed from the wound and treat the affected area. Given the increasingly prevalence of Lyme disease contracted through ticks in BC, you may want to take the tick to medical experts and learn more about this disease.

Hypothermia, the lowering of the body's core temperature, is of constant concern in the backcountry, especially in the alpine and in winter. Recognize the symptoms (slurred speech, stumbling, confused thinking, shivering, weakness, and shallow breathing). With mild hypothermia, assist the victim in getting dry, warm clothing, rehydrated, easily digested food, and active so that the body can rewarm itself. In severe cases, keep the victim immobile and seek emergency evacuation. Most importantly, practice prevention by eating enough food, drinking plenty of fluids, wearing proper clothing, and covering your head and neck, a major source of heat loss.

Heat exhaustion may occur when an individual overheats (normally through physical exertion) or is exposed to a hot environment. This is a definite possibility in the eastern Stein in the summer months. Dehydration (see Water and Nutrition below) and a lack of acclimatization make an individual more susceptible. Be sure to add salt to your food and drink plenty of water. Taking a break during the mid-day and travelling in the morning and late afternoon is also recommended.

WATER AND NUTRITION

Water: Sufficient fluid intake is often overlooked by active people. Your muscles will benefit from proper water levels and your energy level will be higher. This is especially important on hot summer days. As a general rule, active adults should consume at least 2–4 litres of water per day.

Food: Complex carbohydrates and quality proteins and fats are your key for optimum performance and easy packing, as you are striving for a maximum calories per gram ratio (sorry, but espresso does not make the grade). Outdoor retailers now offer many tasty packaged meal options so be sure to check them out. Similarly, the internet, magazines

and books offer a wealth of information on making your own meals using lighweight ingredients found in most grocery stores. Fruit leathers, chocolate, your grandmother's secret gorp mix, dried meats, chocolate, breads, and cheeses help break the monotony for lunches and snacks.

ROUTE FINDING & RIVER CROSSINGS

Several of the routes in this guide require solid route-finding skills. Being able to correctly read 1:50,000 maps and terrain is a skill that requires practice. Plus, in the event of limited visibility due to weather or dense vegetation, you should be able to use a compass to navigate to your destination. Take a course from a reputable company such as Canada West Mountain School or from your local hiking club and read some of the books in the recommended reading section of this book, and go with people who have these skills.

Caution is required when crossing snow and glaciers. None of the summer routes and trails in this guide cross glaciers, but some will take you through seasonal or permanent snow fields. Your greatest concerns in this terrain are avalanches and cornices (overhangs of snow and ice that can give way without warning). Stay in the middle of broad ridges and look for signs of avalanche debris before passing under or across potentially dangerous slopes.

In crossing creeks look for a sturdy log, undo your hipbelt, loosen your pack's straps, and be ready to throw it off. If you do not feel comfortable, try it without the pack first. Try to land on the downstream side if you feel yourself falling. Walking or crawling forward is easier than moving sideways. And, definitely avoid crossing above logjams!

WATER SAFETY

There have been confirmed cases of Giardiasis ("Beaver Fever") contracted in the Stein. This nasty little parasite attaches itself to the inside of the small intestine and, less frequently, the gall bladder of most mammals. It enters water bodies through the feces of a carrier, and symptoms, which normally appear within approximately 15 days, include diarrhea, stomach cramps, lack of appetite, and weakness. This is not to say that the Stein is stricken with bad water—the water is as pure as can be found virtually anywhere. Giardiasis accompanies mammals, so it will be found in any wilderness. Humans contribute greatly to this problem by not properly disposing of their personal waste (see Ethics above) and by bringing their dogs.

To avoid this parasite it is recommended that you treat all water except for that melting directly from a snowpack. There are several water treatment options available these days, ranging from fuel-intensive boiling to portable water filters and chemicals such as chlorine dioxide, which is used by many municipalities in Europe and North America. Do your homework and decide on what will suit you. Personally, I like the compactness and lighweight of chlorine dioxide drops, but some people swear by their filters. It really is a personal preference to a large extent. Iodine is less reliable due to pH and temperature differences, and is not recommended.

RECOMMENDED READING:

- Cox, Stephen, and Fulsaas, Kris, Eds. *Mountaineering: The Freedom of the Hills,* 7th edition, The Mountaineers.

- Hampton, Bruce, and Cole, David. *Soft Paths,* Stackpole Books.

- Herrero, Stephen. *Bear Attacks: Their Causes and Avoidance,* Nick Lyons Books.

- Manning, Harvey. *Backpacking: One Step at a Time,* Vintage Books.

- Meyer, Kathleen. *How to Shit in the Woods,* Ten Speed Press.

- Wilkerson, James. *Medicine for Mountaineering,* The Mountaineers.

RECOMMENDED WEBSITES:

- backpackgeartest.com

- bcmc.ca—BC Mountaineering Club

- bivouac.com

- clubtread.com

- lnt.org—Leave No Trace Centre for Outdoor Ethics

- weatheroffice.gc.ca

- whistlerblackcomb.com—for cams, weather forecasts & current temperatures

- wildernessfirstaid.ca

WHILE IN THE LYTTON AREA:

- Visit the Siska Art Gallery (250-455-2219), 12 km south of Lytton. This gallery features works of local First Nations artists, including soapstone and wood carvings.

- Raft the Thompson River: Fraserraft.com, Hyak.com, Kumsheen.com, Reorafting.com

- Raft the Nahatlatch River: Fraserraft.com, Reorafting.com

- See the Jellyroll & the Lytton Museum (ask at the Lytton Visitor Centre, 400 Fraser Street): Lytton.ca

PART V

Recreational Information

"Without adventure, civilization is in full decay."

–Alfred North Whitehead

LOWER STEIN

Most people's first exposure to the Stein is via the lower canyon. The accommodating weather and terrain, easy access and beautiful scenery make it the obvious destination for a weekend of relaxing exploration.

ECOLOGICAL OVERVIEW: The lower Stein, from the mouth to just west of Stryen Creek's confluence with the Stein and including Van Winkle Flat, is part of the driest and hottest ecological zone of BC, the bunchgrass biogeoclimatic zone. Grassland predominates with bluebunch wheatgrass being the dominant bunchgrass on undisturbed sites. Sagebrush is also common, but is more prevalent on overgrazed areas. Ponderosa pine and Douglas fir are the only trees able to grow in this dry climate.

1. Stein Bridge to Confluence of the Stein and Fraser

Many trails can be found in the area around the Stein Bridge, 5.6 km north of the ferry on the West Side Road. The following two descriptions take you to the mouth of the Stein.

These trails cross Indian reserve property and should be treated with the same respect as any private property deserves. Year-round hiking is possible on these trails, which are suitable for all ages. Time: Each trip, 45 minutes to 1 hour round-trip.

Stein–Fraser Confluence.   ADELBERT BEEKMANS

Winter Villages

The mouth of the Stein has a rich history, for it was on these banks that the Nlaka'pamux lived for millenia. Based out of pithouses—large houses built deep into the ground and often supplemented by cooking facilities, storage areas, and hearths—the native people lived here primarily during the winter months, spending much of the rest of the year hunting and gathering in the mountains. The houses varied in size, with most accommodating 15–30 persons. Some exceptionally large houses held 60–80 people. Apparently, the north bank of the Stein was an ideal winter village site given the close proximity to fishing, hunting and gathering, and the abundance of water, fuel and construction materials. Plus, winter winds were less prevalent here and the soil drained well. To date, approximately 70 pithouse remnants, large circular depressions in the ground, have been recorded by the BC Heritage Conservation Branch.

From South Side of Bridge:

Next to the bridge's south end is a parking area. The easiest approach to gain access to the mouth is to proceed south from the bridge for 0.2 km (0.1 mi), where a gated road intersects the West Side Road.

This road takes you down to the confluence of the Stein and Fraser in only 0.6 km (0.4 mi), and is easy to follow. On a hot summer day, this area offers some respite from the legendary heat of the Lytton area, as there is often a breeze close to the Fraser River.

Confluence and 1986 Stein Festival Site

From the north side of the bridge proceed towards a brick pumphouse building next to the road. A trail on the bank behind the building should be visible. Hop the fence and climb the small slope via the trail for an elevation gain of about 25 m (75 ft). Proceed downstream, crossing the bench you are on for 60 m (200 ft), at which point you will find a road. Follow the road down to a large flat, open bench just above the banks of the Stein. The prayer circle here was part of the 1986 Stein Festival. Numerous camping sites are found in the immediate area.

2. North Shore Trail

Attractions: Accessibility; good views of lower canyon. **Cautions:** Loose footing; steep in places—exercise caution if taking children. **Access:** From first bend in West Side Road 0.5 km (0.3 mi) north of Stein Bridge. **Season:** Year-round. **Rating:** Easy to moderate. **Distance and time:** 2.3 km (1.4 mi); 1 hour–1 hour 30 minutes one way. **Elevation gain:** 30 m (100 ft); 75 m (250 ft) on return. **Map:** 92 I/5.

Finding the beginning of this trail requires following the West Side Road from the north side of Stein Bridge to the first sharp bend in the road 0.5 km (0.3 mi) north of the bridge. Take the rough road that intersects the West Side Road at this point and follow it uphill through a pine forest and underneath the hydro power lines.

ROYAL BC MUSEUM

Alligator lizard
(Elgaria coerulea)

Slender and long (up to 10 cm) in body, it is found in open rock areas, especially near forest. Its primary food sources are insects and spiders. Like the western skink, the alligator lizard can shed its tail, apparently in an attempt to distract a predator.

Go right at the first fork just off the West Side Road. Continue straight uphill, looking for orange markers on the trees. This is the beginning of the trail. The West Side Road should be visible from here. At approximately 0.5 km (0.3 mi) avoid a path on your left that descends to the river. The trail ascends before levelling off 0.6 km (0.4 mi) from the trailhead. You then start descending gently as the trail curves around the side of the hill and moves parallel to the river below. The open Ponderosa pine forest allows for views of the main trail, Van Winkle Flat, and sharp bends of the Stein. You are now approximately 0.8 km (0.5 mi) from the start and 1.5 km (0.9 mi) from the terminus of the trail.

Approximately 0.4 km (0.25 mi) of descent takes you past rock outcrops about 75 m (250 ft) above the river. A couple of minutes past the outcrops is a junction in the trail at a large Ponderosa pine. To continue to the trail's terminus next to the river, take the left fork which descends for 0.8 km (0.5 mi) to the flat bench next to the river. Several campsites are found here. The junction's right fork is a well-beaten game trail that climbs to several viewpoints above (see Bluff Trail description that follows).

3. Bluff Trail

At the junction by the large Ponderosa pine 1.5 km (0.9 mi) from the trailhead and 0.8 km (0.5 mi) from the trail's terminus,

Stryen Creek Bridge.   ANDY MONS

proceed uphill along the right fork. Go left at the first junction 0.2 km (0.1 mi) from the start. A well-defined game trail leads to atop a prominent ridge, 1.0 km (0.6 mi) from the start. Avoid an old trail on your left as you continue uphill for another 0.1 km to the top of the bluff. Fine views of the lower canyon, Van Winkle Flat, and the greater Lytton area are gained from here. Those wanting to explore further can ascend the trail-less ridge, keeping in mind that there is no water in this area.

4. Stein–Stryen Divide

Attractions: Excellent views of Lytton and surrounding area. **Cautions:** Loose footing; some route finding necessary; carry water. **Access:** From rock outcrop 30 m west of Stryen Creek Bridge (see Trailhead to Lower Crossing description, trip # 8). **Season:** April to October. **Rating:** Moderate. **Distance and time:** Approximately 1.3 km (0.8 mi); 1 hour 15 minutes–2 hours. **Elevation gain:** 600 m (2000 ft). **Map:** 92 I/5.

This steep climb to the two small summits on the ridge between the Stein River and Stryen Creek and offers excellent views of the lower canyon, the Thompson and Fraser rivers, Lytton, Botanie Mountain, and Stryen Creek.

JANE MCRAE

Douglas fir
(Pseudotsuga menziesii)

The most common tree in BC. Identification: Symmetrical young trees up to 15 cm in diameter have smooth, grey/brown bark and resin blisters. Older trees have thick (up to 30 cm!) deeply fissured, reddish/brown bark, and heavy limbs. Native people used Douglas fir pitch for torches, branches for harpoon shafts and saplings for dipnets; green saplings are flexible enough to be moulded in to a circular shape.

Approximately 30 m west of the Stryen Creek Bridge is a rock outcrop. Locate a trail just to the east of the rock and begin ascending the lower reaches of the ridge. At first, the ridge is not entirely obvious due to the forest cover. Soon the terrain temporarily flattens and the vegetation opens up. Continue ascending in a southwest direction up the broad ridge line. At 600 m (2000 ft) the ridge narrows. Exercise caution past here; those unsure of their footing should not proceed further.

Atop the first summit, elevation 780 m (2600 ft), the second summit is close at hand to the southwest. Descend 15 m (50 ft) into the gully between the summits and ascend the 25 m (80 ft) needed to gain the second summit. Return to the Stein via the same route used to ascend—the northern slopes are loose.

5. Trailhead to "The Forks," Stryen Creek

Attractions: Enjoyable hiking in pine and fir forests of lower sections of trail; the enchanting forest of "The Forks;" interesting geology. **Cautions:** Active slide area with steep slopes below "The Forks;" bear country; carry water. **Access:** From Stein Trailhead parking lot. **Season:** Late May to October. **Rating:** Easy to moderate. **Distance and time:** About 6.5 km (4.1 mi), 1 hour 30 minutes–2 hours 30 minutes. **Elevation gain:** 640 m (2100 ft). **Maps:** 92 I/5 and 92 I/4.

From the park information display in the Trailhead parking lot, head south into the open fir and pine forest where you will find a decent trail defined by orange markers and flagging tape. After only a few minutes of walking you will start to hike up the gentle slopes on your left and then cross a barb-wired fence. Once on the other side of the fence, go straight up the hill and look for a vague trail that diagonally crosses the slope to gain the open, sparsely vegetated bench above.

Atop the bench, the Stryen Creek basin—with Mount Roach looming above—is visible to the southwest. The trail is fairly easy to follow now as it takes you southward, close to the edge of the bench, and runs parallel to Stryen Creek. In a few minutes you will cross the first of several drainage ditches, some of which are usually dry. Stay left where the trail crosses an old road that drops down towards Stryen Creek and continue along the trail to a larger drainage ditch, which has a small foot bridge across it. Go left on the south side of this crossing and follow the road for roughly 50 m until it intersects another road, at which point a small building is visible a short distance downhill.

Stryen Creek Forks cabin.   DAVID THOMPSON

Go right (uphill) on the newly encountered road, which eventually becomes an easy-to-follow trail. The trail then crosses a rocky area, moves around blowdown, levels off briefly, and crosses more rock in the next 1.2 km (0.8 mi). Soon you come to an open area with a talus slope ahead. Ascend over rocky terrain, including an open slide. The large talus slopes near this area are a good example of cliff face erosion; the talus slopes are the fractured remains of a rock slide from cliff faces above. You are now roughly 0.7 km (0.4 mi) from "The Forks."

Now the terrain becomes more demanding as the trail crosses a boulder field and ascends more steeply. Two switchbacks, elevation 920 m (3050 ft), immediately past the boulderfield are followed by an ascent up steep slopes that are dangerously active. Exercise caution through this section. The trail here is vague in places—some flagging tape identifies the correct route, but it is not consistently marked. A third switchback brings you close to the rise at the top of the slopes, 0.6 km (0.4 mi) from the boulderfield below the slopes. A gradual descent from the rise to "The Forks" junction is easily completed in a few minutes.

You are now 6.5 km (4.1 mi) from the Trailhead parking lot. Several camping sites are close at hand in this beautiful cedar grove forest. See the West Fork description for accessing the cabin, which was constructed in 1932 by Jimmy Johnson and served as a teamsters' stopover for the Lytton Gold Mine.

6. Stryen Creek, East Fork

Attractions: Alpine meadows; good views. **Cautions:** Wet terrain; variable weather; bear country. **Access:** From "The Forks" (see trip #5 for access). **Season:** Late June to September. **Rating:** Moderate. **Distance and time:** To meadows before mining camp, 6.0 km (3.8 mi), 3–4 hours; to lakes, approximately 7.5 km (4.8 mi), 4–5 hours. **Elevation gain:** To meadows, 570 m (1900 ft); to lakes, 720 m (2400 ft). **Map:** 92 I/4.

While quite limited in views for the first 2.9 km (1.8 mi), the East Fork trail of Stryen Creek offers numerous opportunities for alpine exploration. The trail is, for the most part, easily followed until it disappears in the meadowed slopes below Mt. Roach. The beginning of the trail is not obvious due to windfall and erosion. From "The Forks" backtrack to the Stryen Creek trail.

The trail climbs at a gradual pace until 1.2 km (0.8 mi) from the start and then increases in steepness. Another 0.3 km (0.2 mi) brings you to a point above the cascading falls of Stryen Creek's east channel. The trail switchbacks before straightening out, soon offering fine views of Mt. Roach's northeast face. 2.4 km (1.5 mi) from the start is a collapsed bridge across the creek. The bridge offers safe crossing in low water, but exercise caution in spring—it may be impassable at this point.

Having crossed the creek you are now going to follow along its west side. Your destination, the valley east of Mt. Roach, should be apparent now as the east slopes of Mt. Roach and the west slopes of the peak southeast of Mt. Roach form the boundaries of the East Fork. Some views are gained as the trail stays within 100–150 metres of the creek. The trail becomes less obvious and overgrown by the time you reach the corduroy (dilapidated wooden walkway) 0.6 km (0.4 mi) past the bridge. The footing is wet through here, making proper footwear a necessity. Just past the corduroy is a small boulder field. Stay close to the creek through here.

More trees and less identifiable sections of trail make for slower going for the remainder of the distance to the mining camp, 6.0 km (3.8 mi) from the start. Camping can be found in the meadows 0.4 km (0.3 mi) before the mine camp remnants

ANDY MONS

Bracket Fungi

Throughout any forest one is sure to see these semicircular growths on older trees and logs. Actually, these structures are fruiting bodies produced by mold colonies that extend for km within the tree. Rarely recognized for their valuable role in the cycle of the forest, fungi such as bracket fungi are continually changing the landscape by breaking down the trees' cell walls. Ultimately, the tree falls, decomposes into soil, and provides the base for future generations of vegetation. Reproduction is not apparent to uneducated eye, as spores are released from the underside of the bracket fungi.

and just after the mine camp. The lakes at the end of the valley are another 1–2 hours hike and offer good camping.

7. Stryen Creek, West Fork

Attractions: Access to Stein's south divide and Skihist and Pelushkwohap Mountains. **Cautions:** Bushy and rocky trail; bear country. **Access:** From "The Forks" (terminus of trip #5). **Season:** Late June to September. **Rating:** Moderate to difficult. **Distance and time:** To rockslide at 1385 m (4550 ft), 3.0 km (2.3 mi), 1 hour 30 minutes–2 hours; to cabin approximately 4.5 km (2.3 mi), 3–4 hours. **Elevation gain:** To rock slide, 410 m (1370 ft); to cabin about 510 m (1700 ft). **Map:** 92 I/4.

A rough trail still exists on this fork of Stryen Creek and can be followed with some difficulty to the cabin remains 4.5 km (2.3 mi) distant. At "The Forks" junction move towards the bank of Stryen Creek and proceed upstream 60 m before crossing the creek on a large log. 100 m past the crossing turn left and move uphill past the cabin, soon reaching a rock field. The trail then switchbacks 3 times, passes a small section of blowdown, and switchbacks again more steeply in the next 0.6 km (0.4 mi). Continue ascending over rock slides until the trail levels off briefly as you pass by a side-valley 1.8 km (1.2 mi) from the start.

MICHAEL MCINULTY

Exercise caution as you cross the next rock slide and then descend into a brushy area, elevation 1350 m (4500 ft). The remaining 0.6 km (0.4 mi) of measured trail takes you past cabin ruins, and beside the creek, which you must follow to the rock slide at 1385 m (4550 ft). At this point, the valley begins to open up and can be explored much further, especially by those seeking the alpine further south.

Horsefly
(Hybomitra spp)

Few insects are as aggravating as the horsefly, which will sometimes follow you for hours across the subalpine and alpine in hope of getting a bite. They are big (up to 2 cm long) and tough, as they can withstand a severe stomping and come up flying.

"Devoted though we must be to the conservation cause, I do not believe that any of us should give it all our effort or heart... Let us save at least half of our lives for the enjoyment of this wonderful world which still exists. Leave your dens, abandon your cars and walk out into the mountains, the deserts, the forests, the seashores. Those treasures still belong to all of us. Enjoy them to the full, stretch your legs, enliven your hearts—and we will outlive the greedy swine who want to destroy it all in the name of what they call growth."

–Edward Abbey

West fork of Stryen Creek.

LEWIS KAISERSETTER

STEIN RIVER LOWER CANYON

FERRY SCHEDULE

Daily 06:30 -> 22:15

Meal Breaks

9:30 ->10:00
17:00 -> 17:30

Scale 1:75 000   1 cm = 750 metres

Contour Interval: 500 feet (150 meters)

0   .5   1 mile

1 km

♠ Cabin   Trail; Switchback
▲ Campsite   Route

● Lake
vp Viewpoint

Creek; Stream
River

N MN

21°

Botanie Valley

FERRY

LYTTON

↓ Hope

Trans-Canada Hwy.

Thompson River

Hwy. #12

Lillooet

Fraser River

West Side Road

BC Hydro Powerline

Van Winkle Flats

Nohomin Creek

1500 ft (460 m)

Indian Reserve

PARKING & TRAILHEAD

Confluence

Stein Bridge

Lillooet

vp

Seasonal

1500 ft (460 m)

1500 ft (460 m)

"Devils Staircase"

5000 ft (1520 m)

vp

"Christina Falls"

Boulder Field 3000 ft (910 m)

Steep

Stryen Creek

"The Forks"

East Fork

Cord Wood

Bridge Collapsed

West Fork

Mt. Roach 8672 ft (2640 m)

5000 ft (1520 m)

6000 ft (1830 m)

Stein River

Teaspoon Creek

Earl's Cabin

Earl Creek

Akasik Mtn. 8100 ft (2470 m)

2000 ft (6100 m)

Lower Crossing

Klein's Cabin

TRAILHEAD TO STEIN LAKE

The trail system extending from Stein Trailhead to Stein Lake provides access to the accommodating and culturally rich lower canyon, diverse mid-valley forests, and scenic Stein Lake area. Trips in this area vary from simple half-day hikes in the lower canyon to 10 day ventures into the further reaches of the valley. Please tread lightly through this area—it sees the vast majority of use in the Stein, and it is already showing sign of backpackers not practicing minimal impact camping.

ECOLOGICAL OVERVIEW: Extending from the banks of the Fraser River into the middle of the Stein, the Interior Douglas fir zone is the most predominant zone encountered along the Stein Trailhead to Stein Lake trail system. This zone is characterized by widely spaced Douglas fir and Ponderosa pine trees. Cedar groves and stands of northern black cottonwood become more common as one travels west. The much wetter Coastal Western Hemlock zone, which extends from west of Nesbitt Creek to Stein Lake has a more dense forest canopy and ground cover. Mixed stands of hemlock, spruce, cedar, and fir predominate in this zone.

8. Trailhead to Lower Crossing

Attractions: Easy access; spectacular rapids and chutes; steep canyon walls; easy hiking for even non-hikers; reliable weather; numerous camping sites; nonstop river watching. **Cautions:** Hot summer weather (hat and sunscreen are essential); loose footing on talus crossings; carry water since the river is not always accessible. **Access:** From Trailhead, near Lytton. **Season:** March to November. **Rating:** Easy to moderate. **Distance and time:** To west of "Devil's Staircase," 5.3 km (3.3 mi); 2 hours–3 hours 30 minutes; to Earl Creek, 10.8 km (6.8 mi); 3 hours 30 minutes–5 hours; to lower crossing, 13.2 km (8.3 mi); 4–6 hours. **Elevation gain:** 355 m (1200 ft). **Map:** 92 I/5.

Stein Trailhead.   ANDY MONS

Starting at the Trailhead, elevation 225 m (750 ft), on the south side of the Stein, you are surrounded by the Ponderosa pine, bunchgrass, sage, and Saskatoon berry of the interior's dry benchlands. This basically flat trail allows even the non-hiker to appreciate the beauty of the valley. Camping spots are as close as 10 minutes from the Trailhead.

Descending along a clear path towards the river, the roar of the turbulent water grows as you pass through the Ponderosa pine and Douglas fir above the river. You soon come to Stryen Creek, which is also known locally as Last Chance Creek, or *naikzakxn* to the Nlaka'pamux, meaning "to fall a log across," Stryen Creek originates in the alpine south of the Stein's lower canyon. Immediately past the bridge is a large rock outcrop, often called the "Asking Rock," where many of us pause for a few minutes before entering or exiting the valley. According to Harlan Smith, an archaeologist who worked in the Stein area in 1897, native boys and girls came here to wash with fir boughs during their puberty rituals. This site is also the first pictograph panel found on this trail. In late September–October the pools in the Stein below the "Asking Rock" are teeming with spawning pink salmon.

At 1.5 km (0.9 mi) a smooth flat rock outcrop brings you next to the river. This a great spot to fill up your water bottle and cool your feet. The next 2.3 km (1.4 mi) take you along the flat benches of the old river bed, which were formed when the river was much larger and more powerful than it is now. At this point, 3.9 km (2.4 mi) from the Trailhead, the ascent of the "Devil's Staircase" (or "Big Slide" to the native people) section of the trail begins. A trail to the right leads to a large camping area close to the river that features an outhouse and food storage. To continue, go left and begin ascending. Be sure to carry water; for at least 30 minutes there will be none.

Having climbed via two switchbacks to approximately 400 m (1300 ft), you now encounter a large talus field. Careful with your footing here, especially in wet weather (children may require assistance through this section). From the top of the talus slope descend into a rock gully and pass through trees into the wet area of "Christina Creek," 0.6 km (0.4 mi) past the top of the talus slope. The trail continues above the river for 0.3 km (0.2 mi), taking you over another talus slope and above steep slopes that drop precipitously to the river below. The descent should be taken carefully as the footing is loose. A log is on your right near the bottom of the descent and an island in the river is visible.

RICK HEWAT

Saskatoon berry
(Amelanchier alnifolia)

Commonly found in dry openings where it grows in clusters to heights of 2–3 m, the Saskatoon berry is easily identified in April and May when white blossoms envelope it. By July, berries are a dull red turning to a ripe black in early August. In the absence of flowers and berries, look for the Saskatoon's round leaves. Native people used this bush's wood for lining steam pits and protecting spears and arrows.

To experience what is undoubtedly a "power spot" by any definition, cross the log and proceed downstream. Here, at the base of two cliffs, are two large pictograph panels. This location is known as *ts'ets'ekw'* which translates into "markings." **Please show respect for these priceless native artifacts by not touching or marking them. The importance of this matter cannot be overstated.** See Pictographs of the Stein, p.32 for more information on the rock paintings.

Returning to the main trail description, the trail now returns next to the river. Just 0.5 km (0.3 mi) past the bottom of the "Devil's Staircase" is a great view of the river coming into a tight turn. After passing through a cedar grove, you will come to a flood channel. Cross a small seasonal creek and resume a parallel direction to the river. Large boulders and logs near a small island are on your right as you once more move next to the Stein. Proceed to cross a small creek and ascend over a boulder field before reaching the teepee campsite, 8.3 km (5.1 mi) from the Trailhead. A food locker, outhouse, numerous tent sites, easy access to the river, and beautiful views are found at this very popular site, which sadly no longer has the landmark teepee that characterized it for many years. In early spring, a waterfall descends lightly from the steep canyon walls on the north side of the river.

JANE MCRAE

Wolf lichen
(Letharia vulpina)

This bright green lichen is found from valley bottom to subalpine in the Stein. Its name comes from Scanadanavia, where it was apparently used as a poison in wolf bait.

Granitic rock's great strength and the wide spacing of joints within it results in very large blocks and boulders—as shown in this view of the lower Stein River.   DAVID THOMPSON

Lions in the Stein?

If you're prone to hiking with your head down while travelling the lower Stein trail during the warm months, you will probably have noticed tiny, conical pits along the trail. These distinctive structures occur wherever there is exposed dry, sandy, and loose soil. They range in diameter from one to six cm and are often found clustered together. What you may not have realized is that at the bottom of each of these pits is a tiny insect, waiting to seize and consume any other insect unfortunate enough to fall in. Each pit is basically a food funnel whose architect is the larva (juvenile) of an ant lion (family Myrmeleontidae, order Neuroptera). Ant lions are wary, and quick to disappear from their pit when disturbed. However, if you were able to catch one, you would see a small (1–7 mm long) sack with relatively large hollow jaws, through which prey juices are sucked. Tiny legs propel the ant lion backwards, resulting in a "rowing" action through the soil. If a small insect (e.g. an ant) falls into the pit, it will probably slide to the bottom and be seized immediately by the ant lion. Or it will attempt to run up the steep sides of the pit, but the walls will crumble and carry it back towards the waiting ant lion. Indeed, the ant lion deliberately encourages these "mini-landslides" by flicking sand particles onto the pit wall ahead of its struggling prey. Ant lions use smaller, more landslide-prone particles for lining their pit walls, and throw the slightly larger sand particles outside of the pit. If you carefully inspect the pit's periphery, you can probably see the larger, ejected sand grains, as well as the shrivelled corpses of the ant lion's recent meals. The size of the pit is a good indication of the ant lion's present size. Ant lion larvae are remarkably resistant to starvation and can survive for weeks without food. Once the ant lion larva has grown big enough, it pupates in the soil, and transforms into a winged adult resembling a damselfly. Adults mate and lay their eggs in the soil, where larvae hatch out to begin life "in the pits." So, think about these tiny, innovative architects dotting the trail along the lower Stein, and tread lightly.

–Ralph Cartar

To continue past the teepee site, cross the flat, dry benchlands for 0.9 km (0.6 mi) and then ascend a small hill. The trail levels off, allowing views of the river below. Teaspoon Creek lies 0.3 km (0.2 mi) beyond the hill. A cathedral-like grove of cedar trees and numerous camping spots make this a popular and enjoyable rest area, especially in the heat of the summer.

You will then move away from the Stein to cross the creek again over another small bridge with a large boulder on the south side. Move beside a side channel and cross two more channels before resuming a parallel route to the river. A small island should be on your right as you come close to the river again. 1.2 km (0.8 mi) past Teaspoon Creek is

ADELBERT BECKMANS

Earl's cabin

The original Earl's cabin was built by Fred Earl, a trapper and prospector, probably related to the Earl family of the Earlscourt Farm, who died while in service overseas in World War I. Fred reportedly took $12,000 in gold from Earl Creek and left a gold cache, which has not been found despite numerous attempts. Today, the outlines of two other structures and a recent reconstruction of the original cabin are all that remain.

Earl's Cabin, which has several suitable camping sites, outhouse and food locker. The clearing here offers opportunities for wildlife observation. You are now 10.7 km (6.7 mi) from the Trailhead.

A few minutes of easy hiking brings you to Earl Creek. Follow the trail up the south bank to a bridge with a railing. Constructed by the Forest Service in 1978, this bridge can be slippery when wet; caution is required, especially if you are part of a group with children. The trail then follows the bank on the north side for 30 m before moving back towards the flats. A clear and flat trail for the next 1.3 km rewards those coming this far.

At this point the trail comes close to the river where rock bluffs extend to the river's edge. This is a magical spot. The pictographs on the rock walls are made even more impressive by the nearby rapids. From here the lower crossing is only 15 minutes away. Caution is needed in crossing a small boulder field immediately after the rock bluffs. At the crossing campsite, elevation 585 m (1950 ft), you will find a food box, outhouse, and plenty of room for tents. Klein's cabin is situated 200–300 m west of the main campsite.

Making Use of All the Parts

As on the coast, the fibrous bark of western red-cedar was an important material [to the Nlaka'pamux]. It was stripped off the trees in large sheets. The thick outer bark was used as roofing for pithouses, and to line earthen pithouse walls. It was also used as temporary flooring, for sitting and kneeling on in canoes, and piled up, as bedding. Crude vessels were made of it for bailing out canoes. The inner bark was shredded and used for making "slow matches." Cedar fibre, and large, flat sheets of pounded cedar bark were found at Thompson burial sites. Sometimes ponchos, cloaks, bodices, and aprons were made from cedar inner bark, which was rubbed, beaten to soften it, then split into strips of desired width.

–Nancy Turner et al, *Thompson Ethnobotany*
Royal BC Museum, 1990, p.96

Klein's Cabin

One of the early trappers from whom we have learned of the Stein is Adam Klein. His landmark cabin, which he constructed in 1953 with the help of his son, reminds us of earlier times. Klein first trapped in the Stein in 1925 at only 18 years of age, having left his home in southern Saskatchewan after an argument with his brother and father. After learning the ways of the woods under Young Easter Hicks, a veteran trapper of the Stein, Klein worked his own traplines for the next 12 years. Klein's two main lines took him west from Stein Lake to Tundra Lake and south into the Rutledge Creek Valley, trapping marten, muskrat and beaver.

9. Lower Crossing to Ponderosa Creek

Attractions: The ecologically rich mid-valley forests; views of valley & canyon walls. **Cautions:** Loose rock on boulder field crossings; parts are frequently flooded in spring. **Access:** North side of lower crossing, 4–6 hours (13.2 km) from the Trailhead. **Season:** Best April to October. **Rating:** Easy to moderate. **Distance and time:** 7.8 km (4.9 mi); 2–4 hours. **Elevation gain:** About 60 m (200 ft). **Map:** 92 I/5.

BC PARKS

Western hemlock
(Tsuga heterophylla)

A common conifer tree of the coast but less frequent in the interior. Identified by its drooping tree tip, small (1–1.5 cm long) needles, and 2 cm long cone.

The Lower Crossing

An endearing landmark for more than 30 years, the lower cable crossing was replaced by a foot bridge in 2001 as part of BC Parks' efforts to upgrade the Stein's recreational infrastructure. While certainly lacking the character of the old cable crossing, which was an adventure for many hikers, this rather substantial suspension bridge should provide many years of use and be able to withstand the ravages of spring floods.

Heading upstream from the lower crossing, the river and the landscape begin to change. The slow, meandering river of the mid-Stein replaces the turbulent waters of the lower valley. Readily apparent is the difference between the water-eroded, V-shaped lower canyon and the glacier-eroded, U-shaped mid-valley as you head west.

The lower crossing.   RUTH TUBBESING

As you continue westward on the trail on the north side of the bridge, you will move along the side of a hill, passing large Douglas fir and boulders that have fallen from the cliff faces above. Rough camping sites are found here (be sure to set up a food rope) Klein's Cabin is soon visible on the far bank.

ANDY MONS

Ponderosa pine
(Pinus ponderosa)

There is no mistaking the "jigsaw puzzle" bark of the Ponderosa pine.

A large "S" bend in the river occurs just past the cabin, 0.4 km (0.3 mi) west of the lower crossing. Called *stl'imin* (approximate pronunciation is "klemmen")—meaning to "ford the river"—this was the site of the first Stein bridge. Built by Urban Hicks, Walter Issac, and Jimmie Johnson in 1942 to give access to the Silver Queen Mine, the bridge was washed out in 1948. A second bridge was built downstream at the site of the present present crossing after World War II. It too suffered a similar fate in 1968. Next, you will pass a boulder field before moving onto the flat next to the river; the surroundings become wetter through this area. The trail continues to be clearly defined as you move along the river bank. Excellent views of steep cliff faces on the opposite side are found here. Approximately 10 minutes upstream from the lower crossing is a good campsite situated on a sandy section next to the river, which includes a food loft, table and crude pit toilet.

Gently rolling, forested benches with several creeks make up the terrain for the next 20–30 minutes. Fickle Creek and West Fickle Creek are first crossed. These creeks are not dependable water sources. Only 0.7 km (0.4 mi) past West Fickle Creek is Shelter Creek (look through the forest to the north and you will see a waterfall cascading through a notch in the steep valley wall), a reliable source with a. small bridge, followed by Waterfall Creek. As you continue through open forest, the trail comes close to both the river and rock bluffs that extend to the river's edge. Abundant horse tail is evident as you move alongside the slow tranquil river. Look for signs of beaver activity here. Roughly 2.0 km west of Waterfall Creek is Lean-to Creek, which has an outhouse, food locker and room for several tents.

In spring this area can be wet as you cross the several channels of the creek. 10–15 minutes, 0.4 km (0.3 mi), more hiking takes you next to a beaver pond. A large scar on the south side of the valley should be visible from here. Continuing westward, move towards the rock slopes and begin the ascent to "Snake Bluffs," approximately 20 m (70 ft) above the flood plains. These bluffs give great views of the valley bottom. Continue along the bluffs by sidehilling and then carefully descending to the valley bottom. You are now 5.3 km (3.3 mi) from the lower crossing and 2.5 km (1.6 mi) from Ponderosa Shelter. The trail then proceeds towards the river, crossing the floodplains and continuing alongside the river.

Camping on the river banks of the mid-valley.   JAN MAZEREEUW

For 0.5 km (0.3 mi) move next to the river bank on a flat, well-defined trail. A second small ascent is needed, taking you 15–20 m above the floodplains. From this vantage point you can see the clusters of black cottonwood that predominate the mid-valley floor. Aspen, birch, Douglas fir, and western red cedar are also found in this wet area. After descending, move along the hillside, crossing a small boulder field. Due to a re-routing of the trail, the shelter is no longer on the main trail. To locate it, look for a clearly defined junction approximately 0.5 km (0.3 mi) past the bottom of the last climb. This junction is in a scrub forest, approximately 200–300 m away from the river; you cannot hear or see the river from the junction. The old trail moves in a downstream direction from the junction towards the river bringing you to the Shelter, only about 100–150 m from the junction. An outhouse and food storge box are located just past the west channel of Ponderosa Creek, which is only a few minutes from the Shelter.

Ponderosa Creek Bridge.   LEO DEGROOT

New Heights of Ignorance

"I tell my guys if they see a spotted owl to shoot it."

–Jack Munro, president of the International Woodworkers of America, commenting on the spotted owl–old growth forest controversy. April 1990

Note: The spotted owl is an endangered species.

The Cottonwood

Dominating the river and stream floodplains of the Stein is the stately northern black cottonwood (*Populus trichocarpa*), a member of the poplar tree family. The cottonwood is dependent on flooding and the deposition of mud since its seeds need a layer of wet mud absent of other plants. This majestic deciduous tree has minimized its energy output for regeneration and greatly enhanced its chances of successful reproduction by matching its seed release with the spring floods. If you hike the Stein's mid-valley in spring, especially from mid-May through June when the river is at its highest, look for the fluffy and sticky buds, which have the distinct odour of balsam.

The cottonwood has adapted to semi-arid environments by using its extensive root system to collect water, and its thick bark and waxy leaves to minimize moisture loss. Come drier times, it is able to survive by restricting fluid flow to its outermost limbs, in essence pruning itself. The cottonwood was important to the Nlaka'pamux. In addition to using it for dugout canoes and smoking fish, they also harvested the sticky buds. The buds were heated and then squeezed to produce a glue for attaching feathers and arrowheads to arrows, and for sealing cracks in canoes.

10. Ponderosa Creek To Cottonwood Creek

Attractions: Vibrant valley bottom floodplains, the ecological heart of the valley. **Cautions:** Bears frequent the mid-valley in spring and fall; carry water; loose footing in places. **Access:** Depart from Ponderosa Shelter, 21.0 km (13.2 mi) from the Trailhead. **Season:** May to October. **Rating:** Easy to moderate. **Distance and time:** 8.3 km (5.2 mi); 2–4 hours. **Elevation gain:** Approximately 150 m (500 ft). **Map:** 92 I/5.

Beaver ponds, large stands of cottonwood, willow thickets, fir, aspen, and abundant birdlife are found on this section of trail. The trail starts immediately west of the shelter. Ponderosa Creek's four channels are soon met, two with small bridges. Caution is needed when travelling through here in spring. 0.4

Spotted owl
(*Strix occidentalis*)

A confirmed resident of the Stein, this endangered species is becoming increasingly rare in the interior forests of BC thanks to habiitat loss.

LEO DEGROOT

Dragonfly
(order Odonata)

Come summer, the wetlands and river banks of the Stein's mid-valley come alive with the frenzied flying of dragonflies. These insects of ancient design—they date back 350 million years—can be easily observed where the trail comes close to the wetlands between the lower crossing and Cottonwood Creek.

km (0.3 mi) past the main channel are rough campsites and a dilapidated log lean-to close to the trail. This is the starting point for those hiking "Victoria Ridge," trip #30.

Large firs and pine with little ground cover predominate the next 1.0 km (0.6 mi). Little effort is required through this part as the trail is clearly marked and flat. Wet flats and swamp are encountered as the trail takes you close to the river. 1.7 km (1.1 mi) west of Ponderosa Shelter is a rough campsite next to the river. Continuing west, wetlands predominate again on your left. Pass through a large section of blowdown before levelling off for easy hiking through flat, open fir forests.

Soon, you will pass another swampy area. Those with patience and time may find this area to be good for wildlife observation. Past the swamp is a group of culturally modified trees, primarily cedar, just past a fallen fir you must pass beneath. 1.1 km (0.7 mi) of clear trail leads to drier terrain with dense forest cover. Exercise caution as you cross the boulders above the swamps further along. A great view of the valley, peaks, and floodplains is found atop the outcrops called "Swamp Bluffs." You are now 4.2 km (2.5 mi) from Cottonwood Creek and 4.1 km (2.5 mi) from Ponderosa Creek.

The trail quickly drops back to the wet flats. A peaceful river

A typical mid-valley setting east of Ponderosa Creek.   LEO DEGROOT

full of colours and life is then encountered as you come alongside the Stein. The next 3.5 km (2.2 mi) of trail is away from the river, offering enjoyable hiking through flat, open forest. Burnt Cabin Creek and a rough campsite with a few tent sites is your next reference point. Large marshes and wetlands occur again on the river side of the trail as you continue through stands of cottonwood, fir, and poplar. The remaining 1.2 km (0.8 mi) take you through more flats and past a boulder-strewn hillside. Move alongside the hillside while crossing over the boulders.

The junction with the Blowdown Pass trail is the next marker. Those wanting access to the Cottonwood Basin will use this well-marked trail. Another 80 m (270 ft) brings you to the Cottonwood campsite on the creek's east bank, which has several tent sites, a food locker and an outhouse. Excellent views of the valley are found in this area. Cottonwood Falls and a viewpoint 150 m above the valley bottom are well worth the effort. To find the falls, proceed upstream for approximately 10 minutes, moving along the creek's east bank. The viewpoint, about 30 minutes from camp, is located on a ridge just east of the falls and can be reached via the Blowdown Pass trail.

LYNN VALLEY
ECOLOGY CENTRE

11. Cottonwood Creek to "Logjam Camp"

Attractions: Mid-valley forest bottoms and their accompanying wildlife; easy hiking; refreshing Scudamore Canyon. **Cautions:** Bear country. **Access:** From Cottonwood Creek camp. **Season:** April to October. **Rating:** Easy. **Distance and time:** To Scudamore Creek, 3.5 km (2.2 mi); 45 minutes–1 hour 30 minutes. To "Logjam Camp," 8.4 km (5.3 mi), 2–3 hours. **Elevation gain:** minimal. **Maps:** 92 I/5 and 92 J/8.

This easy hike takes you through the Stein's flat valley bottom. Scudamore Creek's canyon makes a fine lunch stop or destination on hot summer days.

To cross Cottonwood Creek, you can take the trail to Cottonwood Falls (described above) and use the cable car crossing or go just downstream from the campsite to the bridge (assuming it has survived another spring flood).

The trail is not obvious on the west side of the creek. Proceed upstream parallel to the creek, following the orange markers. Only 0.2 km (0.1 mi) from the crossing, the trail turns west (left), away from the Cottonwood. While not entirely clear, the

American dipper
(Cinclus mexicanus)

A year-round resident of the Stein, the dipper is common along fast-flowing creeks and rivers. It can be seen diving into the water in search of aquatic larvae, snails and tiny fish. Dippers continually do what appears to be partial deep-knee bends. This unusual movement may possibly be some form of communication between mates.

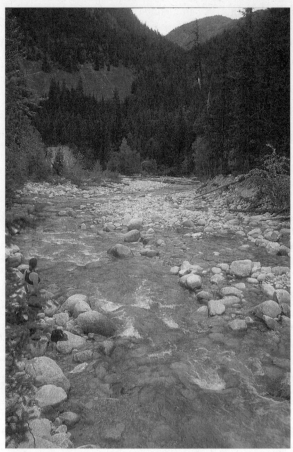

Lower Cottonwood Creek with Kent Falls   LOUISE CHRISTIE
in the background.

trail can be found by looking for trail markers. A flat and clear path soon emerges from the boulders and logs.

Moving westward, away from Cottonwood Creek, the vegetation changes noticeably, as more undergrowth covers the flat forest floors. The Stein River is approximately 1.0 km (0.6 mi) away and will not be rejoined until west of Scudamore Creek. 1.2 km (0.7 mi) past Cottonwood Creek is a small, seasonal stream. Flat and easy trail conditions continue to be the norm for the next 0.6 km (0.4 mi) except for one short ascent and descent.

Just west of the ascent, 2.1 km (1.3 mi) from Cottonwood Creek and 1.4 km (0.8 mi) from Scudamore Creek, is a small dependable stream. Scudamore Creek's roar is soon evident and accompanies you to the cable crossing. Just 0.3 km (0.2 mi) before the crossing is a collapsed trapper's cabin and room for several tents. The cabin was probably occupied between 1920 and 1940, possibly part of an unconfirmed homestead. The trail takes you next to Scudamore Creek and is easily followed. A short climb brings you to "Rowat Crossing," named for Dr. Nona Rowat of Vancouver, who financed the construction of the crossing. You are now 3.5 km (2.2 mi) from Cottonwood Creek.

Scudamore Creek is also known as Battle Creek, in memory of the last battle between the Nlaka'pamux and Lillooet peoples in about 1830. The murder of a Lillooet man by Nlaka'pamux at a potlatch near present day Hope in the 1770s resulted in a series of conflicts between the two nations. The final battle at Scudamore Creek saw a returning group of Nlaka'pamux convincingly beaten by the Lillooet. A peace pact was made in 1850, restoring the normally peaceful relations between them.

A well-defined trail starts at the west end of the cable crossing platform. For 0.5 km (0.3 mi) you wind through blowdown while moving downhill towards the Stein. The trail soon flattens out and enters denser forest. Approximately five minutes more hiking brings you close to the river and at the base of a small hill. Avoid the numerous game trails on the hillside and proceed to move along the side of the hill. You quickly come to an opening in the trees, offering a great view of the slow, meandering river and peaks to the south. The trail becomes more undulating as you move closer to the river.

Another flood plain soon appears on the left side of the trail next to the river. You are now 1.6 km (1.0 mi) from Scudamore Creek. Flood plains, windfall, and cedar groves dominate the rolling terrain for the next 3.3 km (2.0 mi). You will never move further than a few hundred metres from the Stein in this section. "Logjam Camp," which you will discover is appropriately named, is situated next to the river at a large bend in the river, near the confluence of Nesbitt Creek and the Stein. The deep, dark profile of Nesbitt is visible from camp. A food box and toilet are at this popular site which offers good wildlife viewing opportunities. And, be sure to check out the logjam; it is possible to cross to the opposite bank via the logjam, but exercise caution.

No Tree Should Be Without...

Another unseen but vital relationship within forests is found beneath the forest floor. Here the fungi's mycelium—networks of thread-like hyphae—and tree roots work together. The fungi help the tree by extracting moisture and nutrients from the soil, while the tree provides sugar to the fungi. This symbiotic relationship is, in fact, common to all but a few flowering plants. Without this assistance, trees would be small "shrubs," not much larger than a Christmas tree. Fortunately for most trees, dozens of different fungal species are potential partners, ensuring that one fungus is always available. The only evidence we see of this underground work, are the spore laden fruiting bodies (carpophores or mushrooms to most people) by which fungi reproduce. Under the soil, the spores are in the form of truffles, which are distributed on the surface when dug up by rodents, furthering the spread of the fungi.

12. "Logjam Camp" to "Lookout Camp"

NORTHWEST WILDLIFE
PRESERVATION SOCIETY

Cougar
(Felis concolor)

Attractions: Isolation; lush valley bottom. **Cautions:** Flooded sections in spring; frequented by bears—make noise when hiking; uneven terrain through boulder fields. **Access:** From "Logjam Camp." **Season:** May to October. **Rating:** Moderate. **Distance and time:** To "Grizzly Creek," 4.9 km (3.1 mi); 1 hour 15 minutes–2 hours 30 minutes. To "Lookout Camp," 7.6 km (4.9 mi); 2 hours–4 hours. **Elevation gain:** 180 m (600 ft). **Maps:** 92 J/8 and 92 J/1.

This trail offers a great variety of terrain, vegetation, and views. After travelling westwards through forest for approximately 1.0 km (0.6 mi), you rejoin the river. A boulder field must then be crossed. The trail continues next to the river and remains relatively flat. Cross blowdown and then climb a small hill. Look for orange markers when in doubt.

After crossing a boulder field you move back into the forest and have enjoyable hiking. 3.8 km (2.4 mi) from "Logjam Camp," you arrive next to the river having walked through the drier, more open forest of Raven Flats. A steep climb up the hillside follows as you move away from the Stein. The trail

In Search of a Real Male

Cougars, unlike most other mammals, breed year round. Male cougars often follow and fight for the mating role with the desired female. And then they must perform. As with the other large cats, mating is strenuous (the copulation rate is as high as 50–70 times in a 24 hour period!). Why this extreme vigour? Biologists believe that the female assesses the calibre of her potential mate through this high energy process. If she is to produce a large number of healthy young, she requires the finest male available to ensure that her offspring will be strong. A high copulation rate may be part of the criteria she uses in selecting her male partner.

The Deer Mouse

One of the more interesting relationships forest ecologists have discovered is the role of rodents in the regeneration of forests. One such creature you will inevitably meet on an overnight visit to the Stein is the deer mouse. While rodents do hinder the regeneration of a forest by eating many of the tree seeds, they also unknowingly assist the forest. Deer mice and other rodents regularly inoculate the soil by digging up truffles. These under-ground fruiting bodies of fungi have spores that grow new mycelia (the under-ground component of fungi), which are essential to the growth of trees (see No Tree Should Be Without... p.109). While eating a truffle the mouse inevitably drops a few pieces on the ground, making viable spores of fungal inoculum available for the soil. The consumption of the truffle also has delayed benefits. By defecating throughout the forest as they search for food, deer mice spread the still live truffle spores, and companion nitrogen-fixing bacteria and yeast propagules (another fungus) that pass through their intestines after eating truffles. This process is of considerable importance to the fire-regenerated pine and fir forests of the Stein. The heat of a fire often destroys much of the spore inoculum, bacteria and fungi in the soil. By making these valuable tree growth assistants available to the seeds that fall in a recently burned forest, the mice help the process of regeneration.

BC PARKS

Western tanager
(Piranga ludoviciana)

This colourful bird looks like a warbler, but it is not. A common resident of forests, the western tanager is about 15 cm long, all yellow with black wings, white wingbars, and a red head (male). Look for this insect-eating bird in treetops and on the ground.

then levels off with considerable windfall close at hand. Pass through a cedar forest before moving back to the river. "Grizzly Creek" is soon met.

The remaining section of trail to "Lookout Camp" takes you through another pocket of pleasant cedar forest and into the Stein's upper canyon, which was the site of an extensive forest fire in 1996. The trail is in never far from the river as you move upsteam. Some rougher terrain is encountered as you move through windblown trees and small boulders. Not until 1.9 km (1.1 mi) from "Grizzly Creek" does the trail climb considerably, as you move above and away from the Stein. As of October 2007, the last 1.5 km section of trail to "Lookout Camp" is well cleared thanks to BC Parks trail crews. Since this area is still recovering from the 1996 fire, the trail will likely become more overgrown than other parts of the trail (if you don't know what fireweed was before, you will now).

Good views of the canyon and peaks to the west are found after climbing a steep hill that brings you to "Lookout Camp." This vaguely-defined camp has room for a couple of tents and water is a few minutes downhill to the east.

13. "Lookout Camp" to "Avalanche Creek"

Attractions: Scenic upper canyon. **Cautions:** Rough trail with loose footing in places. **Access:** From "Lookout Camp." **Season:** Mid-May to September. **Rating:** Moderate to difficult. **Distance and time:** 2.1 km (1.3 mi); 45 minutes–1 hour, 30 minutes. **Elevation gain:** 150 m (500 ft). **Map:** 92 J/1.

Rougher sections of trail and more demanding terrain are encountered as you leave "Lookout Camp." The next 8.0 km (5.0 mi) of trail to the upper cable crossing are some of the more demanding of the traverse's trail.

Soon after leaving camp you begin to gain elevation and sidehill across rough terrain. Look for orange markers and avoid old game trails. You will continue to move along the northern slopes of the upper canyon, approximately 90 m (300 ft) above the river. The trail then levels off into a dry, fire-scarred forest. Fabulous views of the south ridge's glaciers and peaks to the southwest are visible here. One's pace through here is slowed by the rough terrain and fire debris.

Expect similar terrain and vegetation as you approach "Avalanche Creek." As you get close to the camp, the vegetation opens up and the trail levels off. "Avalanche Creek" is 2 minutes west of camp. Be prepared to be self-sufficient when camping here as there is no food storage or outhouse, although there is a rough stone "toilet" just north of the campsite. The setting is great and there are several suitable tent sites. Rumour has it, from the days of trail construction crews, that boot-chewing rats, underwear-stealing martens and chainsaw-oil-thieving bears prowl this seemingly innocent camp. Recent visits by the author have confirmed that the voracious resident packrats are still present and require that you don't leave anything on the ground, especially packs, boots and clothing—the rats can't get enough salt!

LOUISE CHRISTIE

Yarrow
(Achillea millefolium)

Common in the drier eastern forests of the Stein, this distinctive plant has one or more flat clusters of small whitish flowers, a 20–25 cm tall stem and fern-like green leaves. Reported traditional uses include accelerating blood-clotting when applied to a wound, combating influenza and bladder problems, and serving as an antidote for dysentery

Clearing the Way

Many of the Stein's trails were built under the joint efforts of the Western Canada Wilderness Committee and the Lytton & Mt. Currie Bands. In the 1980s, crews of volunteers cleared windfall, cut trail paths, constructed the cable crossings, marked the trails, and cairned some alpine routes. Leo de Groot, who was involved in almost all of the 1980s trail work, remembers one time in 1986 as being particularly memorable. Having worked continuously for several weeks, Leo, Ken Lay and Gerry Bloomer were the only people left to complete the trail from west of Logjam Camp to Stein Lake. To make an already arduous task worse, they had only ten days and a diminishing stock of food and supplies.

"We eventually had a pattern whereby one person would route-find, another would run the chainsaw and the third would clear the cut deadfall, bushes, etc. off the new trail. Often we had very little route picked out ahead of the chainsaw. At one point, I was flagging the route; Ken was right behind me cutting through the deadfall when I came to a cliff edge. We had to backtrack and decided to give the scout more of a lead!"

At the newly constructed upper cable crossing, they faced an onerous five kilometres of ground with only three days to go. "We ran out of chain oil for the saw so we used the rest of the cooking oil in the saw. Our food stock was also running low; for dinner one night we had plain macaroni. Breakfast consisted of water-fried bannock (doesn't work well) topped with huckleberries. Now without oil for the chainsaw, we had to dip the bar in water every few minutes to cool it down. This worked, but was more time-consuming. Nevertheless, we had the trail to Stein Lake by 1:30 p.m. July 23, a half hour before the helicopter was due in. The helicopter was three hours late, but that didn't matter as it came complete with a warm pizza!"

ANDY MONS

Common Raven
(Corvus corax)

Occasionally seen in the Stein, this much maligned, non-migratory member of the songbird family is large (up to 50 cm in length) and a master of a wide range of sounds. Their amazing intelligence, complex social structure and decidedly colourful personalities make them a joy to watch, especially if you're fortunate enough to catch them playing in updrafts on the edge of a cliff, where they will repeatedly perform twisting somersaults and rolls.

Upper cable crossing.   LOUISE CHRISTIE

14. "Avalanche Creek" To Upper Cable Crossing

Attractions: Great views; enchanting cedar–hemlock forest. **Cautions:** Boulder crossing; flooded sections in spring; pack water. **Access:** From "Avalanche Creek" camp. **Season:** Late May to September. **Rating:** Moderately difficult. **Distance and time:** 6.2 km (3.9 mi); 2 hours 15 minutes–3 hours 30 minutes. **Elevation change:** Descent of approximately 105 m (350 ft). **Map:** 92 J/1.

Your trip through the aftermath of the 1996 fire and above the upper canyon continues for another 3.0 km (1.9 mi) before you begin to descend towards the valley bottom. The first 1.6 km (1.0 mi) from the "Avalanche Creek" camp, elevation 1050 m (3500 ft), is tiring with some elevation gain over rough, rolling terrain covered with Fireweed and young pine trees. Approximately 1.6 km (1.0 mi) from "Avalanche Creek" camp, another camp with a few rough tent sites, food locker, toilet and dependable water supply is found. This is a beautifully situated camp, but beware: The bushy-tailed wood rats here are cunning and ruthless. "Rat Camp" is an appropriate name. You have been warned.

The trail moves up and down as you continue westward. Great views of the peaks and glaciers to the southwest reward you for your efforts. At approximately the 2.8 km (1.8 mi) mark, a boulder field is encountered, which is also as far as the fire burned in 1996. Crossing the boulder field can be a little confusing. The route through this section angles towards the river as you cross the boulder field; just over half way along the field, heading west, the trail/route angles down into the forest below. Look for cairns, orange markers and tape. Those coming from west to east should not encounter the same problems, but keep in mind to angle upwards to the top north-east corner of the boulder field in order to find the "groomed" trail.

Continuing in a southwest direction, the trail drops from about 1050 m (3500 ft) to 945 m (3150 ft) through forested slopes. The going is relatively easy and should present no route-finding problems. Exactly 4.0 km (2.5 mi) past "Avalanche Creek" you will find a log crossing over a stream fed by lakes on the North Stein Ridge far above.

Wetter terrain accompanies the flatter valley bottom trail as you continue in a southwest direction. The trail through here is straight forward as you continue alongside the Stein's north side, travelling through a variety of vegetation and landscapes, including enchanting cedar groves. Camping is possible at the upper cable crossing and just downstream from the crossing is a recommended area right next to the river. Be sure to leave the cable car unsecured after you use it, otherwise you will create significant problems for hikers coming in the opposite direction.

15. Upper Cable Crossing to Stein Lake

Attractions: Ecologically rich coastal hemlock forest; good views. **Cautions:** Bear country; loose footing on some sections; log crossings slippery in wet weather. **Access:** From the south side of the upper cable crossing. **Season:** Late May

BC PARKS

Indian paintbrush
(Castilleja spp.)

15–60 cm high and red in colour. The flowers are of different colours, but are hidden by crimson bracts—similar to leaves—that give Indian paintbrush its distinct appearance.

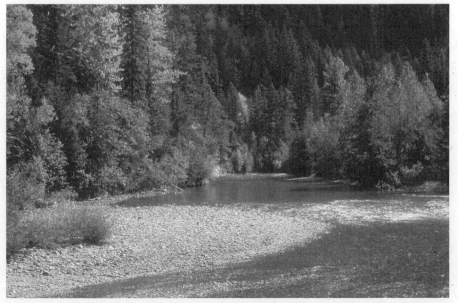

Yet another reason to stop and enjoy the Stein's mid-valley.   LEO DEGROOT

to September. **Rating:** Moderate. **Distance and time:** 4.3 km (2.7 mi); 1 hours, 15 minutes–2 hours. **Elevation gain:** 60 m (200 ft). **Map:** 92 J/1.

With the exception of one or two areas, this section of relatively level trail is clearly visible and presents no problems. The large cedar forests make hiking much more enjoyable on hot summer days. Rolling terrain predominates for the first 2.8 km (1.7 mi).

Having crossed to the south side of the Stein, you soon climb up a hillside covered with western white pine and Douglas fir. Proceed to sidehill, crossing moss-covered boulders as you continue westward passing through one of many cedar groves. A large, solitary boulder is passed 1.2 km (0.8 mi) from the cable crossing. Rolling terrain interspersed with occasional cedar groves predominate for the next 1.6 km (1.0 mi) At this point, you should be at the base of a hill, at the top of which is an excellent view of the North Stein and the main valley to the east. You are now 2.8 km (1.8 mi) from the cable crossing and 1.5 km (0.9 mi) from Stein Lake.

GORDON WHITE

Devil's club
(Oplopanax horridus)

This rather unusual plant's name nicely captures its character. Easily distinguished by its spine-covered stems and large maple-like leaves, Devil's club stands 1–2 m tall and is common in cedar groves and other damp and shady places. This plant will reoccur in your nightmares for years if you are unfortunate enough to bushwhack through it.

Continuing towards Stein Lake, descend from the viewpoint and proceed to sidehill and descend through what can be a confusing hillside. Eventually, you are back to gently rolling terrain. 0.6 km (0.4 mi) from the viewpoint is the main channel of Elton Creek, which has a bridge. More rolling terrain with some uneven footing brings you to the Stein Lake campsite on the lake's south side just east of the logjam. A food box and toilet are found here, but there are few tents sites; in a pinch you can pitch your tent in the helicopter pad clearing above camp.

How is one to live a moral and compassionate existence when one is fully aware of the blood, the horror inherent in life, when one finds darkness not only in one's culture but within oneself? If there is a stage at which an individual life becomes truly adult, it must be when one grasps the irony in its unfolding and accepts responsibility for a life lived in the midst of such paradox. One must live in the middle of contradiction, because if all contradiction were eliminated at once life would collapse. There are simply no answers to some of the great pressing questions. You continue to live them out, making your life a worthy expression of leaning into the light.

–Barry Lopez

LEO DEGROOT

Bear biologists continue to debate why a bear decided to flatten this trail builders' tent in the Stein in the late 1980s. Possibly, the tent offended his architectural sensibilities. Maybe it simply was in his way. Or, perhaps he was curious as to what would happen when he jumped on it. The bottom line: When a bear takes its course of action, stand clear.

Hiking through the pine-fir forests of the Stein.   LEO DEGROOT

Winging It

One of the more populous and yet rarely seen group of mammals in the Stein are bats (order Chiroptera). These often maligned creatures of the night can frequently be found over water bodies in pursuit of flying insects; the logjam at Stein Lake is perhaps the best viewing site, hosting several dozen bats when insects are abundant.

The most distinguishing feature of bats is their wings, which are basically arms with enormously elongated forearms and fingers. The airlift necessary for flight is made possible by a skin which extends out to the finger tips and back past the forearm to the knee or ankle. The bats found in the Stein weigh 5–20 g and have a wingspan ranging from 25–45 cm.

Perhaps the most fascinating attribute of these essentially blind creatures is their navigational system, called echolocation, a process similar to sonar. While flying, a bat emits through its nose or mouth a continuous series of high frequency squeaks—inaudible to the human ear—that reflect off objects and return to the bat's ears. The brain then interprets the information for distance and direction and forms an image of the surroundings.

The bats' hectic midnight feeding frenzies (up to 500 insects an hour!) are an entertaining showcase of their highly effective navigation system and dexterous flight. Moths, beetles, mayflys, and mosquitoes, to name but a few, are normally caught directly in the mouth and less frequently on the wing (literally). Some large insects may be transferred to a tail pouch for later eating. Come autumn, reduced insect populations and colder temperatures mean that some bats such as the silver-haired bat (Lasionycteris noctivagans) migrate south, while others such as the more common little brown bat (Myotis lucifugus) and big brown bat (Eptesicus fuscus) hibernate for the winter. The accumulated fat layers of summer—up to one third of their normal body weight—enable bats to survive until spring while sleeping in confined underground colonies. During hibernation, bats undergo a dramatic transformation as their heart rate slows to about 25 beats per minute (it is normally 400 per minute and over 1000 in flight!) and their temperature cools from 36–41° C to approximately 6° C. This regime appears to serve bats well, since many of them live as long as 30 years.

"Never doubt that a group of thoughtful, committed citizens can change the world; indeed, its the only thing that ever has."

–Margaret Mead

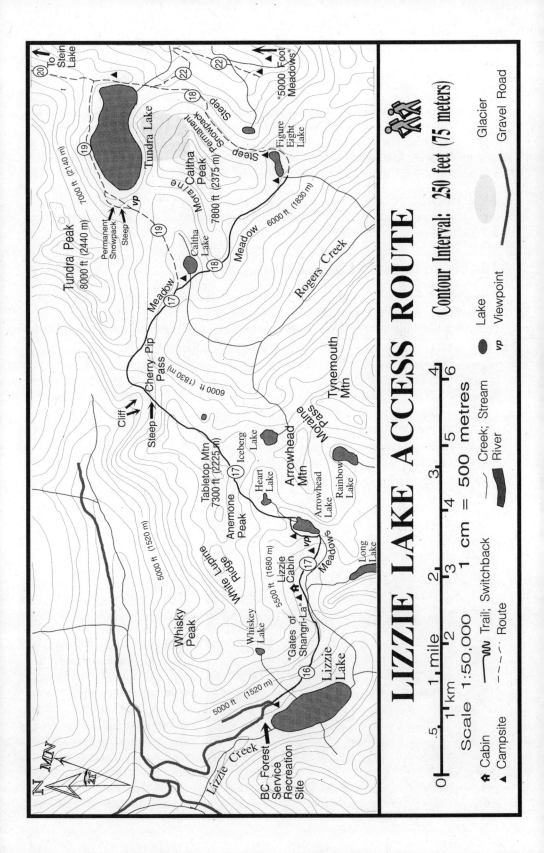

LIZZIE LAKE ACCESS ROUTE

Contour Interval: 250 feet (75 meters)

Scale 1:50,000   1 cm = 500 metres

	Cabin		Creek; Stream
	Campsite	**vvv**	Trail; Switchback
	Lake	---	Route
vp	Viewpoint		River
	Glacier		Gravel Road

LIZZIE LAKE TO STEIN LAKE

The alpine between Lizzie Lake and Stein Lake offers some of the most attractive scenery and hiking to be found in the Stein. The terrain is demanding, however, and the weather can change quickly and be rather wet. Be prepared for all type of conditions when visiting this area. And, now that the Lizzie Creek road is now longer passble by vehicle, you need to allocate more time for hiking the road.

ECOLOGICAL OVERVIEW: The mountainous terrain between Lizzie Lake and Stein Lake is predominantly alpine tundra. This zone is characterized by several types of vegetation cover including heather meadows, sedge marsh and lichens.

16. Lizzie Lake to Lizzie Cabin

Attractions: Enchanting old-growth forest; accessible alpine meadows. **Cautions:** Unpredictable weather; muddy terrain—proper footwear recommended. **Access:** Lizzie Lake. **Season:** June to September. **Rating:** Moderate. **Distance and time:** 3.0 km (1.9 mi); 1 hour 15 minutes–3 hours. **Elevation gain:** 300 m (1000 ft). **Map:** 92 J/1.

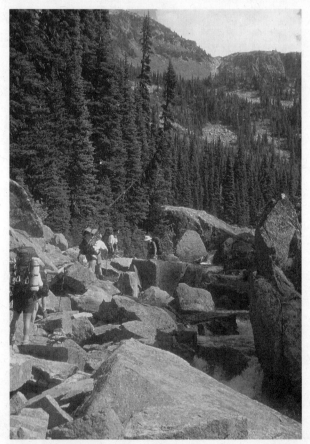

A popular recreation destination, the Lizzie Lake area is now only accessible to those willing to undertake the 12 km (and, elevation gain of 1050 m (3500 ft)) hike from the start of the road, where the roadbed was washed out in October 2003, to Lizzie Lake (see Road Access section). See Matt Gunn's *Scrambles in Southwest BC* and Bruce Fairley's *Climbing & Hiking in Southwestern BC* for information on the peaks in this area. Camping sites are located near the lake's edge.

The hardest part of this trip is finding the start of the trail. The perpetual windfalls (hmmmm, do the adjacent clear-cuts have anything to do with this?) often obscure the trail. From the parking lot move towards the lake along a rough trail and take a left after approximately 90 m (300 ft). Proceed to move through the windfall, avoiding

Passing through the Gates of Shangri-la.   LOUISE CHRISTIE trails on your right for the next 120–180 meters (400–600 ft). At first you will move away from the lakeshore and then travel parallel to it, once past the windfall, approximately 0.6 km (0.4 mi) from the beginning.

The trail begins to climb at this point. Several streams and muddy sections will be crossed as you continue to ascend from the lake at 1305 m (4350 ft) to the cabin at 1590 m (5300 ft). The gain in elevation brings a thinning of vegetation and occasional glimpses of the lake below. Be sure to check out the Englemann spruce through here. About 1.6 km (1.0 mi) (1 hour–1 hour 30 minutes) from the start, the trail levels off at approximately 1590 m (5300 ft) and you soon come to a boulder field within close proximity to the creek. You are now 0.8 km (0.5 mi) from the cabin.

LEO DEGROOT

Moving along, the slopes on your left steepen and meet the rock slopes from the south to form the "Gates of Shangri-la." To many, this point is like a doorway to another world. The remainder of the trip follows alongside the creek's north bank and crosses talus slopes for 0.2 km before entering open forest. Numerous camping sites are found near the cabin, which was built in 1968 by Tom Anderson, G. Richardson, M. Juri, and D. Nickerson and is open to the public—please show respect for the cabin and its belongings.

17. Lizzie Cabin to Caltha Lake

Attractions: Great alpine scenery; accessible peaks. **Cautions:** Volatile weather; poor footing in wet conditions; pronounced fog in poor weather. **Access:** Immediately east of the cabin. **Season**: Mid-July to September. **Rating:** Moderate to difficult. **Distance and time:** To Caltha Lake, 7.2 km (4.5 mi); 4 hours 30 minutes–8 hours. To Tundra Lake, 8.4 km (5.2 mi); 5 hours 30 minutes–10 hours. **Elevation gain:** To base of Tabletop Mtn., about 390 m (1300 ft); to Caltha Lake, 195 m (650 ft); to Tundra Lake, 360 m (1200 ft). **Accumulative elevation change:** To Caltha Lake, 705 m (2350 ft); to Tundra Lake, 870 m (2900 ft). **Map:** 92 J/1.

Those wanting to set foot in the Stein, but not able to go further, will find this trip to be worthwhile. Strong hikers can make the round-trip in a day, but beware, the terrain is demanding and the weather can change quickly.

White-tailed ptarmigan
(Lagopus levcurus)

The white-tailed ptarmigan is a fixture of most alpine areas. Its excellent camouflage is attributable to its spotted brown and white plumage, which turns all white come winter. It is able to sustain itself in the harsh alpine environment by feeding upon insects, flowers, buds, and seeds.

One example of ptarmigans' excellent adaptation to their alpine habitat is how they take advantage of snow's excellent insulative properties by creating temporary snow cave type dwellings. Biologists have found evidence of ptarmigans occupying a snow shelter for several days if conditions are particularly bad topside.

Arrowhead Lake.   LOUISE CHRISTIE

ROYAL BC MUSEUM

Red crossbill finch
(Loxia curvirostra)

Identified by its chunky build, short tail, distinctive black crossed bill (which is used to extract seeds of conifer cones), and absence of white wing bars found on similar pine grosbeak and white-wing crossbill. Adult males are varying shades of red; females are yellowish-grey.

Immediately to the east of the cabin is a well-beaten trail that takes you across the main channel of the creek. Several trails now appear, most of which proceed in a southerly direction towards the small hill south-southeast of the cabin. The trails quickly flatten out as you come onto a meadow-covered basin, which offers suitable campsites in the drier times of August and September. Approximately 10–15 minutes from the cabin, there is a fork in the trail: Take the left fork (the right fork takes you to the Long Lake area) and move in a southeast direction towards the outflow of Arrowhead Lake (1800 m (6000 ft), which is obvious on the rockface to the east-southeast of your present position. This route's first boulder field crossing is required to gain the lake. Caution is necessary here in wet weather. The 210 m (700 ft) gain in elevation to the lake from the cabin offers rewarding views to the west, including Garibaldi Park.

Once across the outflow, continue along the west side of Arrowhead Lake. The trail takes you to the the north end of the lake and past a flat spot east of a rock outcrop, which provides rough camping sites. Rumour has it the packrats at this site are quite assertive so be prepared if camping here.

Advance towards the base of a slope to the northeast that forms the north border of a basin in which Heart Lake rests. The trail is clearly defined and well-marked with cairns. You should now be past the west end of Heart Lake and on a bench above it. To continue, climb more or less straight up in a northerly direction, following cairns, or move along the spine of a ridge lying on a southwest-northeast axis. Either way, you soon come to a well-beaten path continuing in a northeast direction.

A bench below Tabletop Mountain is reached at an elevation of 2010–2040 m (6700–6800 ft). Rogers Creek and Caltha Lake immediately west of the Stein divide are visible from here. The trail continues in a northeast direction along the base of Tabletop, crossing relatively flat, boulder-strewn benches and ridges. The numerous cairns are well-constructed and visible through here and have helped the author more than once in hiking through this area in complete fog.

Soon you begin to drop down to Cherry Pip Pass, 1875 m (6250 ft), situated between the east fork of Lizzie Creek to the north and Rogers Creek to the south. From the pass, move in a north-northeast direction towards the base of Tundra Peak. After climbing approximately 90 m (300 ft) to roughly 1950 m (6500 ft) start heading in an east-southeast direction across the talus slopes of Tundra Peak. Numerous cairns and boulder-hopping here—slow-going for some. Your destination, Caltha Lake, is now 30 minutes–1 hour away. The grassy meadows and boulder fields you are crossing are home to many marmots and pikas.

Eventually you will come onto the rolling meadows north of Caltha Lake. The outflow end of the lake offers the most accommodating camping spots. To actually reach the Stein Divide, continue due east and then northeast to the ridge that forms the western boundary of Tundra Lake. The meadows on this approach are open and the going is easy.

Tundra Peak, directly to the north of Caltha Lake, is a moderate scramble for those wishing to gain a good view of the surrounding areas. Ascend from the southeast via a ridge that lies to the west of Tundra Lake and watch for loose rock. Approaches from the southwest can be frustrating due to the false summit to the southwest of Tundra Peak. Allow a half day for a return trip from Caltha Lake.

ROYAL BC MUSEUM

Mountain huckle-berry/mountain bilberry
(Vaccinium membranaceum)

This densely branched, coarse shrub is found on mountain slopes and in the subalpine. Leaves: 2–5 cm long. The purplish-black berries were harvested by native people both as a food and as a purple dye.

MICHAEL MCINULTY

Black fly
(Simuliu spp., family simuliidae)

What backpacking trip would be complete without a few blood-thirsty insects in constant pursuit? These 2–4 mm long flies, often black in colour, are sometimes encountered in the western reaches of the Stein in June and July.

Busiest around sunset, black flies tend to light on dark-coloured clothing, so choose your wardrobe accordingly.

18. Caltha Lake to Tundra Lake via Figure Eight Lake

Attractions: Great views of alpine and Rogers Creek; remoteness. **Cautions:** Volatile weather; loose and slippery rock. **Access:** From Caltha Lake's west side. **Season:** Mid-July to September. **Rating:** Difficult. **Distance and time:** To Figure Eight, 4.7 km (2.9 mi), 1 hours 30 minutes–3 hours; to Tundra campsite, 12.2 km (7.6 mi), 5–10 hours. **Elevation gain:** 105 m (350 ft). **Accumulative elevation change:** Approximately 405 m (1350 ft). **Map:** 92 J/1.

This trail & route takes you into the Stein watershed via fairly rugged terrain for the average hiker. A shorter, less scenic alternative to this route is to hike along the north shore of Tundra Lake (trip #19). The Figure Eight route is more demanding due to its greater length, requisite route-finding, and steeper terrain, although some find the boulder-hopping on the north side of Tundra Lake to be rather intimidating.

In the 1990s, a rough trail from Caltha Lake to Figure Eight Lake was inadvertently created by the appreciable number of hikers travelling through this area. In general, this trail is easy to follow, but in foggy and/or snowy conditions, you may very well need to travel by compass and altimeter so be prepared.

Figure Eight Lake.   LOUISE CHRISTIE

Cross the outflow at the west end of Caltha Lake and move south towards the west side of the first rock bluff/outcrop and then in a southeast direction across the rock. You then pass a small rock outcrop before coming to level terrain and then past another outcrop to the south. Continue across this undulating terrain in a southwest direction and then proceed south across meadow-covered slopes. You should now be at an elevation of 1890 m (6300 ft). Views of peaks to the south are gained from here.

Maintain your elevation as you continue south and then in a southeast direction across several small ridges. You will need to slowly gain an elevation of 1935 m (6400 ft) as you get closer to the basin in which Figure Eight Lake resides. The final section before Figure Eight Lake is more difficult as you come to a ridge north of the basin of Figure Eight Lake. Here you must move in an east-southeast direction (the target, the divide to the east, is obvious from here). Soon you are at the lake's western outflow where there is suitable terrain for several tents (elevation, 1950 m/6500 ft) The meadow-covered benches above the south side of the lake can also be used for camping, but be careful as this sensitive vegetation is easily damaged.

To continue to the east side of Tundra Lake, move along the south side of Figure Eight Lake to its east end, crossing the permanent snow pack and rock next to the lakeshore. Move up the lake's north side, aiming for Caltha Peak to the north. Your immediate objective is to get above the steeper sections of the south-facing slopes of Caltha Peak you are about to cross, as you begin hiking in a northeast direction. Care is needed as you move to the slope via a rocky ridge. Avoid

LEO DEGROOT

Hoary marmot
(Marmota caligata)

These bushy-tailed alpine residents are close relatives of woodchucks/ground-hogs. They're normally found in colonies in boulder-strewn meadows that provide them with the food they need to fatten up for a long winter hibernation, which lasts from September–October to late April or May. Their only natural predators are grizzlies and golden eagles.

going low since there are steep slopes leading to the tarn below. You want to move along at approximately 2030 m (6700 ft). Several small snowfields may need be crossed as you move across the face towards the ridge that runs east of Caltha Peak. Exercise caution when crossing the snowfields in this area in the morning. If the snow is frozen it makes for treacherous travel and possible fatal results with the cliffs below.

Approximately ⅔–¾ across the face you should be directly underneath a large bluff. Start angling slightly downwards here towards the small ridge to the east. Move through the bushes and trees at the ridge's bottom (avoid going below here since it steepens considerably), and continue moving at your new elevation of approximately 2000 m (6600 ft). You are now 1 hour 30 minutes–2 hours from the south shore of Figure Eight and 1 hour 30 minutes–3 hours from Tundra Lake.

The remaining section can be confusing, requiring careful route-finding. Descend towards the next grouping of trees and bush to an elevation of roughly 1950 m (6500 ft.). You soon come to a small, but recognizable boulder-laden ridge, which lies below the east ridge of Caltha Peak. Tundra Lake should be visible at this point. Numerous streams, glacier-polished bedrock and steep sections of moraine make the next part difficult, especially in wet weather. Continue sidehilling at about 1950 m (6500 ft) in a northwest direction towards a little gully where a creek runs, and then descend gently to the meadows on the southeast side of Tundra Lake, adjacent to the lake's outflow. Suitable campsites are located on the top of the ridge north of the outflow. Cross the outflow—be sure to fill your water containers here—and then make the 90 m (300 ft.) ascent up the ridge to the camping area. Fabulous views and an undeniable sense of isolation rewards those making it to this special place. Water can also be obtained from the snowpack and tarns close by. Your best option for storing food at this site is to bury it in the talus slopes directly below camp.

Note: for those travelling east to west, the above section can be particularly challenging route-finding. After crossing the outflow of Tundra Lake, aim towards the glacier on the north side of Caltha Peak, which will involve scrambling up and across the bedrock benches where the glacier once resided. Your best bet is to gain the slopes just below the bottom of a step rock face on the east ride of Caltha Peak, at an elevation of 1980 m (6600 ft.). Once at the base of the rock face, you are in a position to begin sidehilling towards Figure Eight Lake; be sure to not lose any elevation through this section as there are cliff bands below.

19. Caltha Lake to Tundra Lake via North Shore of Tundra Lake

Attractions: Relatively quick travel between Tundra Lake's east side and Caltha Lake. **Cautions**: Steep snow and meadowed slopes; bouldered lakeshore; loose rock slopes. **Access**: From the ridge west of Tundra Lake, 30 minutes east of Caltha Lake. **Season**: Mid-July to September. **Rating**: Difficult. **Distance and time**: 2.2 km (1.5 mi); 2 hours 30 minutes–4 hours. **Elevation gain**: 105 m (350 ft). **Map**: 92 J/1.

This is the shorter, less scenic route to the east side of Tundra Lake. To begin, gain the ridge west of Tundra Lake. From here, you have two options: **1)** To avoid crossing the relatively steep snowpack below, proceed north up the ridge to 1950 (6500 ft), and then descend to the lake's northwest corner. **2)** Descend across the permanent snowpack and steep meadows to the lake edge. Following the stream down may be worthwhile.

Once at the northwest corner, move along the shoreline. Approximately 0.7 km of boulder hopping brings you to a point where you must ascend 60–90 m (200–300 ft) above the lake in order to avoid a shrub-covered bluff that extends to the waterline. Continue sidehilling at this elevation as you must stay above another smaller vegetated bluff in the north-east corner of the lake. Your elevation should be close to that of the ridge on the lake's east side, 1890 m (6300 ft) Maintain this elevation to the northeast corner of the lake, cross a small creek, and then move south along the ridge to the campsites situated among the small trees.

20. Tundra Lake to Stein Lake

Attractions: Fantastic ridge walk with views of Stein Lake, Stein's south divide, and North Stein. **Cautions:** Loose rock and steep slopes; scarcity of water; exposed in poor weather. **Access:** From east side of Tundra Lake. **Season:** Mid-July to September. **Rating:** Difficult. **Distance and time:** To Puppet Lake, 4.0 km (2.5 mi), 4–6 hours; to Stein Lake, 10.5 km (6.5 mi), 8–11 hours. **Elevation change:** Loss of 885 m (2950 ft). **Accumulative elevation change:** To Stein Lake, 1425 m (4750 ft). **Map:** 92 J/1.

This section of the traverse is demanding for all but the most hardened backpacker. You may want to consider breaking the trip in two, with an overnight stop at Puppet Lake. Be sure to drink and carry plenty of water; on the ridge there is only the permanent snowpack and Puppet Lake.

The "normal" approach is to gain the saddle on the east-west lying ridge (elevation 2010 m/6700 ft) north of the Tundra Lake camp, A fairly well-defined trail takes you in a northerly direction up the ridge directly north of camp. At about 120 m (400 ft) above Tundra camp, you should be close to the small tarn shown on 92 J/1, elevation 2010 m (6700 ft). From here, err on the higher western part of the slope so as to avoid some of the steeper snowfields and rocky slopes. Your immediate goal—the saddle next to the ragged peak above—should be obvious from here. Stock up on water here—this is your last chance for several hours.

You are now 45 minutes–1 hour from the Tundra Campsite; 15–30 minutes of scrambling over loose, steep, rocky slopes brings you to the saddle, elevation 2160 m (7200 ft). Above

Hiking from Tundra Lake to Stein Lake.   JANE MCRAE

the saddle is a jagged peak which has a large snowfield on its north side. At this point, the most engaging scenery of the traverse is before you as you travel this ridgetop.

Alternatively, to avoid the rough, rocky route via the saddle described above and below, you can sidehill to the meadows below the ridge and then easily ascend the ridge just west of Puppet Lake. Start by climbing northward on the same ridge used to approach the saddle. At the tarn shown on 92 J/1 sidehill in a northeast direction, descending to roughly 1800 m (6000 ft). Steep shaley slopes eventually give way to trees and bush, making for slow going. Eventually, the open meadows greet you with easier travel, flower-laden slopes (in season) and easy access to the ridge approximately 210 m (700 ft) above.

Returning to the ridgetop description, drop down and then climb up to the next peak, staying on its south side. The remainder of the ridge to the peak west of Puppet Lake is fairly obvious and relatively gentle. To make the 210 m (700 ft.) descent to Puppet Lake, follow the trail on the ridge west of the lake which takes approximately 20 minutes. Suitable tent sites are found on the outlet next to the lake and food rope trees can be found.

Note: A handful of groups have descended to Stein Lake by moving parallel to Puppet Creek to roughly 0.3 km (0.2 mi) west of Stein Lake. Large sections of deadfall west—northwest of Stein Lake may be avoided by moving due east at approximately 1200 m (4000 ft) to the northwest corner of Stein Lake. From there, move alongside Stein Lake's north shore to the logjam. Count on 5–7 hours travel, one way. Keep in mind that this route requires appreciable bushwhacking, especially in the lower sections, is more difficult than the standard route via the ridge, and is not recommended.

Continuing to Stein Lake via the ridge top, the route is obvious and the open terrain east of Puppet Lake makes for pleasant travel. Moving east of Puppet Lake, follow the trail to the north side of the next peak's western side and once on top, angle into the next dip in a southeast direction staying on the south side. Elton Falls and the Klackarpun Icefield should be visible to the south at this point. Maintain your position on the south-facing meadows at approximately 1920 m (6400 ft) as you move past the third to last peak on the ridge. In this parkland-like terrain, look for orange markers on trees indicating the beginning of the marked section of trail to Stein Lake. You are now at least 1 hour and 15 minutes from the peak west of Puppet Lake and more than 3 hours from Stein Lake.

Maintain an elevation of 1920 m (6400 ft) while sidehilling along these dry slopes. About 0.5 km (20–30 minutes) of travel brings you to within 15 m (50 ft) of the dip between the last two peaks. Scramble up to the gap and then continue sidehilling eastward. Approximately 0.5 km more sidehilling is required to gain a slight shoulder where the trail begins to head downhill at a southeast angle. You will now follow the eastern ridge, being sure not to stray off course to the steep slopes to the south and north. The loose footing and absence of water on this section of trail add to the difficulties. And, keep in mind that despite the best efforts of trail maintenance crews, this section of trail is difficult to maintain so be sure to allow enough time to keep on the the trail while sidehilling, as it is easy to wander off it.

A descent of 750 m (2500 ft) via switchbacks and a seemingly never-ending trail eventually brings you to a point where the trail partially flattens out and the roar of the

Looking westward to Caltha Peak.   LOUISE CHRISTIE

North Stein River is apparent. Soon, the trail swings west-southwest. The Stein River is no more than 300 m away, for those who are severely dehydrated at this point. The remaining 2 km to the cable car below Stein Lake requires 20–30 minutes travel. ATP, the cable car was difficult to operate and is scheduled to be fixed by BC Parks. If you cannot make it work, go upstream to the logjam at the mouth of Stein Lake and cross to the campsite on the south side of the lake, which has a food locker and toilet. Extra tent sites can be found in the helicopter clearing above the camp.

STEIN LAKE AREA

The following routes are for those seeking a rewarding day trip from the Stein Lake or Tundra Lake campsites.

ECOLOGICAL OVERVIEW: The Stein's western subalpine and alpine is by far the wettest region of the watershed, receiving up to 200 cm of precipitation annually. Indicative of this high rainfall and snowfall is the coastal western hemlock zone east of Stein Lake. Mature stands of trees in this zone provide excellent wildlife habitat, especially for grizzly bears.

ROYAL BC MUSEUM

Rufous hummingbird
(Selasphorus rufus)

Look for this dull red (male) bird wherever wild flowers grow, both above and below treeline. Having the fastest metabolism in the bird world, hummingbirds are perpetually on the move in search of flower nectar. And, come fall migration time, they make for an amazing sight in the alpine as they shoot past an unsuspecting hiker or climber at speeds of up to 80 km/hr.

21. Stein Lake to Elton Lake

Attractions: Spectacular views; fabulous alpine. **Cautions:** Carry water; steep slopes in lower sections can be dangerous — be sure to follow the ridge; exposed in poor weather. **Access:** From Stein Lake campsite on south side of lake. **Season:** Mid-June to September. **Rating:** Difficult. **Distance and Time:** 3 km (1.9 mi), 3–5 hours one-way; full-day round trip. **Elevation gain:** 795 m (2650 ft). **Map:** 92 J/1.

Spectacular Elton Lake is perhaps the most picturesque lake in the Stein; its Klackarpun glacier backdrop, size, and solitary island make it both beautiful and unique.

Note: As you climb the lower section of the ridge be sure to take note of several reference points to assist you in the descent — to wander off to the east or west of the ridge can be dangerous.

From the Stein Lake campsite, proceed directly up the slopes behind camp, in a southerly direction. Your first goal is to identify the ridge that runs in a northeast — southwest direction from the northeast end of Stein Lake to west of Elton Lake; Elton Creek runs parallel to this ridge on its east side for the lower half of the ridge. 10–15 minutes of ascent from the lake should bring you to a point where the ridge is evident. At 1380 m (4600 ft) a second ridge to the east joins this ridge. Make note of it so that you take the correct one on the descent.

Continue ascending as you move in a southwest direction through, around, and over bush and rock. At approximately 1500 m (5000 ft), views of the peaks surrounding Elton Lake become more visible. The slope flattens at about 1800 m (6000 ft), at which point you begin to sidehill in a southeast direction towards what is now an identifiable basin that Elton Lake lies within. This final section is straight forward as you hike across the rolling terrain northwest of the lake.

22. Tundra Lake to 5,000 Foot Meadow

Attractions: The ecologically rich meadows west of Stein Lake; isolation. **Cautions:** Grizzly country; volatile weather. **Access:** From Tundra Lake campsite on east side of lake. **Season:** Mid July to September. **Rating:** Moderate. **Distance and Time:** 5.3 km (3.3 mi); half-day one way, full day round-trip. **Elevation change:** Descent of 350 m (1175 ft). **Map:** 92 J/1.

The objective of this trip, an unusual flat meadow surrounded by glaciated mountains, is well worth a visit. From the Tundra Lake campsite, descend to the outflow of Tundra Lake and continue down on the east side of the creek. Heather soon gives way to granite slabs over which the creek cascades to a small pool 75 m (250 ft) below. Cross the boulder field and ascend a grassy gully directly opposite for about 20 m (75 ft). (Do not try to follow the creek down to the meadow; it drops too steeply.) There is excellent camping in the shade of large whitebark pines near several small ponds. From here climb a snow-filled gully to the south, then begin descending in an easterly direction.

Be careful not to descend any gullies on the north side of the ridge towards the creek until you can clearly see the way down into a small heather basin below. The creek cascades into this basin before splitting into two channels to join the stream from the 5000 foot meadow. (The elevation here is actually 5075 feet, 1550 m.) Walk down to the junction of the two streams, then turn right (southwest) and follow the creek back into the meadow. Stay close to the water's edge until entering the meadow by the remains of a beaver dam, then stay along the drier foot of the hillside.

The stream meanders through the meadow with a drop of only 30 m (100 ft) over 1.2 km (0.8 mi). To the south, mountain streams rush from melting glaciers. Hummingbirds are common here, probably because of the varied flower displays. Several small ponds lie 90 m (300 ft) above the meadow floor at its southern end, set among whitebark pines. Camping here is sheltered, but for fresher water you may prefer to camp by the stream to the southeast.

From this point you may either retrace your steps or complete a circuit that offers good views of "Cline" and Skookjim mountains and Stein Lake. To take this circuit, sidehill west from the ponds across a large boulder field to where a cascading creek disappears under the rocks. Hike up along this creek to a bluffy area at 1750 m (5750 ft) and then along the gully on the north side of

BC PARKS

Mayfly nymph (naiad)
(*order Emphemeroptera*)

Found in fast-flowing rocky streams, this 1.5 cm long insect has a green, brown, and transparent body with slim legs and three filaments on the end. It is smaller than the similar damselfly and stonefly larvae.

the slabs (the creek is on the south). This opens out into a cirque with a small lake at 1850 m (6080 ft) which may remain snow-bound until August. The flat ground along the lake outflow, if free of snow, has room for several tents. However, the sun sets very early in this location and cool evenings can be expected, with winds blowing over the divide 150 m (500 ft) above. An alternate camping place is directly above on the divide.

To gain the divide, ascend the 60 m scree gully to the north of the lake into a long draw, usually snow-filled. At the top, pick up the route to Tundra Lake described in trip #18 (p.124). (You can reach the divide near Figure Eight Lake by climbing out of the draw onto the lip of the cirque, then hiking south to the lake.)

Magnificent Elton Lake.   LEO DEGROOT

Looking south to Elton Lake from the ridge above Stein Lake.   DAVID THOMPSON

SIWHE CREEK–CATTLE VALLEY

Rarely visited (and harder to access now that road cannot be driven to its terminus—see Road Access), the subalpine and alpine accessed from Texas Creek's East Fork and the Siwhe Creek trail provides fabulous ridge walks, stunning scenery and relatively dry, open wilderness exploration.

ECOLOGICAL OVERVIEW: The subalpine and alpine of this area is characterized by two biogeoclimatic zones: Engelmann spruce-subalpine fir and alpine tundra. The open parkland of the subalpine zone is easily identified by clumped Englemann spruce and subalpine fir trees interspersed with meadow, grassland, and heath. An excellent example of this is found in upper Cattle Valley. Most of the terrain is alpine tundra, characterized by herbs, lichens, mosses, and dwarf shrubs.

23. East Fork of Texas Creek to "Brimful Lake"

Attractions: Relatively easy access; open ridge walks; panoramic views of Cottonwood basin; clear trail. **Cautions:** Trail muddy and wet in sections; questionable water. **Access:** From East Fork of Texas Creek. **Season:** June to early October. **Rating:** Easy to moderate. **Distance and time:** 6.5 km (4.0 mi); 2–4 hours. **Elevation gain:** 390 m (1300 ft). **Map:** 92 I/5.

Be sure to gain the proper road access for this trail. At the final branch of the East Fork of Texas Creek, 22.3 km (14.0 mi) from the West Side Road turnoff, take the right branch and cross Texas Creek. The trail begins at the end of the road, 0.2–0.3 km past this last junction.

MICHAEL MCINULTY

Dusky shrew
(*Sorex monticolus*)

These primarily nocturnal insectivores are rarely seen, despite their perpetual quest for food. Look for the dusky shrew's small burrows and trails in the snow and amongst the grassy shores of moist areas from valley bottom to alpine.

This unmarked, but visible trail climbs through the forest, crossing several muddy sections with corduroy crossings in the lower section. Ascending from the road at 1710 m (5700 ft) to the pass at 2330 m (7000 ft), you will stay on the East Fork's north slopes. The predominantly subalpine fir forest gives way to meadows and the trail levels out before switchbacking up the boulder-strewn slopes below the pass.

Once you gain the obvious pass, you must be sure to scramble up the slope to your left, as the trail is not obvious at this point. Continue in a southwest direction at an elevation of 2100 m (7000 ft) across the meadows. After approximately 0.8 km (0.5 mi), you will begin moving in southerly direction along the western side of the peak directly north of "Brimful Lake." The rest of the trail is straightforward: Continue around the peak and move in southeast direction once past the peak's southwest ridge. "Brimful Lake" should be visible from here. The final section involves a gradual 75 m descent from the shoulder of the ridge and a ramble across the vast meadows to the west side of the lake, where you will find camping sites, a food locker and toilet. Numerous day hikes are possible from the lake, site of the 1985 and 1987 Stein Festivals.

BC PARKS

Western anemone
(Anemone occidentalis)

Found in subalpine and alpine meadows, western anemone (tow-head baby) has hairy stems, a fluffy seed head, and a white flower with blue on the outside. This early blooming flower stands 15–40 cm in height.

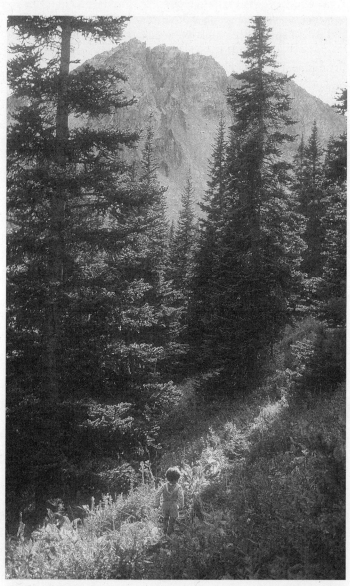

Brimful Lake Trail.   WILDERNESS COMMITTEE

24. East Fork of Texas Creek to Stein Divide

Attractions: Stunning scenery; easy terrain. **Cautions:** Exposed in bad weather; questionable water. **Access:** From East Fork of Texas Creek. **Season:** June to mid-October. **Rating:** Easy to moderate. **Distance and time:** 1.8 km (1.1 mi); 1.5–2.5 hours. **Elevation gain:** to meadows, 300 m (1000 ft). Map: 92 I/5.

Despite the increased access time to get the trailhead (see Road Access), a visit to this unique area is well worth the effort, especially since the number of visitors will be few due to the road being inaccessible by vehicle for the last 12 km. If you enjoy open ridge walks, great scenery and relatively dry alpine, check out this gem of an area. The warmer weather and drier climate of this part of the Stein means that this area is normally accessible earlier in hiking season than the cooler and wetter alpine to the west.

Finding the beginning of the trail is the only hard part of what is otherwise a very enjoyable hike. Be sure to follow the East Fork of Texas Creek to its final branch, 22.3 km from the West Side Road turnoff, and take the left hand road of the final branch for another 0.3 km (The right hand road takes you to the "Brimful Lake" trailhead, trip #23).

At the road's terminus you are in a clearcut normally abundant in fireweed (and later in the year, blueberries!). Locate the trail at the end of the road and follow its switchbacks up towards the southwest corner of the cutblock. Here, at the edge of the forest, is a cascading stream and blue spraypainted markings on the trees. You are approximately 90 m (300 ft) elevation above the road at this point. Past here, the trail becomes more apparent.

The trail continues uphill, moving away from the creek in an easterly direction through a beautiful Englemann spruce and subalpine fir forest carpeted with moss and lichen. After roughly 0.5 km (0.3 mi) of easy hiking, the forest opens up and to your right is a small valley with a moraine on its jagged southern slopes, elevation 1890 m (6300 ft). Move in an east-southeast direction along the north side of the flat boulder field by following a wet trail through the meadows adjacent to the boulders (you can avoid most of the wet trail by crossing over the bottom corner of the talus slope and regaining the trail on the southeast corner of the boulder field).

After five minutes of travel, you begin to climb as the trail gains elevation up the east side of the small valley you are

BC PARKS

Indian hellebore
(Veratrum viride)

Found in shady, moist forests from sea level to alpine, Indian hellebore is a tall (1–1.5 m), unmistakably tropical-like plant with large ribbed leaves. The greenish-yellow flowers bloom between May and August, depending on the location. All parts of hellebore are extremely poisonous.

Devils Lake

Devils Lake is an area of powerful spirits according to Indian legend. Even today, native people blacken their faces when passing by the lake in order to avoid being recognized by the devil who lives in the lake. One story reported by Judge Thomas Meagher of Lillooet tells of the devil, an old woman with long hair, floating around the lake on a log chanting strange songs. Other accounts tell of herds of goat turning into stone, young maidens dying while swimming, and a bull with a dog on its head attempting to swim the lake and disappearing about halfway across.

hiking through. Soon the destination becomes apparent: The dip in the ridge at the south end of the valley. Open meadows and views of the Stein's eastern southern divides reward you upon reaching the top, elevation 2070 m (6950 ft). You are now 1–2 hours from the trailhead and 30 minutes from the Siwhe Creek–Stein divide. Camping is possible in the meadows surrounding the tarn you soon encounter. "Devils Lake," not yet visible, lies in the basin to the east-southeast.

To reach the divide, proceed in a southwest direction across the meadows to what should be a clearly distinguishable ridge that connects the meadows you are leaving with the peaks to the south; Siwhe Mountain—the jagged peak that dominates the surrounding summits—is a valuable reference point. From this divide, elevation 1980 m (6600 ft), you can descend into Cattle Valley or proceed along the ridge to "Earlobe Lake," "Blueberry Hollow" and the Ponderosa Creek drainage, with the option of ridge-walking to Cottonwood Creek's confluence with the Stein River (see trips #28 & #29).

25. Siwhe Creek to Stein Divide

Attractions: Scenic canyon; access to "Devils Lake;" good trail with only a few rough sections. **Cautions:** Loose footing on boulder field crossings; questionable water. **Access:** From West Side Road, 24.1 km (15 mi) north of Lytton ferry. **Season:** June to early October. **Rating:** Moderate. **Distance and time:** To "Devils Lake," roughly 12.5 km (7.8 mi)/ full day; 4–6 hours from lake to Stein divide. **Elevation gain:** 1455 m (4850 ft). **Map:** 92 I/5.

This well-cleared trail is a lengthy and scenic access route to the Siwhe Creek–Cattle Valley alpine normally gained via Texas Creek. The Hance family takes their cattle to (where else?) Cattle Valley via this trail. The lower section of trail crosses the Hance's farm and reserve property; ask permission before parking and crossing their property (from the 24.1 km access point at the sharp switchback on the West Side Road drive 2.5 km north, at which point a rough road leaves the West Side Road and quickly brings you to a gate and house).

Wolf spider
*(Pardosa spp.,
family lycosidae)*

This primarily grey-brown spider (with a 10–15 mm long body) is appropriately named. Being a ground-dwelling spider, it does not construct a web. Rather, it moves across the forest floor or rocky slopes in pursuit of insect prey which it pounces upon. For a spider, this species has good eyesight (several cm) and quick movement, which assists them in their active pursuit of their next meal. Look for females carrying a white egg-case attached to their abdomen. Once the young spiders hatch, they subsist on their yolk-sacs until they go their own way.

Starting at the sharp switchback, enter the fields and move north to the visible Siwhe Creek canyon. Measured distances start at the canyon edge. Move west uphill along the banks of the canyon. After 0.3 km (0.2 mi) of easy ascent a road from the south (left) is met. Continue moving alongside the canyon edge via the road, which is above the remains of a flume (wooden water channel). 0.5 km (0.3 mi) from the start, the road ends and a trail continues left up the bank and crosses a foot bridge.

90 m past the bridge, the beginning of a water channel is encountered. At this point you are well above Siwhe Creek, which can be heard, but not seen. Avoid a trail on your left 0.3 km (0.2 mi) past the beginning of the water channel and continue along the rolling terrain. The next 1.1 km (0.7 mi) has a well-cleared trail that descends into a small gully and eventually to the edge of a clearing. Here is an excellent example of forest succession, as the trees are slowly reclaiming this former field. Good views of Siwhe canyon to the west and the Fraser River to the east are found here.

Cross the field in a westerly direction to the cabin remains in the southwest corner. Regain the trail roughly 50 m into the forest and and resume a roughly parallel route to the water channel. 0.5 km past the cabin is a fork in the trail—go right here. The next 0.8 km (0.5 mi) of trail is easily followed as you continue through scrubby forest before descending to Siwhe Creek. 120 m along the creek is a sturdy bridge that crosses the creek. Avoid this crossing and continue upstream on the south side of the creek. As indicated above, the water from Siwhe Creek is of questionable quality due to the presence of livestock further upstream.

The trail now moves close to Siwhe Creek and begins to ascend more steeply for the next 3.4 km (2.1 mi). 0.5 km (0.3 mi) past the bridge the canyon narrows and then broadens 0.2 km (0.1 mi) further. An easy 0.2 km (0.1 mi) of hiking brings you to a sturdy bridge. Cross here to the north side of the creek. Now sidehill across rocky terrain as the trail continues to ascend. Brief views of the steep canyon walls above are possible through here. After moving alongside the creek, two boulder slopes with loose footing are crossed before entering a small forested section of trail with an island in the creek below. You are now 4.9 km (3.1 mi) from the start of the trail.

The trail then steepens considerably as it switchbacks four times, climbs, and then switchbacks four more times. More boulder slopes closer to the creek are crossed before a side valley to the south becomes visible, elevation 1290 m (4300 ft). The trail has been measured only as far as here. Beyond this point, 6.9 km (4.4 mi) from the start, the trail continues to ascend in the gradually opening valley. Windfall becomes more pronounced and some confusion is possible given the numerous cattle trails through here, especially west and north of "Devils Lake." Rough camping sites are found on the north shore of "Devils Lake," elevation 1695 m (5650 ft) and in the forested area below and east of the lake. The numerous trails through the meadows north of the lake may be confusing when moving between the lake and the Stein Divide to the west. Be sure to allow time for the bushwhacking you'll inevitably encounter. At the divide, you are at the terminus of trip #24 and at the starting point of trips #26–#28.

26. Stein Divide to "Brimful Lake" via "Rainbow Ridge"

Attractions: Good views; open ridge walk. **Caution:** Loose footing in places; exposed in bad weather. **Access**: From Siwhe Creek to Stein divide (terminus of trips #24 & 25). **Season:** Late June to early October. **Rating:** Moderate to difficult. **Distance and time:** 6.0 km (3.8 mi); 4–6 hours. **Elevation gain:** To the northern slopes of the peak east of "Brimful Lake," 165 m (550 ft). **Accumulative elevation change:** 480 m (1600 ft). **Map:** 92 I/5.

This route is an excellent way of gaining views of the alpine and side valleys of the eastern Stein; a 1–2 day round-trip from the East Fork of Texas Creek is recommended. Keep in mind that the slopes along the ridge and above "Brimful Lake" are comprised of loose rock and are moderately steep in places.

Ridge-walking near Brimful Lake.

Start at the terminus of trips #24 & #25 on the Siwhe Creek–Stein Divide, elevation 1980 m (6600 ft), and locate a small peak northwest of the ridge that forms the divide. After a quick 150 m ascent of this peak, proceed in a westerly direction. The route is obvious from here: The ridge lies west and presents no problems. Stay to the south side as you move into the saddle.

Once at the saddle, proceed up the slopes of the next peak, veering to the left of the smooth rock faces. Here you have two options: **1)** Move straight up through the Krummholtz to the top, for a 30 m elevation gain. **2)** Sidehill at 2090 m (6900 ft) on the south slopes of the peak for approximately 300 m. This route is not obvious but is easy, allowing quicker access to the ridge top.

You are now 15–30 minutes from the peak east of "Brimful Lake." Moving southwesterly up the boulder-strewn ridge, fabulous views of the Cottonwood basin to the east will greet you at the top. From this point, elevation 2280 m (7600 ft) and 60 m (200 ft) below and north of the summit, the lake is easily accessed. Sidehill down the west-facing slopes of the peak, angle to the middle of the slopes in a southwest direction, and then in a northwest angle to the lake's northeast corner. Be sure to stay on the northern end of this peak's western slopes — the slopes further to the south are loose and steep. Allow 1 hour–1 hour 30 minutes for the 285 m (950 ft) descent.

27. Stein Divide to "Brimful Lake" via Cattle Valley Headwaters

Attractions: Great scenery; open alpine; accommodating routes. **Cautions:** Exposed in bad weather; loose rock; carry water. **Access:** From Stein divide (terminus of trip #24). **Season:** Late June to early October. **Rating:** Moderate to difficult. **Distance and time:** Roughly 5.0 km (3.3 mi); 4–6 hours. **Elevation gain:** 390 m (1300 ft). **Accumulative elevation change:** 735 m (2450 ft). **Map:** 92 I/5.

This route makes a round-trip from Texas Creek to "Brimful Lake" and back a possibility. It is not as difficult as the "Rainbow Ridge" route and is arguably more scenic.

This route begins on the western slopes of Cattle Valley's upper meadows. It is important to find the correct slope to ascend — the 1:50,000 map (92 I/5) is essential. Locate "Brimful Lake" on the 92 I/5 map. Directly east of the lake is a peak which has a ridge that extends southeast into Cattle Valley. It is this ridge with a pronounced round top on its east side that you must ascend.

At the 1950 m (6500 ft) elevation level on the round summit's north slopes, begin ascending the meadow-covered slopes in a southerly direction, sidehilling rather than climbing straight up. After 60–90 m (200–300 ft) elevation gain you should find the slopes easier to directly ascend. You should now be moving in a westerly direction. About 1 hour from the valley bottom and 285 m (950 ft) higher, you are now atop the round summit. From here, the going is easier. Move in a northwest direction into the dip and ascend the slopes to the west, passing over boulders and bedrock. The 2250 m (7800 ft) peak directly above "Brimful Lake" rewards your efforts with a great 360° view.

To descend to "Brimful Lake," walk directly south to the talus slopes of the ridge connecting the peak you just ascended, dropping 75–90 m (250–300 ft) over a distance of approximately 300 metres. You are now above moderately steep slopes, which contrary to initial appearances, are relatively easy to descend. Move in a northwest direction, aiming for the south end of the lake. Allow 20–40 minutes for the descent.

Shaping the Land

The majestic, jagged peaks and gentle alpine meadows near "Devils Lake" are more than just spectacular scenery. Here one also finds many excellent examples of the glacial erosion processes that have shaped the landscape. During the ice ages, the ice sheet covered all but the highest peaks and crests above about 2600 m. The scouring action of the glaciers enlarged cirques (steep-sided, bowl shaped valley heads) and troughs at the expense of lands between the highest points, giving rise to the distinctive, steep-sided peaks (Stein, Siwhe and Skihist are typical glacial hornes) and ridges (aretes) so prominent today. Ridges and summits below about 2600 m were overridden by ice streams. They are distinguished by their rounded profiles and provide for excellent ridge walks—the ridge north of "Earlobe Lake" being perhaps the best example in this area. Also easily identified are two of the more obvious cirques in the Stein: "Brimful Lake" and "Earlobe Lake." At each of these cirques the strong scouring action of the glacier's head carved out a deep bowl. The melting of the glacier at each of these cirques resulted in the lakes (tarns) found today.

STEIN WILDERNESS ALLIANCE

Mountain goat
(Oreamnos americanus)

This alpine resident is found on steep, rocky terrain, feeding on grasses. Pellet-like droppings and rough game trails on ridge tops are the most common signs of these shy ungulates. Although not as plentiful as in the past due primarily to hunting and habitat impacts, these distant relatives of the chamois of Europe and mountain antelopes of Asia can be spotted in the more remote alpine areas of the Stein.

28. Stein Divide to Upper Ponderosa Creek

Attractions: First class ridge walk; fabulous scenery; isolation; access to Siwhe and Stein Mtns. **Cautions:** Carry water; exposed in poor weather. **Access:** From Stein to Siwhe Creek divide (terminus of trip #25). **Season:** Late June to early October. **Rating:** Moderate to difficult. **Distance and time:** To above "Earlobe Lake," 2.5 km (1.5 mi), 1 hour 30 minutes–3 hours; to Meadow Lake, 12.0 km (7.5 mi), 6–10 hours. **Elevation gain:** To above "Earlobe Lake," 270 m (900 ft); to Meadow Lake, 30 m (100 ft). **Accumulative elevation change:** 1170 m (3900 ft). **Map:** 92 I/5.

This route is suitable for a day-trip to "Earlobe Lake" and persons seeking the remoteness and beauty of the upper Ponderosa Creek basin. Be sure to fill up several water containers before starting this trip, as there is no water until "Earlobe Lake" or further south. Starting at the divide between Cattle Valley and Siwhe Creek (terminus of trips #24 & #25), proceed south-southeast atop the dry, open ridge dividing the two valleys. You will soon reach the first rise within 15–20 minutes of easy hiking. Views of "Devils Lake" and the surrounding peaks are found at the top, a gain of 110–120 m (350–400 ft).

Continuing along, initially gradual slopes give way to steeper terrain as you proceed towards "Earlobe Lake." While there are no problems in route finding or terrain, resist the temptation to avoid the next small ascent by sidehilling on the west side of the final small summit to the northeast of "Earlobe Lake"— the bush and loose footing of the slopes makes for slow travel. You are now 1–2 hours from the start, at an elevation of 2130 m (7100 ft) and are approximately 120 m (400 ft) above the lake. For the most rewarding views, especially of the main Stein valley and Skihist and Petlushkwohap peaks, continue along the ridge, ascending one small peak, dipping slightly, and then ascending a small summit northeast of "Earlobe Lake."

To continue to "Blueberry Hollow" and the rest of the upper Ponderosa Creek basin, descend from the peak in a southwest direction to the base of the summit directly south of Earlobe. From here the sloping, boulder-strewn meadows of "Blueberry Hollow" can be crossed. Camping sites are found by the lake in the northeast corner of this valley. Moving past "Blueberry Hollow," stay on the west side of the valley, sidehilling around the base of the summits to the west.

Approximately 1.5 km (1.0 mi) of travel from above "Earlobe Lake" brings you to the slopes of the peak more or less west of the aforementioned lake on the east side of the hollow. At these slopes, you begin to "round the corner," as the west side of the basin opens up. Descend in a southwest direction through the meadows, which give way to open forest. You are now 3–4 hours from the start and 3–4 hours from Meadow Lake. Your goal is the boulder-laden slope below the jagged peaks to the west. Be sure to fill your water bottles at the stream in the forest before climbing the slopes.

You should now be at the base of the talus slopes, at approximately 1950 m (6500 ft), with the jagged peaks above. These peaks form a distinctive ridge along the western boundary of this valley, clearly identifiable on the 1:50,000 map. Ascend the loose and relatively steep slopes to roughly 2100–2150 m (7000–7200 ft) in a southwest direction. Gain the visible notch in the peaks to the southwest and then proceed along the ridge top, being sure to take the western ridge (an eastern ridge branches off in a southeast direction towards Ponderosa Creek). Atop the summit of this ridge, elevation 2240 m (7400 ft), the goal of this route, Meadow Lake, which lies in the southwest corner of this valley, should be visible. Angle southwest to the saddle between the peak you are on and the summit to the southwest and then descend across the meadows to the lake. Several suitable camping sites are found close to the lake, which is the perfect base for exploring this wonderful wilderness.

ROYAL BC MUSEUM

Clark's nutcracker
(Nucifraga columbiana)

This 30 cm long jay has a grey body, black and white wings, and is most easily distinguished from the grey jay by its long black beak, which is used to tear open whitebark pine cones. It is often found in subalpine forests. In the Stein, the Blowdown Pass area is frequented by many Clark's nutcrackers.

In order to survive on its seasonal food supply of whitebark pine seeds, this vocal subalpine resident collects 10,000s of seeds and stores them in as many as 2500 different caches, normally on south-facing rock ledges and tree trunks up to 15 km from the food source. Months later, they can remember where about 80% of their cache locations are located.

Earlobe Lake.   LEO DEGROOT

29. Upper Ponderosa Creek to Cottonwood Creek

Attractions: Great views & ridge walk. **Cautions:** Carry water; steep slopes with loose footing in places; route-finding required; some bush. **Access:** From terminus of trip #28. **Season:** Late June to early October. **Rating:** Difficult. **Distance and time:** 7.5 km (4.8 mi); 6–10 hours. **Elevation gain:** 240 m (800 ft). **Accumulative elevation change:** 1800 m (6000 ft). **Map:** 92 I/5.

MICHAEL MCINULTY

Whitebark pine
(Pinus albicaulis)

Found from subalpine to timberline, thriving on rocky, exposed terrain. Easily identified by its high elevation habitat, five needled sheath, and thick cones. The seeds found in its cones are the primary food source of the Clark's nutcracker.

Do not travel this ridge walk–bushwhack unless you are experienced in route-finding, in good shape and have a sense of humor. The rewards of the route are near its beginning—unparalleled views of the Stein River and the alpine regions surrounding the watershed. After this high point (literally!), the route becomes an enjoyable ridge walk in parkland terrain before descending through fir and pine forest. Total elevation loss: 1560 m (5200 ft). Ensure that you have enough water for this dry trip.

Start from Meadow Lake at the terminus of trip #28 and proceed directly west to the distinctive meadow-covered face of the summit directly northwest of the lake; this summit is not as jagged and pronounced as those to the south. Now hike in a westerly direction along the ridge. Some parts of this ridge require moving carefully around jagged rock outcrops. Finally at the top, you are 45–90 minutes from the lake and 240 m (800 ft) higher. If this view does not move you....

From this vantage point, the route to Cottonwood Creek and the Stein River should be obvious. The ridge connecting the peak you are on extends west and then southwest into Cottonwood Canyon. Be sure that this route is clear in your mind before continuing. Loose rock and steep slopes demand slower hiking at first; err on the north side. Once into the first dip with trees atop the ridge, well-defined game trails can be followed on the north side of the ridge which then flattens out and opens up offering enjoyable rambling with good views. About 2.3 km past the 2250 m (7500 ft) peak northwest of Meadow Lake and still on relatively open and flat terrain, an important change in the terrain becomes apparent. To continue west is to encounter steep slopes on the eastern side of Cattle Valley Creek. The goal is to connect onto the forested ridge that descends in a southwest direction towards the lower Cottonwood Canyon.

Before dropping onto this forested ridge get a rough target of peak(s) in the distance to use as a reference point. A compass bearing is also worthwhile. The first 0.5 km (0.3 mi) of travel involves a steep descent down shrub, tree and blowdown-laden slopes, interspersed with a myriad of game trails. Below 1500 m (5000 ft) be sure to maintain your reference points so as to continue in a southwest direction (important!) towards the Cottonwood's lower canyon. The final 450 m (1500 ft) of descent is steep in places. Ideally, you will connect with the Blowdown Pass trail, elevation 960 m (3200 ft), which is situated on the east side of Cottonwood Canyon. Once on the trail, you are only 30–60 minutes from Cottonwood camp, elevation 690 m (2300 ft).

BC PARKS

Long-tailed weasel
(Mustela frenata)

This primarily nocturnal weasel is found throughout the valley in pursuit of small mammals and birds. Size: 40 cm long. Summer coat is cinnamon brown above and white below. A consummate rodent hunter (40% of its food supply in summer and the primary source in winter), this all-terrain hunter combines hyper energy levels, intelligence, brawn and boldness to pursue prey—such as snowshoe hares—up to five times its weight.

30. "Victoria Ridge"

Attractions: Ponderosa Creek basin alpine; great views of Stein Valley. **Cautions:** Drink plenty of water before starting and carry as much as you can; demanding hiking requiring solid route-finding skills. **Access:** From Ponderosa Creek, if ascending, or terminus of trip #28 if descending. **Season:** June to October. **Rating:** Difficult. **Distance and time:** Approximately 4 km (2.5 mi); 4–5 hours one way, a **long** day for a round-trip. **Elevation gain:** 1500 m (5000 ft) **Map:** 92 I/5.

This inconspicuous ridge offers both access and exit from the alpine of the Ponderosa Creek drainage. Be prepared for considerable vertical gain, bush, narrow ridges, and dry conditions. (In other words, this is another route for those with a well-developed sense of humor.) Stop frequently to assess the situation and note landmarks for your descent.

Begin on the western side of the four channnels of Ponderosa Creek at a dilapidated log shelter, just off the main trail. Proceed northwards, staying within 150–200 m of the creek for approximately 0.5 km. The terrain quickly steepens as you leave the valley bottom and begin ascending the valley's northern slopes. Your first goal is the lower reaches of the ridge at 1200–1500 m (4000–5000 ft). The 1:50,000 map shows a distinct knob at 1350 m (4500 ft), the stopping point for those wanting views of the valley but who are limited for time. At this point, the sheer-sided canyon of Ponderosa Creek is visible.

Proceed in a northwest direction along this rough ridge, being careful not to venture off to the east or southwest. Old blazes may be found in the denser timber of the narrowing ridge as you continue to climb. Eventually the forest cover thins out as you move above the 1800 m (6000 ft) level. The summit, 2100 m

(7000 ft), is gained by scrambling up the final section of rock. Camping is found at Meadow Lake further northwest along the ridge, less than 1 hour away. Water is most easily obtained by descending north to a small pond. To continue to Cottonwood Creek proceed to the aforementioned lake and then follow trip #29. Cattle Valley and Texas Creek are reached via trip #28.

A Healthy Appetite

One insect that has recently gained recognition for its appetite is the mountain pine beetle (family Scolytidae). This small (5–10 mm long) beetle has dramatic population explosions, resulting in the destruction of large numbers of pine trees. A conflict between two consumers of pine trees—mankind and pine beetles—inevitably ensues.

Weak trees which can be overcome by beetles are usually widely scattered in a healthy forest. Central to the maintenance of healthy pine forests are fires, which normally thin forests, leaving only the strongest trees.

If fires do not occur, however, a portion of the forest may become stagnant. Competition between the trees for nutrients, water and space is intense, and eventually a closed canopy of dense pine trees develops. At this point, the trees are susceptible to insect infestation.

Pine beetles eventually move into the stagnant forest area and begin to proliferate. The outbreak builds slowly and eventually peaks. When the supply of suitable trees diminishes, the beetle population decreases, the dead trees fall and decompose to provide nutrients for future forests, and the forest begins a process of regeneration.

Unfortunately, this beetle has become one of the forest service's and industry's favorite excuses for clear-cutting large tracts of forest. The "salvage logging" operations so common in the Interior are based upon the premise that the timber infested by the pine beetles will create fire hazards and otherwise remove valuable timber from industry's pocket book. This perceived threat is based on an economic point of view.

Insect infestations, like other natural disturbances such as disease and fire, are in fact part of the natural cycle. Left alone, the forests will regenerate naturally. One need look no further than the Stein to see forests that have been regularly exposed to these disturbances. Despite these stresses, the forests are doing just fine without man's intervention.

ROYAL BC MUSEUM

White-crowned sparrow
(*Zonotrichia leucophrys*)

Commonly seen in small flocks in most habitats, feeding on the ground searching for insects and seeds. This 15 cm long sparrow is identified by its black-capped head, which has three stripes across it, and greyish breast.

HERB JOHNSTON

Somewhere in Blueberry Hollow.   LEO DEGROOT

COTTONWOOD BASIN

While somewhat spoiled by a mine access road, the Cottonwood area has plenty of accommodating terrain. Plus, for those wanting a shorter, less demanding one-way traverse through the Stein, Blowdown Pass and the road and trails that connect with it allow you to experience the Stein's alpine, subalpine, mid-valley, and lower canyon in a pleasant four–seven day trip. See the Road Access section for a description of the access to Blowdown Pass.

ECOLOGICAL OVERVIEW: The Cottonwood Creek drainage encompasses three of the Stein's six biogeoclimatic zones. Most hikers will access this area via Blowdown Pass, which is in the alpine tundra. The subalpine zone—Englemann spruce-subalpine fir—lies between the alpine and the lower elevation Interior Douglas fir forests which extend from the valley bottom up Cottonwood Creek to just north of the junction and to an elevation of roughly 1350 m (4500 ft).

31. "Kidney Lakes"

BC PARKS

Meadow vole
(Microtus pennsylvanicus)

Seldom seen, but almost always present in grassy marshes and meadows is this rodent-like creature. The meadow mole is active primarily in the morning and late afternoon feeding on grasses and sedges. Come winter, they live off their stockpile collected during the fall.

Attractions: Accessible alpine lakes. **Cautions:** Slippery terrain when wet. **Access:** From outflow (west) end of "Blowdown Lake." **Season:** Early to mid-June to October. **Rating:** Easy to moderate. **Distance and time:** 1.0 km (0.6 mi); 30 minutes–1 hour. **Elevation gain:** About 30 m (100 ft). **Map:** 92 J/8.

For a short, scenic trip from "Blowdown Lake," this route is worth considering. Move in a southwest direction from the lake's outflow, crossing the meadows which give way to forested slopes and boulder fields adjacent to the ridge you will move along the north side of. Maintain an elevation of 2010 m (6700 ft). You should be close to the prominent northwest pointing extension of the main ridge you are moving alongside. This protrusion, a valuable reference, lies south of "Blowdown Lake" and is visible from the lake.

Talus slopes and boulder fields extend out from the ridge at this point and the forest thickens. Having come around the boulder slopes of the ridge's extension, move in a southerly direction, ascending steepish meadows for an elevation gain of 30 m (100 ft) to the plateau that sits slightly above the small tarns (small alpine lakes). Here at approximately 2040 m (6730 ft) is your destination, several small tarns.

32. North Fork of Scudamore Creek

Attractions: Remote alpine; the scenic North Scudamore; opportunity for numerous day-trips. **Cautions:** A 1:50,000 map is essential; some bushwhacking and loose, rocky slopes; do not attempt in bad weather. **Access:** From outflow (west) end of "Blowdown Lake." **Season:** Late June to late September. **Rating:** Moderate to difficult. **Distance and time:** To lake north of pass, approximately 4.0 km (2.5 mi), 3 hours–4 hours, 30 minutes; to "Cirque Lake," 6.0 km (3.8 mi), 4–6 hours. **Elevation gain:** To pass, about 120 m (400 ft). **Map:** 92 J/8.

Note: In the 1990s, a trail was built in the valley bottom of Blowdown Creek that gives easy access to the "Cirque Lake" area (description below). The following route description for "Cirque Lake" has been retained in this book's 2nd edition so that hikers camping in the Blowdown Pass area can still access this gem of an area. The trail is accessed from close to the recommended parking area, whereas the route is accessed from "Blowdown Lake."

MICHAEL MCINULTY

Red-tailed hawk
(Buteo jamaicensis)

Common in open country, where it can be seen soaring above meadows. Gains prey — primarily rodents — by gliding down in surprise. A red-tailed will pursue other birds, frogs, salamanders, and even fish. The red-pink tail, which is broad in flight, is the best means of identification.

The South Blowdown–North Scudamore area is an intriguing subalpine and alpine mosaic of ridges, tarns, meadows, wildlife, and forests. From the outflow of "Blowdown Lake" proceed in a southwesterly direction through the meadows which give way to forested slopes interspersed with boulders, maintaining an elevation of 2010 m (6700 ft). Your first reference point is the outflow from the "Kidney Lakes" (see previous description for access to the lakes). At this point the bush is thick and the slopes steep. The easiest route of travel is to descend to approximately 1890–1920 m (6300–6400 ft) and then sidehill in a southwest direction, eventually crossing a large boulderfield (talus slope).

Maintain this elevation except for a quick scramble up one or two meadowed slopes. Open forest with numerous wet sections from small creeks draining melting snowpack above are crossed. Approximately 1.0 km (0.6 mi) of sidehilling brings you to gentler slopes rising to a small plateau nestled against the large ridge alongside which you are travelling. Here are several small tarns at 2040 m (6730 ft) and open spaces — a great lunch spot or camping site in drier months. To reach the lake north of the pass requires 15–20 minutes of easy rambling through the meadows.

Pushing on to the not yet visible "Cirque Lake" which lies in the north fork of Scudamore Creek (neither the north Scudamore nor "Cirque Lake" are indicated on the 92 J/8 topo map), the pass requires a climb of 90 m (300 ft) from the lake north of the pass to the pass proper at 2025 m (6750 ft). Your objective should now be visible to the southwest. To descend to "Cirque Lake," 30 minutes–1 hour away, go to the right of the vegetation-free gully (shown on the 1:50,000 map) and descend through a vegetated gully, bolstered with solid footing. Descend to 1950 m (6500 ft) and then cross the meadows to the lake. This section can be wet with many streams draining the snowpack until late in the season. At the lake there are several suitable dry campsites. Numerous day-trips are possible from here.

Trail to Cirque Lake

Be sure to closely follow the Road Access description for the Blowdown Creek Logging Road so that you have the correct starting point for this recently constructed trail, which takes roughly 2–3 hours and is easy to moderate in difficulty. The trail starts on the west side of Blowdown Creek and on the south side of a large clearing on the road; in the fall of 2007 the trailhead was marked by flagging tape. The trail initially goes uphill in a southwest direction and then takes you in a southeasterly direction for the next 1–1.5 hours.

A flat section of grassy meadows is soon encountered, followed by a lightly forested section, as you travel this well-defined trail along the west side of Blowdown Creek. 15–30 minutes from the trailhead, you encounter a talus slope that can be slippery when wet. After this tedious section, the trail then winds for approximately 30–45 minutes through a pleasant forest interspersed with many small creeks. Approximately 1–1.5 hours from the start, you will cross a small bridge spanning one of the larger creeks in this drainage. At this point, the trail begins to take you in a southwesterly direction towards the pass.

If visibility is good, you should soon see that you are in the southwestern branch of Blowdown Creek. The trail begins a gentle ascent then more steeply for last 15–20 minutes before levelling off in beautiful plateau area with tarns and views. You are now close to the pass leading to "Cirque Lake" in the North Fork of Scudamore Creek. Follow the above described route to "Cirque Lake" if in doubt as to how to proceed up and over the pass. This plateau is also the starting point for accessing the ridge walk to the Silver Queen Mine area (trip #33).

33. Silver Queen Mine Ridge Walk

Attractions: Fabulous ridge walk over relatively easy terrain. **Cautions:** Drink and carry lots of water; rough terrain with loose footing places; hike this route in the longer days of July to August. **Access:** From lakes 0.8–1.0 km east of the pass between Blowdown Creek drainage and North Scudamore Creek (see trip #32). **Season:** July to late September. **Rating:** Moderately difficult. **Distance and time:** About 11.5 km (7.0 mi.); full day. **Elevation gain:** to meadows, 165 m (550 ft). **Map:** 92 J/8.

The starting point for this trip is in Blowdown Creek's southernmost branch, where the "Kidney Lakes" and North Scudamore routes are found. From the tarns, which are approximately 0.8 km–1.0 km east of the pass between Blowdown and Scudamore and at elevation of between 2040 m (6800 ft) and 2190 m (7300 ft), head south over this distinctly benched area with several broad flat sections. Your first goal is to climb to the col between the valley you are presently in and the South Fork of Cottonwood—it should be visible to the east-southeast of your position. This route is relatively straightforward as you work around the lakes; be sure to drink a lot of water here and top up your water bottles.

Once at the col, descend to the valley bottom, which has some very pleasant meadows that make for excellent camping. From the meadows, head down the drainage for approximately 1.5 km and keep on the south side of the creek. Your goal is to find more gentle talus slopes that allow access to the ridge; those further up the valley are steep and lead to a section of ridgetop with slabs and bush that is best avoided. To reach the ridge you must hike up through the forest and then open slopes for an elevation gain of roughly 300 m (1000 ft).

Once on the ridge, the route is obvious. At 1980 m (6600 ft) the ridge broadens, followed by a gradual elevation gain of 150 m (500 ft) over approximately 2 km to the 2145 m (7150 ft) peak above the uppermost lake of the Silver Queen Mine area. See the Silver Queen Mine to Stein River route description if in doubt as to how to descend to the lake below; at this point, however, thirst may overtake all rational thought processes.

34. Summit South of Blowdown Pass

Attractions: Most accessible views of main Stein Valley from Blowdown Pass. **Cautions:** Exposed in poor weather; loose footing in places. **Access:** From final bend in road west of Blowdown Pass. **Season:** Mid-June to late September. **Rating:** Moderate. **Distance and time:** 1.2 km (0.8 mi); 2 hours round-trip to viewpoint, 3.0 km (1.9 mi), 4 hours round-trip via Kidney Lake return. **Elevation gain:** 270 m (900 ft). **Map:** 92 J/8.

Diversity of Life

Biological diversity is the wealth of life on earth, the millions of plants, animals, and micro-organisms, the genes they contain, and the intricate ecosystems they help build into the living environment. Biological diversity is the end result of four billion years of evolution …. Estimates of the global number of species range from five million to thirty million. Of these, only 1.4 million species have been given names. The unknown diversity of the world is an unexplored frontier…. According to some sources, 15–20% of all species on earth may disappear by the year 2000 if human consumption and destruction patterns don't change. This is an extinction rate 1000 times greater than the natural rate.

–A Statement by WWF (World Wide Fund For Nature)
The Importance of Biological Diversity, pp.3–4.

From the final bend in the road west of Blowdown Pass move south up a broad gully to an open snow/boulder field. Excellent views are soon gained from the top of this ridge, with the best vantage point being at the 2400 m (8000 ft) peak. Those wanting a half-day loop trip will continue along the ridge to the steep slope above "Kidney Lakes" and descend to the Lakes. From the "Kidney Lakes," "Blowdown Lake" is only 30 minutes northeast (see Trip #31 if the route is unclear).

35. Gott Peak

Attractions: Views, views, views! **Cautions:** Exposed in poor weather. **Access:** From Blowdown Pass. **Season:** Early June to September. **Rating:** Moderate. **Distance and time:** Straight up from the pass, 2 km (1.3 mi), 2–3 hours round trip; via the ridge, 4 km (2.5 mi), 3–5 hours round trip. **Elevation gain:** 360 m (1200 ft). **Map:** 92 J/8.

An obvious destination for anyone visiting this area is Gott Peak. On a clear day the views are incomparable. Two basic routes are possible to gain Gott itself: **1)** From the pass, ascend directly north and then northwest up a broad open slope to the first summit at 2415 m (8050 ft). From here drop into the dip between the two peaks and scramble up the southeast ridge of 2545 m Gott Peak, with fine views all the way. **2)** For an enjoyable half-day trip that gives you more views of the intriguing main Cottonwood Valley, proceed over the pass and along the road for approximately 1.5 km east to a point below the ridge where a discernable saddle (dip) 60 m (200 ft) above is evident—it is easily distinguished on the 1:50,000 map.

A quick scramble up these marmot-mad meadows brings you to the ridgetop and fabulous views of the Cottonwood. This can be the starting point for trips to the "Three Summits," "Marmot Gardens" and Gott Peak. To attain Gott, proceed in a westerly direction, erring on the south side of the barren, open ridge. You soon come to a ridge

Avalanche Lilies

One of the Stein's most colourful alpine floral displays is found on Gott Peak's southern slopes. Soon after snow melt, usually mid to late June, a sea of yellow encompasses these slopes as the early blooming avalanche lilies lead the way of the alpine flowers. Besides providing colour to the alpine, avalanche lilies are also an important food source for grizzly bears. In any remote avalanche path or slope that is home to avalanche lilies and sweetvetch, to name but two, you may find a grizzly digging up the roots of the flowers, which are an essential carbohydrate source for these bruins of the higher country.

where to continue means cutting across the slopes in a westerly direction. Continue gaining elevation towards your immediate target—the peak directly west of you, 360 m (1200 ft) above the saddle. Once at this unnamed peak, Gott Peak is easily gained by descending to the dip between the two peaks and scrambling up Gott's southeast slopes. Descend via the meadow-covered southwest slopes.

36. "Three Summits"

Attractions: Relatively easy access; good views of the Cottonwood Basin. **Cautions:** Carry water; exposed in poor weather; cornices on north side of ridge. **Access:** From Blowdown Pass. **Season:** Late June through September **Distance, time, and elevation gain:** "Summit 1:" Moderate hike. 5.3 km (3.3 mi); 2–3 hours; 240 m (800 ft). "Summit 2:" Moderate hike. 6.0 km (3.8 mi); 2 hours 30 minutes–3 hours 15 minutes; 300 m (1000 ft). "Summit 3:" Strenuous round trip. 14.8 km (9.2 mi). 480 m (1600 ft). **Map:** 92 J/8.

This high ridge gives closer views of the Cotttonwood area of the Stein that can be obtained from other trips in this section. You do not have to hike all the way to "Summit 3," and in fact the full trip may be too strenuous in hot weather for many day hikers. Backpackers may aim for a small lake south of Summit 3 and use it as a camping base for more leisurely explorations. Fill your water bottles before ascending.

From Blowdown Pass move eastward down the road for 1.5 km (1.0 mi) and then sidehill northeastward to the distinct saddle which lies above the road at 2100 m (7000 ft). This landmark is obvious on the 1:50,000 map. Take special note of the cornices along the ridge. Moving eastward, the ridge is very broad at first, but it narrows above steep scree slopes. Ascend "Summit 1" directly; do not sidehill to the south. The walk to "Summit 2" takes about a half hour. Glimpses of the South Fork of the Cottonwood and of the road can be obtained from rocky outcrops. (The hanging valley to the northwest is "Marmot Gardens," trip #37.) The view to the south and east is dominated by the mountains on the Stein/Mehatl and Stein/Kwoiek divides. In the distance to the east is Mount Lytton and the lower canyon.

BC PARKS

Avalanche lily
(*Erythronium grandiflorum*)

The ascent of "Summit 3" presents no technical difficulty but means a loss 120 m (400 ft) in elevation, followed by an ascent of 180 m (600 ft). Because of a lingering snow patch on the steep slope to the northeast, you should make the first 90

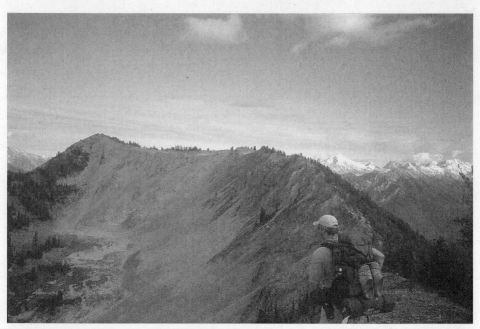

Looking east on the ridge west of Silver Queen Mine.   GORDON WHITE

m (300 ft) of descent to the southeast; then head north and northeast to "Summit 3." For most people, "Summit 3" will be the turnabout point. Only experienced mountaineers should continue, for ahead lies a narrow ridge of unstable, rotten rock. To camp by the small pond at 1995 m (6650 ft) you must descend 180 m (600 ft) from the ridge between "Summits 2 and 3." Do not attempt to descend to the road from this pond; there are cliffs and dangerous slopes below.

37. "Marmot Gardens"

Attractions: Numerous exploration opportunities; accessible, but rarely visited. **Cautions**: Rough terrain in places; careful of cornices on ridge at start of trip; bear country — exercise caution. **Access:** The ridge west of "Summit 1" (see above description). **Season:** Mid-June to late September. **Rating:** Difficult day trip, moderate overnight backpack. **Distance and time:** 8.0 km (5.0 mi); 4–5 hours one way, full day return. **Elevation gain:** To ridge, 120 m (400 ft); to "Marmot Gardens" 400 m (1300 ft) **Map:** 92 J/8.

"Marmot Gardens," a large hanging valley, lies north of "Summit 1" and is accessed via the north Cottonwood Creek valley. Your starting point is the ridge just west of "Summit 1" (see trip #36), where the scree slope is less steep (on the 1:50,000 map these slopes' contour lines are distinctly further apart than the rest of this ridge's north slopes). Proceed to descend in a northeast and then northerly direction down the slope. "Marmot Gardens" is now due north of your present position and is attained by crossing the valley and ascending to the lower meadows.

38. Blowdown Pass to Cottonwood Junction

Attractions: Fine panoramas; accessible alpine; the enchanting North and South Cottonwood Creeks. **Cautions:** Snow storms not uncommon in the alpine in the summer months; wet forest sections. **Access:** From Blowdown Pass. **Season:** Mid-June to late September. **Rating:** Easy–moderate. **Distance and time:** To Silver Queen turnoff, 5.4 km (3.3 mi), 1 hour 30 minutes–2 hours; to Junction: 13.5 km (8.4 mile), 4 hours. **Elevation change:** Descent of 1170 m (3900 ft) **Maps:** 92 J/8 & 92 I/5.

From Blowdown Pass many different areas of the Stein can be accessed. This route follows the mining exploration road into the South Fork of Cottonwood Creek and ultimately to the junction of the Cottonwood branches. You will descend from the pass at 2145 m (7150 ft) to 1460 m (4800 ft) at the mine turnoff. Take this route when accessing the Silver Queen Mine area. Route-finding is not a concern since the road is clearly visible. Just below the pass on the east side are vast meadows with fine camping in the southwest corner close to the base of the ridge to the west. Continuing along, in dry conditions a shorter route can be gained by dropping from the road you are on to the old road which cuts across the meadows, intersecting the more recently constructed road 2.8 km (1.8 mile) further down.

From the pass, follow the road which lies on the hillside above the forementioned meadows. Past here the road begins to curve and switchback. Roughly 0.3 km (0.2 mi) below the intersection between the old and new roads, a creek crosses the road. The adjacent meadows here offer many fine camping spots. You are now 3.2 km (2.0 mi) from the pass and at an elevation of 1860 m (6200 ft).

The remainder of the road to the mine turnoff is punctuated with meadows above and below the road, avalanche paths, and fine views. Several streams cross the road making for wet travel in the early summer. 8.6 km (5.4 mi), 1–2 hours, from the pass is a bridge that crosses the Cottonwood, leading to the Silver Queen Mine diggings. Rough camping sites are situated on the north side of the creek. To continue to Silver Queen Mine, see trip #39.

The Pika

The pika is a model of cold weather adaptation. Living in the cold subalpine and alpine weather, this relative of the hare and rabbit (thus, the nickname, "rock rabbit") has a small body (averaging 15 cm in length), round ears and short legs and tail. This body configuration serves to minimize heat loss by exposing the least amount of surface to the cold. Also, a thick fur insulates the pika from head to toe including the inside of the ears and the bottom of the feet so that frost and sharp rocks are not a problem. Plus, the pika's body temperature is 2–3° C higher than other small mammals. As a result, this cold winter body is so efficient that it cannot withstand temperatures above 28° C for more than a couple of hours. Hence, on hot summer days you will find pikas inside their cool rock dwellings, escaping the heat outside.

0.5 km (0.3 mi) east of the Silver Queen Mine turnoff, the road descends to the creek and proceeds up the south side. At this point look for a well-marked and cleared trail. The going is slower as you move through flowered meadows and bush. The remainder of the distance to the junction is straightforward as you follow the trail above the creek, never varying more than a few hundred metres distance from it. The descent is gradual until reaching the slopes above the confluence of the north and south forks of Cottonwood Creek, where you descend about 120 m (400 ft), passing an old trapper's cabin only 0.3 km (0.2 mi) from the creek crossing. Once on the banks of the main creek move downstream approximately 100 m to the crossing—a large log with a rope railing. A beautifully situated camp with a food cache and rough tent sites is found here, elevation 1065 m (3550 ft). Check out the spruce here—there are some big ones. To continue the trek to the Stein River and Cottonwood Creek camp see trip #41.

39. South Cottonwood Creek to Silver Queen Mine

LOUISE CHRISTIE

Sky-pilot
(Phacelia sericea)

Often found in dry, rocky, open terrain in the alpine and subalpine, this 30 cm tall perennial's distinctive purple to dark-blue, bell-shaped flowers have long orange or yellow stamens that give it a "fuzzy" appearance.

Attractions: Open, parkland covered ridges; excellent views of the Stein. **Cautions:** Carry water when climbing in this dry area. **Access:** From the South Fork of Cottonwood Creek, 5.4 km (3.3 mi) east of Blowdown Pass on the mining exploration road. **Season:** Late June to September. **Rating:** Moderate. **Distance and time:** 5.5 km (3.4 mi); 1 hour 30 minute–2 hours 30 minutes to the upperlake. **Elevation gain:** To the upper lake, 390 m (1300 ft). **Map:** 92 J/8.

For a great ridge walk and access to the tiring but rewarding "Angel's Walk" (see trip #40), take this route. While the road has damaged the area considerably, it does provide relatively easy access to the alpine. You must wade across the south fork of Cottonwood Creek as the bridge is no longer usable.Fill your water bottles here. The road soon switchbacks. After the third switchback a road which accesses diggings on the west side of the mine area intersects on the right. Continue straight ahead. A steady climb for another 20–45 minutes brings you to a basin at 1770 m (5900 ft) in which resides a boarded up mine shaft, mine tailings, etc.—all the ugly stuff of an old mine.

To continue to the uppermost lake, proceed along the road you were travelling following as it curves around to the east, passing mining debris and switchbacks three times. Just past the first switchback, a road intersects from the left followed by a levelling off of the road and another road on your left. Past this road only 200–300 m are several more roads intersecting the main road. You should be able to see a lake with several adjacent buildings down below and to the east.

Continuing forward, proceed to a basin with a meadow-strewn ridge forming a backdrop and a lake in the basin's western half. A forest is on the northern fringes of the basin. The road continues to the uppermost workings in the southeast corner of the basin. Small caves are visible above the road's terminus. You are now at an enchanting spot which makes an excellent base camp for exploring this area. On the northwest corner of the basin, just into the woods, is a suitable camping site. In drier months, fine camping is found on a small flat meadow, 45 m (150 ft) above the road's terminus. See the next trip description (#40) to continue beyond here.

Golden eagle
(Aquila chrysaetos)

A resident of high mountain ridges and open tundra, the large Golden eagle (wingspan up to 2 m) can be seen soaring over its range without rest for several hours. Favourite snacks: Marmots, snowshoe hares, ptarmigan, jays, and crows. Look for these majestic birds gliding over the meadows near Blowdown pass.

40. Silver Queen Mine to Stein River

Attractions: Fabulous views of North Scudamore, main Stein. **Cautions:** Steep slopes with loose footing and abundant windfall; carry lots of water—fill up at the upper lake; exposed in poor weather. **Access:** From upper lake in Silver Queen Mine area (see previous description). **Season:** Mid-June to late September. **Rating:** Difficult. **Distance and time:** 10.6 km (6.6 mi), full day. **Elevation change:** Descent of 1450 m (4800 ft) **Maps:** 92 J/8 and 92 I/5.

Appropriately titled the "Angel's Walk" (mere mortals need muscular thighs and healthy knees) by the late Father Damasus, a contributor to *Exploring the Stein River Valley*, this is one of the

"I hope and pray that this area will be reserved ...for people who will treat it gently and share it with others. A hundred years from now I can imagine a doctor prescribing a trip through the Stein for one who needs to regain a basic rhythm of life and a faith in human nature too. The Stein Valley would be a living testimony to the truth that one generation of this province considered the needs of the next. They would find to their joy one resource of our province that cannot be renewed or restored — the beauty of this land as it came from the hand of God."

–Father Damasus

Varied thrush
(Exoreus naevius)

Similar in size, shape and appearance to the much more common robin, the Varied thrush is distinguished by its orange-coloured breast, which has a dark band across it, an orange eye-strip and orange bars on the wings. It is most commonly found in forests, especially on the forest floor where it searches for insects, worms, fruits, and seeds.

more scenic routes in the entire watershed. It is also demanding. Do not travel this knee-burner unless you are experienced in route-finding. Starting at the highest lake in the Silver Queen Mine area (see the end of trip #39), proceed to the southeast corner of the basin you are in and ascend the slopes near the end of the road in a southeast direction. A flat area is quickly reached — a fine camping spot once the ground has dried from the winter snowpack. Continue in a southeast direction up the next slopes, which give way to a southwest-northeast lying ridge offering great views of Stein and Siwhe Mountains to the east, the "Three Summits" and Gott Peak to the northwest.

You must now move in a southwest direction up the ridge to the 2130 m (7150 ft) peak south of the lake. The route along this ridge top is easily followed and has good footing. Approximately 1 hour from the lake, you are now on top of the peak. Views of the North Scudamore and south ridge of the Stein are gained from here. For those making a day-trip from Blowdown Pass, this may be your destination. If based near the uppermost lake, you may want to ramble westward along the open ridge top. Be sure to take note of the terrain here — it is classic parkland landscape that is found on warm, dry, and steep southern slopes; whitebark pine and subalpine fir trees predominate interspersed with meadow, heath, and grassland.

To begin the "Angel's Walk" proper, move due south and then east along the distinct ridge top. Your first destination is the small summit east-southeast of the 2145 m (7150 ft) starting point, roughly 1 km distant. Overall, err on the south side of this ridge. 45 minutes–1 hour travel from the 2130 m (7150 ft) peak, this small peak, elevation 2100 m (7000 ft), is the meeting point of several ridges. Continuing along, move directly east into the small dip west of the next small peak, losing 60 m (200 ft), and then southeast along the ridge top to a small, distinctly round-topped summit, elevation 2010 m (6700 ft). Views of the main Stein valley become more frequent now.

Once atop this small rounded peak the route should be obvious as you want to continue in a southeast direction to the next peak at 1980 m (6600 ft). The easiest route is to stay close to the east side of the ridge top since it is more open and has rough game trails. Atop this broad ridge, you are at an important junction. The ridge splits here with one arm extending southwest towards the Scudamore basin, another in a northeast direction into Cottonwood Canyon, and the other (the one you want to take) dropping in a southeast direction towards Cottonwood Creek and the Stein.

From the 1980 m (6600 ft) peak, descend in an easterly direction about 0.5 km to where the southeast tending ridge is apparent and then proceed in a southeast direction along this ridge. Now the route-finding becomes more difficult as you enter into the western pine, subalpine fir and Engelmann spruce forest. Continuing in a southeast direction (Kent Lake and Creek which lie between Petlushkwohap and Skihist Mountains to the south are your best reference point) stay on the west side of the vegetated slopes up to the ridge top which is apparent with the drops to east and west. Eventually the ridge flattens out before continuing a gradual descent and then climb of 5–10 minutes to the final peak at an elevation of 1680 m (5600 ft).

Now move along the eastward-pointing ridge (well-defined on the map) dropping about 300 m (1000 ft) to the 1350 m (4500 ft) contour. From here move in a southeast direction being sure to avoid moving easterly into the Cottonwood Canyon. Prolific windfall and loose footing make for slow travel in the final 690 m (2300 ft) of descent. Use Kent Falls as a reference point when moving down the tree-covered slopes. Eventually you will come out near Cottonwood Creek with the main Stein trail no more than 10 minutes away. Follow the orange markers to the crossing downstream to reach Cottonwood camp, situated on the east side of Cottonwood Creek.

41. Cottonwood Junction to Stein River

Attractions: Great views of the Stein from just above Cottonwood Camp; the quickest and easiest way to connect the Stein River and alpine regions. **Cautions:** Loose footing on the slopes above Cottonwood Creek camp; questionable water from Cattle Valley Creek. **Access:** From Blowdown Pass, 13.5 km along the road and trail (see trip #38). **Season:** Early June to October. **Rating:** Moderate. **Distance and time:** 8.5 km (5.3 mi); 4–6 hours. **Elevation change:** Descent of 390 m (1300 ft). **Map:** 92 I/5.

Leaving the upper Cottonwood, you hike towards the Cottonwood's lower canyon while travelling along a well constructed trail. The views are limited on the northern three quarters of the hike, but are quite spectacular on the southern end above the Cottonwood Canyon and the Stein.

The first 4.5 km (2.8 mi) is straight-forward as the well-marked and cleared trail rolls along the east side of the Cottonwood,

BC PARKS

Fireweed
(Epilobium angustifolium)

Found from valley bottom to subalpine, especially in old burns and clearings. Easily identified by its height (up to 1.5 m), pink-purple flowers and tall, slender profile. Native people harvested the vitamin C rich shoots of fireweed.

never more than 90 m (300 ft) above the river. Several small side creeks make for muddy sections in places. 1 hour 30 minutes–2 hours travel brings you to Cattle Valley Creek, elevation about 990 m (3300 ft). A rough camp with space for several tents is found on the creek's east side. Crossing the creek's channels on a recently constructed bridge 150 m upstream from camp—look for the orange markers. You are now 3.6 km (2.2 mi) from Cottonwood Creek camp.

The trail now ascends above the steep canyon walls further downstream. Numerous steep switchbacks made slower by loose footing take you out of the Cattle Valley Creek depression and up to gentler terrain at roughly 1080 m (3600 ft) A well-established trail

Divorce is Out of the Question

Everybody knows the old adage about it being hard to see the forest for the trees. In the Stein River Valley, it can sometimes be hard to see the trees for the lichens.

Check this for yourself by pausing a moment along the trail. If you've chosen your stopping place well, and if you look closely, you'll see that what you had always assumed were just tree trunks and tree branches are also actually patchwork quilts of living lichens. On some trees you may have a hard time finding bark that isn't covered by lichens of a dozen or more kinds.

The same is true of the Stein's boulders and rocky outcroppings. These are not the cold, inanimate things they may at first seem; their surfaces are very much alive with lichens of every imaginable hue and texture. Isn't it time you slowed down to take a closer look?

The first thing to know about lichens (pronounced "LIKE-ens") is that they are fungi. There are approximately 100,000 different fungi, most of which are microscopic. Of those large enough to be seen by the naked eye, some familiar ones include the meadow mushroom, the morrel, and the bread mould.

Unlike flowering plants, but like most animals, fungi don't produce their own carbohydrates; to survive they must "eat." Some fungi eat decaying matter. Others eat plants. Others again, eat animals—even living people. Loosely defined, a lichen is a fungus that eats algae. Though some kinds of algae, including seaweed, can be large, the ones that lichen fungi associate with are very small. So small, in fact, that they live inside the weft of fungal threads that is the lichen.

Most fungi live hidden away inside the hosts they feed on. You'll see them, if at all, only during the few weeks of the year when they develop fruiting bodies such as mushrooms. Because lichen fungi, however, actually envelop their food host, they themselves are able to grow exposed to view. Think of lichens as living fungal greenhouses wherein algae simultaneously grow and provide food for the host fungi. In essence, both of the "partners" benefit: The lichen fungus has a reliable food source and the algae gains a home.

Not that lichens necessarily look much like

sidehills above the Cottonwood Canyon for the next 1.1 km (0.7 mi). Since leaving Cattle Valley Creek you have either climbed or been on the level above the canyon. Look for a small pond on the east side of the trail below a small rock face where you begin to descend to the Stein 360 m (1200 ft) below.

0.6 km (0.4 mi) past the pond, you descend into a small basin and climb up the south side, at the top of which is a flat rock outcrop, "Unnecessary Knob," elevation approximately 780 m (2600 ft). Keep parallel to the canyon at first and then move in a southeast direction. As you come onto the top of a rough and steep rocky section look for cairns and orange tape and slowly descend down the slopes. Once below the steepest slopes aim for a large fir tree in the middle of a boulder field and then angle towards the Cottonwood Canyon. Kent Falls should be visible across the valley.

greenhouses—though at times they seem to resemble just about everything else. In general, however, it is convenient to distinguish seven different groupings, namely the dust lichens, the crust lichens, the scale lichens, the leaf lichens, the club lichens, the shrub lichens, and the hair lichens. A little careful lichen-looking along the trails of the Stein should turn up all of these.

In the valley bottom, you won't have to look far to find the Wolf Lichen (Letharia vulpina)—a little, shrubby, sunshine-coloured thing very common over Douglas-fir and Ponderosa pine. The Wolf Lichen contains vulpinic acid and is mildly poisonous. In Scandinavia, it was once mixed with ground glass and sprinkled over wolf bait—apparently to good effect. Hence the name. Closer to home, the Thompson Indians are said to have used this species as a body and face paint, and as a dye for their animal skins. A colourful species no matter how you cut it.

Underfoot, watch for the Freckle Lichen (Peltigera apththosa), one of the largest of all leaf lichens. Just look for what resemble emerald green (turquoise when dry) scatter rugs laid out here and there over the forest floor. Peppered over their upper surface are numerous tiny "freckles"—technically "cephalodia." These are actually tiny colonies of nitrogen-fixing cyanobacteria; for here is a lichen that is made up of not two, but three different organisms. What is more, each of these derives from a separate kingdom of life. The only kingdoms not represented in the Freckle Lichen are the Animal Kingdom and the Protista.

As you climb higher, the branches of the trees become heavily laden with hair lichens. These belong mostly to the genus Bryoria, and come in many different species. To tell them apart, notice their different colours, their different sizes, and their "dandruff," or "soredia." (Some will have it, while others won't.) Farther north, these same hair lichens are the main winter food of the mountain caribou. In earlier times, they also provided a winter staple for the native peoples who gathered them (especially Bryoria fremontii) to steam with berries as a kind of vegetarian Salish pemmican. An acquired taste, you can be sure.

–Trevor Goward

You must now switchback down the slopes, encountering more boulders and varying degrees of steepness. The dry open forest becomes thicker and the trail flattens out as you descend the last 0.4 km (0.3 mi) to the junction with the main Stein trail. Look for a sign indicating "Stein Lake 30 km, Blowdown Pass 20 km". Cottonwood camp is only 100 m away, situated on the creek's east side. Cottonwood Falls, one of the focal points of the valley and a refreshing stop on hot days, is only 10 minutes travel upstream from the camp on the Cottonwood's east bank.

Cottonwood Falls.   LEO DEGROOT

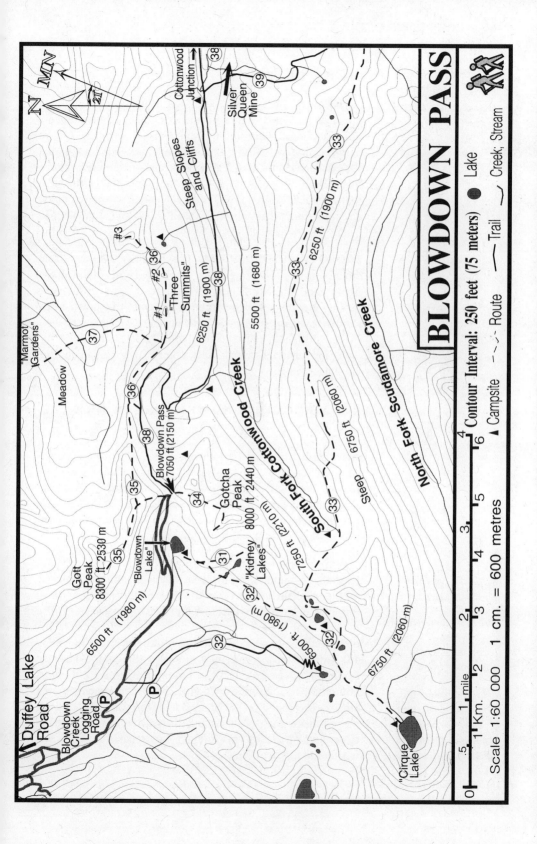

BLOWDOWN PASS

Contour Interval: 250 feet (75 meters)

● Lake
— Trail — Creek; Stream
-·-· Route
▲ Campsite

Scale 1:60 000   1 cm. = 600 metres

Duffey Lake Road
Blowdown Creek Logging Road
"Marmot Gardens"
Meadow
Gott Peak 8300 ft 2530 m
"Blowdown Lake"
6500 ft (1980 m)
6500 ft (1980 m)
"Kidney Lakes" 7250 ft (2210 m)
Gotcha Peak 8000 ft 2440 m
Blowdown Pass 7050 ft (2150 m)
"Three Summits"
6250 ft (1900 m)
South Fork Cottonwood Creek
6750 ft (2060 m)
6750 ft (2060 m)
5500 ft (1680 m)
6250 ft (1900 m)
North Fork Scudamore Creek
Steep
Steep Slopes and Cliffs
Cottonwood Junction
Silver Queen Mine
"Cirque Lake"

N MN 21°

NORTH STEIN

The North Stein is best described in one word—wild. Be prepared for a bushy entrance and exit, unbelievable numbers of mosquitoes, rough terrain, and volatile weather. This is bear country, so be sure to make your presence known and keep a clean camp. As trip reports posted on the internet have made clear, a trip down the valley bottom of the North Stein to the Stein Lake area is NOT recommended unless you enjoy a lengthy bushwhack through Devil's club and slide alder in prime grizzly habitat.

ECOLOGICAL OVERVIEW: The majority of the terrain covered in the following route descriptions are in the alpine tundra zone. The North Stein's high snowfalls are conducive to heather meadows, which are characterized by evergreen dwarf shrubs, rowberry, blueberries, and heathers. The lower reaches of the North Stein include coastal forest species such as Pacific silver fir, western hemlock, huckleberry, white rhododendron, and false azalea.

42. Van Horlick Road to Van Horlick Pass

Attractions: Flowered meadows; isolation. **Cautions:** Cold, wet weather; bear country. **Access:** From terminus of east fork of Van Horlick Creek Logging Road. **Season:** Mid-June to October. **Rating:** Moderate. **Distance and time:** About 2 km (1.3 mi); return day trip (bushwhack) to pass. **Elevation gain:** 285 m (950 ft). **Map:** 92 J/8.

While a short route to the Stein's alpine, this trip involves at least 30–60 minutes of bushwhacking and is wet in the lower section near the creek. From the road end, head south down through thick woods to the creek and then follow the creek. You may find some flagging tape and signs of a rough trail here, but don't count on any kind of marked route. After approximately 1.0 km (0.6 mi), move in a southeast direction. The bush eventually gives way to rocky terrain. Large meadows greet you at the pass, elevation 1875 m (6250 ft). Numerous camping sites can be found on the Stein side of the pass. The ridge to the northeast may be ascended without technical difficulty to the summit at 2250 m (7500 ft). Be prepared for cold, wet weather in this area.

BC PARKS

Spring beauty
(Claytonia lanceolata)

An easily recognized 10–20 cm tall flower with two broad leaves and white or pale-pink flowers. Found from valley bottom to alpine in meadows and open woods. Blooms in early spring at lower elevations, mid-summer in the alpine.

What a Beauty

The corms of this plant were formerly an important "root" food for the Nlaka'pamux…. They were usually dug from late May to late June, during or immediately after flowering; at this time the corms could be easily located. One could also dig them later in the summer or fall if he knew where to dig. Ranging from pea-sized to golfball-sized, the corms are usually found from 4–8 cm below the surface. The older the plant, the larger its corm….Formerly, they were cooked in underground pits, like avalanche lily corms, or steamed in watertight baskets using red-hot rocks….The corms could also be dried immediately after they were dug. They were often cooked, then mashed and formed into little loaves, about 3–4 cm thick, then dried on mats.

–Nancy Turner et al, *Thompson Ethnobotany*
Royal BC Museum, 1990, page 240.

43. North Stein Viewpoint

Attractions: Views that no camera can bring back. **Cautions:** Rough, exposed terrain. **Access:** From Van Horlick Pass. **Season:** Mid-July through September. **Rating:** Easy to moderate. **Distance and time:** 1.6 km (1.0 mi) one way; 5.6 km (3.5 mi) round trip via meadows; 30 minutes, one way; 2 hours round trip via meadows. **Elevation gain:** 300 m (1000 ft), 490 m (1600 ft) via meadows. **Map:** 92 J/8.

From the meadows on the south side of the pass, proceed south towards a distinct summit. You may find it easiest to follow a small creek upstream in a southwest direction to its source at a small tarn not shown on the 1:50,000 topographic map. The rounded summit is easily gained, rewarding you with excellent views of the North Stein.

44. North Stein Meadows

Attractions: Abundant flora and fauna, especially flowers in early summer. **Cautions:** Bear country. **Access:** From Van Horlick Pass. **Season:** Mid-July to September. **Rating:** Moderate. **Distance and time:** 4.3 km (2.7 mi) round trip; 4–5 hours round trip. **Elevation gain:** On return to pass 210 m (700 ft). **Map:** 92 J/8.

From Van Horlick Pass descend southeasterly about 100 m (350 ft) to the extremely flat upper meadow. The only other prominent feature here is a canal-like stream whose banks, unlike the lush enclosing valley sides, support few flowers because of their poor drainage and lingering snow. The stream and its banks provide home and food for various small mammals. As the creek begins to cascade to the lower meadow, the vegetation changes from short sedges to chest-high hellebore. In the distance the peaks around Stein Lake are evident. There are large displays of Indian paintbrush (both red and white) and mimulus along the mossy banks. A small pond is home to numerous frogs.

The meadows end where the valley drops steeply to the North Stein 300 m (1000 ft) below. From here you can see the effects of avalanches that have swept down the east ridge and dislodged trees on the opposite side of the valley.

45. North Stein Ridge from Van Horlick Pass

Attractions: Spectacular views; wildlife. **Cautions:** Carry water; volatile weather; exposed terrain. **Access:** North of Van Horlick Pass. **Season:** Mid-July to September. **Rating:** Difficult. **Distance and time:** 12.8 km (8.0 mi) round trip; full day round trip. **Elevation gain:** 510 m (1700 ft) or 750 m (2500 ft) depending upon the route chosen. **Map:** 92 J/8.

In order to avoid the steep hike up the northeast ridge from Van Horlick Pass, start in the middle of the moraine north of the pass and hike in a northeast direction parallel to the ridge. Eventually you will reach rocky meadows at roughly 1710 m (5700 ft), at which point you will continue ascending up relatively easy terrain until you reach a knob at 2060 m (6750 ft). Now you have a choice: Less energetic hikers can sidehill east-southeast to the 2025 m (6750 ft) saddle; others may wish to make the steep climb to the 2265 m (7550 ft) ridge above. Once on the ridge, head southeast over huge granite blocks to the main summit. The panorama to the south from here includes a vertical silver thread that is Elton Falls.

ROYAL BC MUSEUM

Mountain chickadee
(Parus gambeli)

From June to September, this chickadee frequents the semi-open coniferous forests of the subalpine. Distinguish it from the similar black-capped chickadee by noting whether the cap is solid black; if the cap is broken by a white eye-line, then it is a mountain chickadee.

Looking south from the North Stein Ridge.   RANDY STOLTMANN

From the saddle, continue southeast to a second, gentler 2250 m (7600 ft) summit. The third summit to the south may be avoided by sidehilling along flowered slopes at the 2190 m (7300 ft) level on the west. Descend into another broad saddle at 2175 m (7250 ft), where snow-melt to the east should provide water; good camping is found by the lakes on the east side of the ridge. Mountaineering routes begin here. You may return to the pass by reversing your approach, but a good alternative is to descend 150 m (500 ft) before contouring northwest along a shoulder through meadows at the 1980 m (6600 ft) level. This traverse below the steep cliffs and scree slopes leads back towards Van Horlick Pass. Because of the steepness of the slopes, avoid descending directly to the meadows visible below.

46. Van Horlick / Scudamore Divide

Attractions: The rarely visited Scudamore basin; wildlife; spectacular views. **Cautions:** Exposed; rough terrain; route finding skills are essential. **Access:** From north of Van Horlick Pass. **Season:** Mid-July to September. **Rating:** Moderate to difficult. **Distance and time:** 16 km (10.0 mi), full day. **Elevation gain:** 275 m (900 ft) to Scudamore meadows; 610 m (2000 ft) for full descent. **Map:** 92 J/8.

As with the initial access for trip #45, start in the middle sections of the moraine north of Van Horlick Pass and move in a northest direction parallel to the northeast ridge. Eventually, you will ascend to the bottom of a large meadow. Cross the creek and meadow and pass into an open basin punctuated with large boulders approximately 2.4 km (1.5 mi) from the pass. A shallow tarn (not shown on the 1:50,000 map) at 2040 m (6800 ft) gives wonderful reflections of the mountains to the west. Ascend 60 m (200 ft) east to the divide between Van Horlick Creek, which you are in, and Scudamore Creek (Stein divide). On the Scudamore side there is good camping, and water is available from snow-melt.

Two or more routes are possible from here. A high route, which provides outstanding views, climbs north from the divide, following the ridge-top to a high point at 2205 m (7350 ft). A lower, more sheltered route (sometimes snow-bound until August) leads through the meadows east of the ridge at about the 2100 m (7000-ft) level, passing a small tarn at 2100 m. A

Grey wolf
(Canis lupis)

Combine the cunning and fearlessness of a highly skilled hunter with the endurance and toughness of ultra marathon runner, and you have the makings of one of the most amazing athletes of the animal world, the wolf. Consider this: Naturalist Adolph Murie observed a pack in Alaska that traveled 60 km (40 mi) — the distance from Stein Lake to the Trailhead — each day in search of food. Similarly, wolves have been observed breaking trail in 1.66 m (5 ft) of snow for 35 km (22 mi), stopping only for brief pauses but no rest. And, they put it all on the line: Autopsies of wolves in the north have revealed that over 50% of these canines had survived one or more traumatic injuries (fractured skulls, broken legs and ribs), likely, from hunting big game such as moose.

few hundred paces farther north is a second tarn set in a deep hollow. Descend to this tarn (which has no outflow) and climb the shoulder on the north side to join the high route on the ridge above. This ridge then dips gently to 2145 m (7150 ft) before ascending the final bump that offers a fine panorama for a lunch spot.

Hikers camped in the North Stein may wish to return from here; it is feasible to descend 150 m (500 ft) into the pass to the northeast and then sidehill to three small lakes at about 2175 m (7250 ft). The lakeside has room for two or three tents, but is exposed. The broad ridge above may be hiked in either direction. A return via the ridge, rather than across the meadows, will probably be the quickest.

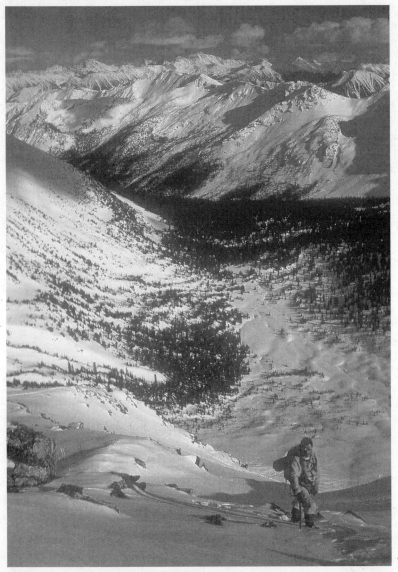

The Scudamore Creek drainage in winter.   LEO DEGROOT

NORTH STEIN RIVER

Duffey Lake Road

East Fork Van Horlick Creek

7750 ft (2360 m)

Meadow

vp

46

6000 ft (1830 m)

Meadow

7000 ft (2140 m)

Scudamore Creek

Meadow

Meadow

Meadow

P

Road

Scree

46

46

7250 ft (2210 m)

Meadow

vp

45

42

Van Horlick Pass

6750 ft (2060 m)

Meadow

43

vp

44

45

vp

45

45

Cliff

6500 ft (1980 m)

North Stein River

Meadow

Avalanche Slope

Willow Thicket

7250 ft (2210 m)

6000 ft (1830 m)

4750 ft (1450 m)

6000 ft (1830 m)

N   MN

21°

0	.5	1 mile	2	3	4
1 Km.	2	3	4	5	6

Scale 1:50 000   1 cm. = 500 metres   Contour Interval: 250 feet (75 meters)

▲ Campsite   Creek; Stream   Glacier
--- Route   ● Lake   *vp* Viewpoint

KAYAKING THE STEIN

To see how much skill levels and attitudes have advanced in the sport of whitewater kayaking in recent years, one need look no further than the Stein. It wasn't until September 1989 that the first complete descent of the Stein River—from below Stein Lake to the confluence with the Fraser River—was completed by Robin Barley, Eric Ridington and Ian Taylor. At the time, this descent was a significant achievement and light years beyond what early whitewater pioneers such as Klaus Streckman envisioned back in the 1970s. Word quickly spread, and the Stein became a classic for advanced river runners from around the world, as several dozen groups flew into Stein Lake during the 1990s and early 2000s to begin their adventures down this free-flowing, wild river that features two canyons, a scenic mid-valley float and generally easy portages.

Access for this trip was inevitably going to change when the Stein became a provincial park in 1995. However, it wasn't until BC Parks began enforcing the ban on motorized access in the park, including floatplanes and helicopters, in the early 2000s that the "normal" approach via floatplane to Stein Lake was no longer an option. Does this mean that a full descent of the Stein is no longer an option for kayakers? No. Boldness and creativity were harnessed by Corey Boux, Braden Fandrich and David Norell in the summer of 2003, as they pioneered what apparently was the first descent of the North Stein. The one catch is that you need to be a very strong creek boater to paddle the North Stein. With skills and mindsets changing so rapidly in this sport, it may be a matter of time before then North Stein and Stein Rivers become a double shot classic.

North Stein

One of the least visited areas of the Stein, the North Stein is a rugged tributary that features the postcard beauty of a glacially-sculptured valley surrounded by glaciers and snow-capped peaks. On average, it receives more snowfall than other parts of the Stein with the exception of the western alpine near Tundra Lake. Access is via Van Horlick Pass, off the Duffey Lake Road (see Road Access for details).

From the end of the overgrown road in the east fork of Van Horlick Creek to the put-in on the North Stein River requires approximately 10 km of kayak hauling. Once over Van Horlick Pass, there are several kilometers of hiking with kayaks along the lush and gentle valley bottom before it is possible to start a gentle float down the North Stein River for roughly 10 km. Several logjams are encountered in this scenic initial section, but little in the way of difficult paddling.

The final few km of the North Stein before the confluence with the Stein River is another story, as increased volume and steepness give this section a decidedly different character. Most of the rapids are of drop-pool character, and scouting and portaging are reported to be relatively easy, which is surprising given the North Stein's deserved reputation as a densely vegetated valley bottom of slide alder and Devil's Club, best left to the resident grizzlies. The original descendants, who paddled the North Stein in late July during an average snow pack year, portaged 4 of the 19 drops. Given the need to avoid pushy higher flows and vertebrae-compressing lower volumes, choosing the right level is critical.

Upper Canyon

From the confluence of the North Stein and Stein to the beginning of the upper canyon is approximately 7 km, the first few km of which are often obstructed by logs and other hazards. The remainder is class II with several sections of class III–IV rapids. Once in the canyon, the fun begins. Extending for about 8 km and dropping as much as 80 m/km (400 ft/mi) in some sections, the upper canyon becomes more continuous, but less severe as one moves downstream. There are over 24 distinct drops in this section, along with 6 class V rapids and 2 as yet unattempted class VI waterfalls, so scouting is important.

Middle Stein

This 30 km section of class II is where you get to relax before tackling the lower canyon. Great views, solitude and abundant wildlife make the mid-valley an enjoyable float; there are a few logjams that must be negotiated, especially the ever growing collection of wood at "Logjam Camp." Just before the lower crossing there is a short section of class III, a convenient warm-up for the rapids ahead.

Lower Canyon

Just below the lower crossing, the river becomes an almost continuous series of rapids for 15 km, as the gradient averages 20–40 m/km (100–200 ft/mi). In August–September levels, the rapids are generally IV, with roughly 12 class IV+–V drops, any of which can be easily portaged as the trail is close at hand on the south bank. Two sections worthy of respect are the "Devil's Staircase" and the "Devil's Escalator." The latter starts roughly 3 km downstream from the teepee campsite—a well-known landmark, despite the teepee no longer being there, see p.99—on the south side of the river. A 5 metre drop starts this section followed by 150 m of class IV+–V. The "Devil's Staircase," farther downstream, is 150 m of class V drops. Once at the Trailhead parking area, 4 km of class III–IV paddling remains before the confluence with the Fraser is reached.

Day paddlers can carry their boats for roughly an hour to the lower end of the "Devil's Staircase," while those less inclined to play the mule can put in just upstream from the Trailhead. You can take out near the Trailhead parking lot, at the Stein Bridge (and miss the final few hundred metres of paddling down to the confluence with the Fraser, which can be a fair bit of bump and grind in lower flows), or continue to the Fraser and then hike with your kayak back to the road along the south side of the Stein (see Lower Stein hiking description, pp.85–86). August to September is generally the best time to paddle the lower Stein; in the higher levels of May and June, especially in deep snow pack years, the lower canyon is best viewed, but not paddled.

Running the upper canyon.   ROBIN BARLEY

WINTER RECREATION
Ski-touring

As the winter snowfalls begin to accumulate in December, the Stein transforms into a ski-touring destination. A seemingly endless array of terrain and abundant dry snow make this relatively unexplored area worth visiting. The following is a brief overview of the more easily accessed skiing areas within and adjacent to the Stein. None of the described areas can be accessed without at least five hours of travel up the logging roads or trails that give access to these areas, however.

Ski-touring requires special equipment, skills and knowledge. Avalanche safety, proper equipment and intermediate skiing ability are requisites for all persons intending to visit the Stein's slopes in the winter. In other words, this section is only for experienced backcountry skiers.

Texas Creek

From Texas Creek's East Fork, access is gained to the alpine areas surrounding "Brimful Lake" and the Siwhe Creek–Cattle Valley divide. The relatively low snowfall of the Lillooet area will normally allow you to drive at least part way up Texas Creek. Proceed to the final junction of the East Fork, 22.3 km (14.0 mi) from the West Side Road (see Road Access section for details). At this junction you can gain the "Brimful Lake" area via the right fork, which crosses the creek and extends for approximately 0.3 km (0.2 mi), or the Siwhe Creek–Cattle Valley divide via the left fork, which also terminates within a few hundred metres. From there, a great variety of skiing can be accessed.

The "Brimful Lake" access route crosses some steep slopes that should be avoided in times of higher avalanche hazard. Proceed to the col to the west, elevation 2085 m (6950 ft), which is clearly identified on the map. Once at the pass, "Brimful Lake" can be gained directly by proceeding southwest and then south until at the small ridge north of Brimful. Alternately, a safer route in higher avalanche conditions is to proceed west and then southwest from the pass for about 1.5 km (1.0 mi), losing roughly 200 m (670 ft) elevation before climbing in a southeast direction to Brimful.

The Siwhe Creek–Cattle Valley access begins by gaining the southwest corner of the cutblock above the road's terminus. A trail should be identifiable at the beginning of the forest. The trail proceeds east through forest for about 0.5 km (0.3 mi) before opening up. To the southeast is a col that provides access to the numerous slopes around "Devils Lake" and Cattle Valley. If the slopes are of questionable stability, use the forested valley southwest of the previous route. Starting at the top of the same cutblock, head southeast, quickly gaining elevation and soon entering a forested valley, which extends up to the col at the south end, elevation 2055 m (6850 ft).

Blowdown Pass–Cottonwood Creek

Access is via Blowdown Creek. The 14 km (8.8 mi), 900 m (3000 ft) ascent from the Duffey Lake Road to "Blowdown Lake" requires at least six hours of steady climbing. Several avalanche tracks from the slopes to the east intersect the road so be sure to assess the conditions. The greatest avalanche danger is found beneath Gott Peak's southwest slopes. If the snowpack is questionable, move south to the open forest and meadows below the road. Cornices are normally quite pronounced on the ridge between Gott Peak and "Summit One" as are the ridge tops between Blowdown Pass and "Cirque Lake."

Within this area you will find excellent skiing. Numerous peaks, ridges, and slopes are found in the North Scudamore

The Opportunist on the Move

Especially broad-ranging in its perpetual quest for food (its latin name is Gulo gulo, meaning "glutton glutton"), the elusive wolverine will cover a territory of up to (an unbelievably big!) 2000 square km. This fierce and aloof carnivore is highly opportunistic. When it is not able to kill small mammals such as muskrats and beavers, fierce fighters in their own right, the wolverine will sometimes drive even bears and cougars from their kills! In winter, the deep snow slows down bigger animals, allowing the wolverine to hunt mountain goat, deer and moose.

In ski-touring the Stein's alpine, one is almost assured of seeing wolverine tracks that appear to go forever across the ridgetops. Wolverine tracks are easily identified by their 10—18 cm length and five toe marks. If you are fortunate enough to cross tracks with this increasingly rare animal, look for a one metre long, thickly furred, dark brown creature with a broad light stripe along each side and a proportionally small head. Nicknamed "skunk bear" because of its bear-like appearance and disagreeable musk, which is used to mark its kills and carrion, the wolverine is one animal that cannot tolerate man's presence. Protection of large wilderness areas is essential if this amazing weasel is to survive.

MICHAEL MCINULTY

Snow crane fly
(*Chionea spp.*)

One insect you are almost assured of seeing on the snow is the crane fly. This 5–12 mm long wingless insect looks like a spider at first glance, but it has only six legs, whereas spiders have eight.

LEO DEGROOT

Researching the skiing section of this book was, of course, strictly serious work.

area, while closer to "Blowdown Lake" there are several summits and slopes worth visiting. East of Blowdown Pass, the southwest-facing slopes below "Summit One" provide for some good tree-skiing. If the snowpack is stable, an ascent of Gott Peak followed by a ski down its southwest slopes is a possibility. On poor weather days the avalanche tracks off the road west of "Blowdown Lake" provide short, steep powder runs.

Van Horlick Creek–Scudamore Creek

Van Horlick Creek's east fork provides access to attractive terrain in the North Stein and Scudamore Creek. Allow 5–7 hours to ski the 15.3 km (9.5 mi) from the Duffey Lake Road to the end of the east fork.

The east fork branches off from the mainline, 8.9 km (5.5 mi) from the Duffey Lake Road. At the terminus of the East Fork, elevation 1620 m (5300 ft), Van Horlick Pass, elevation 1875 m (6250 ft), lies only 2.0 km to the south and is easily gained from the road end.

Northeast of the end of the east fork road is another pass that gives access to the headwaters of Scudamore Creek. To reach this pass, ski to the top of the cutblock at the east fork road's end. Pick up a gully in the forest at the south corner of the cutblock and follow it straight up to treeline. Avalanche danger at the top can be avoided in the trees on the north side. From the top of the gully, contour north into an attractive basin offering good campsites. The pass is at the top of the basin and leads over into Scudamore Creek. Good ski slopes abound on both sides of the pass. Total time from east fork terminus to the pass with Scudamore Creek: About 3 hours.

Another access to this same general area lies north of Van Horlick's east fork. About 6.3 km (3.9 mi) along the mainline is a branch road that climbs for approximately 4.0 km (2.5 mi) to 1650 m (5500 ft). The slopes further southwest reportedly offer fine skiing. Further exploration into Scudamore Creek may be possible via the col at 1820 m (6075 ft).

Springtails

On warm winter days in the subalpine and alpine, the shuffle of one's skis may send the "fleas of the snowpack," springtails (order collembola) jumping in every direction. These small (2–6 mm long) wingless insects would not be noticed if it were not for their leaping ability. Springtails have an abdominal tail called a furcula which extends forward and is secured and released by a catch mechanism. When the springtail wants to move, its catch mechanism releases the fucula, resulting in a springing action, propelling the springtail 10–15 cm into the air. These primitive insects actually spend most of their time on the ground eating pollen, fungus and leaf debris. Once the adults are mature (November to March), they climb up vegetation and rocks to reach the snow surface, where they mate in swarms covering areas up to several square km in size.

Lizzie Lake

Access to the Lizzie Cabin alpine is gained via the Lillooet Lake and Lizzie Creek roads. In exceptionally cold winters the Lillooet Lake Road may not be passable; contact the Squamish District Forestry office, (604 898-2100), for road conditions. From the Lizzie Creek–Lillooet Lake junction, you face approximately 15 km (9 mi), 1260 m (4200 ft) of ascent to Lizzie Cabin. Average time: Seven hours. The Lizzie Lake Road presents few avalanche dangers except for the predictable, road-blocking slide from the north slopes approximately 6 km (3.8 mi) from the start.

Once at Lizzie Lake, the cabin is most easily reached by crossing the lake to its southeast corner and then ascending through the forest in a east-northeast direction, staying within 100 m (330 ft) of the creek depression to the southeast. You should reach the bench west of the "Gates of Shangri-La," elevation 1560 m (5200 ft). From here, the cabin is easily found by following the creek for approximately 10–15 minutes.

MICHAEL MCINULTY

Ruffed grouse
(*Bonasa umbellus*)

One of the more frequently seen residents of the Stein's valley bottom is the ruffed grouse. Listen for the male's distinct drumming call during breeding season from March to May.

Like other members of the dog family, the grey wolf's tracks consist of four toes, with toenails normally showing, and a distinct heel pad, when clearly shown.

The Lizzie Creek Cabin, which was built in 1968 by volunteers, sees greater stress upon it come winter. Your help in maintaining this public use cabin is essential if it is to continue serving everyone. Please clean up after yourselves, pack-out all garbage and food (the resident rat is well fed), hang up the foam pads, and close the shutters and doors securely when you leave. Also, the volunteer-cut firewood supply is limited, so please use the stove sparingly.

Avalanche hazards of special note are the slopes immediately east of the cabin, Arrowhead Mountain's northwest-facing slopes, and the south-facing slopes between Cherry Pip Pass and Caltha Lake (the south slopes of Tundra Peak were appropriately nicknamed the "Terminator" by John Baldwin). Also beware of the large talus slopes found in this area, especially in the early months of winter—telemark skiers should consider bringing knee cap protection.

On bad weather days, and of course, for the deepest powder, good tree-skiing is found north of the cabin, while directly below Arrowhead Lake fantastic tree skiing is reported. White Lupine Ridge, which extends south from Anemone Peak, provides excellent skiing and can be reached by skiing directly up the forested slopes behind the cabin. Watch for avalanche danger when exiting the trees at the top. Further along this ridge, the 2100 m (7000 ft) col between Anemone Peak and Tabletop Mountain leads to a large snowfield on the northwest side and more great slopes. The open country around Arrowhead Lake, Heart Lake, and Long Lake is worth exploring. The peaks and slopes east and southwest of Long Lake make for enjoyable touring, especially in times of high avalanche hazard. Those wanting a more challenging and lengthy ascent will consider Cloudraker to the southwest—a very long day-trip or comfortable two-day return trip from the cabin.

Food for thought:

One loop trip that may be worth trying in times of relatively stable snow pack is via Lizzie Lake and Cherry Pip pass. Gain the pass from the Lizzie drainage. Descend from the pass to the valley to the north (your major concern here will be the volatile slopes of Tundra Peak above) and gain Bellevista Ridge. Proceed north to Meadow Dome and then descend to the logging road west of Meadow Dome. The road then switchbacks down to within 1 km of the start of the Lizzie Creek Road.

A longer and much more ambitious venture is found on the south divide of the Stein Watershed. This trip has was first completed by myself and two friends in March–April 1990 and has now been completed by several groups. We were able to complete the entire trip from Lillooet Lake to the Fraser River via Log Creek in eight days, with generous help from the weather gods. Count on at least seven days travel and allow for up to two weeks as your exit routes are limited and lengthy if the conditions don't cooperate.

Starting at Lizzie Creek, move east to Caltha Lake and then southeast to Figure Eight Lake, south of Tundra Lake, where the divide portion of the trip begins. Some route-finding is required as you travel in a southeast direction to the glacier east of Mount Skook Jim, elevation 2580 m (8600 ft). Proceed east of Mt. Skook Jim along the glaciers which sit on the north side of the divide. Crevasse Crag and Mount Klackarpun are easily climbed along this section. The views are truly incredible from this section—perhaps the most spectacular of the entire trip.

The crux of the trip begins approximately 5.0 km east of Mount Klackarpun and extends to roughly 2.5 km west of

Deep Sleep

One of nature's least understood mysteries is a bear's ability to go into a dormant state for up to six months. Surviving off the accumulated fat layers, bears consume approximately 1 kj (5000 calories) per day during hibernation. How they can maintain this high metabolic rate for such a long time without eating or drinking is not entirely understood. Some insights have been gained through recent research, however. Apparently bears convert their urea—a by-product of the burning of food and normally unloaded as urine—into proteins. Thus, muscle mass is maintained and toxic buildups of urea are avoided. Similarly, females nurse their cubs during dormancy without drinking. If the mother bear is to produce milk, she requires water. The metabolizing of fat, which produces water, may be the source of fluids the sow needs.

BC PARKS

Wolverine
(Gulo gulo)

Biologists studying wolverines in the Yukon have found finely ground caribou bones in their stomachs. The jaw strength to achieve this is truly remarkable, putting the wolverine alongside the hyena and shark for one of the most formidable set of jaws on this planet. Sign of wolverine is found throughout the Stein, especially in the winter as their distinctive 5-toed tracks are easy to identify. Despite having spent hundreds of days in their habitat, the author has yet to see one, so if you do happen to cross paths with one, consider yourself very lucky.

the terminus of the Rutledge Glacier. Moderately steep snow slopes necessitate climbing and downclimbing several sections as you move along the ridge proper until above the three lakes in the basin above the north arm of Mehatl Creek. Once north of the eastern most of the aforementioned lakes, move on the south-facing slopes of the divide. A ramp south-southeast of the easternmost lake brings you over the divide and into the Rutledge Creek drainage.

At this point the route-finding becomes easier. Sidehill in an easterly direction to the Rutledge Glacier, which you then ascend to the south side of Kwoiek Peak in order to gain the Kwoiek and Chochiwa Glaciers. The easiest exit is via the tongue of the Chochiwa Glacier that extends eastward into Log Creek. A logging road reaches to within about 3.5 km of the west end of the Log Creek's valley bottom. The Nahatlatch River mainline is eventually gained via this road.

Winter hiking

The Stein's lower canyon offers year-round hiking opportunities. Normally this dry area receives no more than 10–15 cm of snow, allowing for relatively easy travel. Beyond the lower crossing, however, the snowfalls are greater and skis or snowshoes may be needed. Ensure you have lots of warm clothing—the sun does not warm the valley bottom for long in the winter. Wildlife viewing can be worthwhile at this time of year as mule deer, grouse, chickadees, nuthatches, and dippers frequent the lower canyon.

Winter camping in the lower Stein.   DAVID THOMPSON

PART VI

The Politics Of Wilderness Protection

PAT MORROW

Nlaka'pamux elders Hilda Austin and Mabel Joe at the 1985 Stein Voices for the Wilderness Festival.

"Vision without action is merely a dream. Action without vision just passes time. Vision with action changes the world."

—Joel Barker

PROTECTION OF THE STEIN: DEMOCRACY IN ACTION

Introduction

When Premier Mike Harcourt's government designated the Stein River Valley a provincial park in October 1995, a lengthy wilderness protection and First Nations rights campaign of over 20 years had finally come to a successful conclusion. While one could conclude that we have another great addition to our protected area system and leave it at that, there are several important lessons to be gained from the Stein's protection, however, especially in these times of increasing cynicism and disillusionment with our governments and mainstream political parties.

The Early Days

In December 1973, Roy Mason of the BC Mountaineering Club made the first public effort to protect the Stein when he submitted a private brief, which was endorsed by the BC Wildlife Federation and supported by a similar submission by the Federation of Mountain Clubs of BC, to the provincial government requesting a moratorium on resource development in this untouched watershed.

Skeptical of the ensuing provincial government study, the FMCBC conducted its own study, which was in the words of the Parks Branch Director, "an outstanding… private proposal." Unfortunately, the newly-elected Socred government ignored the recommendations of both the FMCBC report and its own Stein Basin Moratorium Study's recommendation that the Stein's timber be removed from the annual allowable cut. Adhering to its traditional "multiple-use" approach, the government announced in May 1976 that the Stein was to be logged.

In response to this decision, concerned citizens came together in March 1977 to form the Save the Stein Coalition. Representing more than 15 conservation and recreation organizations whose membership totaled more than 45,000, the Coalition came to be the stalwart of the fight to protect the Stein for the next eight years. With the coalition's release of *Exploring the Stein River Valley* (Roger Freeman and David Thompson) in 1979, the Stein's profile and accessibility gained a tremendous boost. Newspapers and magazines began reporting on this issue and public interest in this previously unknown wilderness increased greatly.

At the same time, the Coalition convinced the Forest Service to create the Stein River Public Liaison Committee. Unfortunately, as has been the case with most of the public advisory processes in BC, the Committee's terms of reference were woefully deficient in allowing for any affect on decisions at the political level. Equally time-consuming and challenging for the Coalition members was their successful fight to stop Ken Morris, a mining developer, from building an access road into the watershed.

In 1984, the Stein Advisory Committee released its Stein River Resources Folio. With the debate gaining momentum, the FMCBC released *Wilderness or Logging: Case Studies of Two Conflicts in BC* (Trevor Jones). This thorough study raised serious concerns about not only the volumes of the merchantable timber within the Stein, but also the profitability and subsidization of the proposed logging.

"It is a long time since British Columbians hiked through timbered valleys or paddled by tree-lined shores. So long in fact that they accept tree stumps, logging slash and drowned shorelines as standard. There are no lakes under 2500 feet in altitude within 100 miles of Vancouver that have not been logged to the shoreline, dammed or both. Not one. Not Pitt, nor Alouette, Chilliwack, Bunsen, Buttle, Dickson, Sproat, Stave, Weaver, Alta, Horne, Nahatlatch, Alice, Norton—none. There is only one major valley within 100 miles of Vancouver that has not been logged, flooded or both. Only one. It is the valley of the Stein River. It's just that simple. By the year 2000—just 27 years from now—there will be three million people within a 3 hour drive of the Stein basin. How can we afford not to preserve this area....?"

–Roy Mason, December 4, 1973
From the first submission made to the provincial government on the
future of the Stein River Valley by the Federation of Mountain Clubs of BC

Support Grows

When the Forest Ministry announced in February 1985 that road-building would begin as soon as possible, one of the more significant developments in the protection campaign soon followed, as local First Nations became part of a growing grass roots movement. Not only was support growing greatly in numbers, but the issue broadened to include native rights, for the Stein is part of the traditional territories of the Lytton and Mt. Currie First Nations. This intertwining of wilderness protection and aboriginal title was reflective of society's growing awareness of the interconnectedness of these two issues.

Integral to this burgeoning protection campaign was the first "Voices for the Wilderness" festival. Sponsored by the Lillooet Tribal Council and publicized by the recently formed Western Canada Wilderness Committee, the festival brought together 500 people at Brimful Lake in the Stein's northeast alpine for three days of speeches and music in August 1985. The festivals grew over the following years, with attendance reaching 30,000 – 40,000 at the Mt. Currie site, and were instrumental in greatly boosting the profile of the Stein issue.

Recognition of the native people's concerns was achieved when the provincial government's 1986 Wilderness Advisory Committee recommended that "{a} road should not be constructed through the Stein River Canyon without a formal agreement between the Lytton Indian Band and the Provincial Government." This recommendation plus the growing ground swell of public support convinced the government that the Stein was a major wilderness protection and human rights issue worthy of further consideration.

Meanwhile, in the mid to late 1980s, other wilderness campaigns such as Gwaii Haanas (South Moresby in Haida Gwaii or Queen Charolette Islands) and Meares Island (Clayoquot Sound) were being firmly established on the national agenda, heightening awareness of unsustainable forestry practices, the need for wilderness protection and indigenous people's concerns. Under the courageous leadership of Lytton Indian Band Chief Ruby Dunstan and Mt. Currie Indian Band Chief Leonard Andrew, the campaign intensified and gained an international dimension as the Chiefs visited New Zealand in 1988 to address shareholders of Fletcher Challenge, the forestry company intent on logging the Stein.

Thanks to the growing success of the festivals, the Wilderness Committee's public education and trail-building work with the Bands, publication of Stein: *The Way of the River* (Michael M'Gonigle & Wendy Wickwire, 1988), plus the grassroots outreach efforts of smaller organizations such as the Stein Wilderness Alliance, the political viability of logging the Stein was becoming less and less realistic. This was reflected in Fletcher Challenge's declaration of a one-year moratorium on logging plans for the Stein in April 1989. In the spring of 1989 the Lytton and Mt. Currie Indian Bands unveiled plans for a Stein Tribal Heritage Park, which would include a cultural interpretation centre at the mouth of the Stein. Permanent protection was finally secured in 1995, as Stein Valley Nlaka'pamux Heritage Park was created thanks in part to recent work of organizations such as BC Wild, which was actively engaged in the Harcourt government's comprehensive land-use planning initiatives. These multi-stakeholder processes were designed to address the province's growing number of land-use disputes by moving beyond the time- and resource-intensive valley-by-valley conflicts of the 1980s.

Safeguarding BC's Parks & Wilderness Areas

The 1990s were a pivotal decade for securing protection of wilderness areas, as the Harcourt and Clark governments created dozens of new parks, including the Khutzeymateen, Carmanah, Tatsheshini, Muskwa-Kechika, and Kitlope. By the end of the decade, more than 12% of the province's land base was designated as protected areas. This rapid expansion of BC's park system was unprecedented and helped address many long-standing issues. Less well known is that the many of these new parks are largely devoid of significant low

---

BC's Protected Areas

- As of spring 2007, BC has over 800 parks and protected areas covering just over 13% of BC's land base.

- Each year there are over 18 millions visitors to BC parks.

- The parks system is a model of sustainable economic activity, as it generates over $170 million in tax revenues each year, more than six times BC Parks' budget; in 1999, the last year the provincial government tracked the economic benefits of our protected areas, the economic benefits generated were estimated at $500 million.

- According to a survey conducted by the BC government in 2002, over 80% of British Columbians polled said that parks are important because the protect natural environments and wildlife.

- BC has only one park ranger for every eight parks.

- There are currently no government-funded interpretive programs for park visitors, making BC one of only two jurisdictions in North America lacking this basic service.

elevation, old growth forests. As of 2006, only 4% of these ecologically vital forests are protected, and given the forest industry's and government's continued high volume, low value approach to forestry in BC, we need to move quickly to secure protection of more valley bottoms in order to give wide-ranging species such as the grizzly bear and wolf a chance to survive. Connecting the province's protected areas through connective corridors is also essential, otherwise our parks will become islands of extinction.

Maintaining the ecological integrity and accessibility of BC's protected areas system is a challenge that must be addressed, as recent governments, including the Clark and Campbell governments, which cut BC Parks' budget and staff by more than 40% between 1996 and 2001, have significantly reduced our capacity to safeguard our parks. Equally disturbing are current efforts by the Campbell government to commercialize many of our parks through private development, including backcountry lodges and mechanized access. The opposition from recreational and environmental organizations to these proposed developments has been strong, but considerable work still needs to be done, including restoring BC Parks' funding and changing provincial laws to ban private developments and resource extraction within all protected areas.

One need no look no further than the Stein as a good example of how neglected our parks are becoming, as trail maintenance is sadly lacking, despite the best efforts of the woefully understaffed Parks ministry. Eleven years after the 1996 forest fire in the upper canyon, BC Parks was finally able to allocate some of its limited resources to clear this section of the main trail.

Resolving First Nations' Longstanding Issues

Some progress was made in the 1990s in addressing First Nations concerns, but the glacial speed of land-claim negotiations and continuation of resource extraction in aboriginals' traditional lands while discussions continue are of serious concern. The Campbell government has received praise from some native leaders for giving higher priority to resolving many First Nations issues, including making a greater commitment to accelerating the land claims negotiations. Hopefully, more land claims will be resolved in the coming years, and additional work is undertaken to assist aboriginal communities in building their capacity and overcoming the many challenges they are grappling with, including healing the scars of the residential school experience and safeguarding their culture.

> "What more do these people want? They take our lands. They take our culture. They take away our traditions. They take away our language. They anglicized us. They tried to fit us into a society that we really don't belong to. Now they gonna go and strip our land. They're going to take everything that we have. That's the last little bit of Stein we have, out there in the Stein Valley! If we allow them to go in there we might as well take the last bit of skin we got left on our bodies. And after that what else do they want—our lives?"
>
> –Chief Ruby Dunstan of the Lytton Band
> at the Stein Voices for the Wilderness Festival, August 1987

How You Can Help

If we are to address critical issues such as global warming and the loss of cultural and biological diversity, we must draw upon the lessons of past successes. Protection of the Stein and many other wilderness areas in BC was achieved as a direct result of democracy in action, as hundreds of British Columbians donated their time and money and tens of thousands more wrote letters and signed petitions.

With the future of our planet looking increasing bleak, there never has been a more important time in our history for individuals to put aside their cynicism and apathy, take action and demand that our governments make the necessary changes. As noted in the first edition of this book, it is the people who will lead the change, not the politicians. In fact, virtually all the successes in environmental and human rights throughout human history have been a direct result of the expression of democratic rights.

You can make a difference by: Writing to our elected representatives to encourage them to adopt Ecosystem Based Management forestry practices (which is a critical component of a truly sustainable society sometimes referred to as the Conservation Economy), restore funding for our parks, protect wilderness areas, address First Nations' concerns in a timely and meaningful manner; and by supporting conservation groups. And, for all you who wrote letters, signed petitions, and supported those organizations that helped protect the Stein, thank you—this magnificent wilderness area would not be a tribal heritage park if you hadn't take action.

A few organizations you may want to learn more about:

- Wilderness Committee:1-800-661-9453 wildernesscommittee.org
- World Wildlife Fund Canada:1-800-26-PANDA wwf.ca
- Ecotrust Canada: (604) 682-4141 ecotrustcan.org
- ForestEthics: (604) 331-6201 forestethics.org
- David Suzuki Foundation: (604) 732-4228 davidsuzuki.org
- Sierra Club of Canada—BC Chapter: (250) 386-5255 sierraclub.ca/bc
- Canadian Parks & Wilderness Society—BC Chapter: (604) 685-7445 cpawsbc.org
- Raincoast Conservation Society: 1-877-655-1229 raincoast.org
- Rivers Without Borders: (867) 668-5098 riverswithoutborders.org
- Ecojustice: 1-800-926-7744 ecojustice.ca

LEO DEGROOT

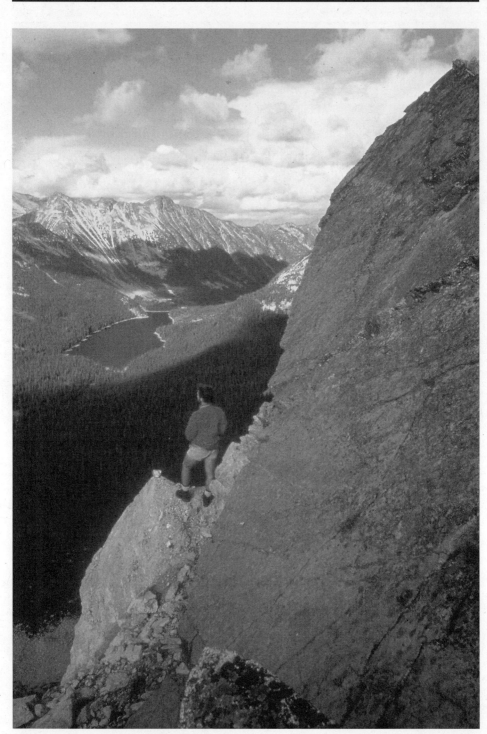

Looking northeast to Devils Lake.

JACQUES ANDRE

PART VII

References

Selected Bibliography

General

- Freeman, Roger, and Thompson, David. *Exploring the Stein River Valley*, Douglas & McIntyre, 1979.
- McGonigle, Michael, and Wickwire, Wendy. *Stein: The Way of the River*, Talon Books, 1988.
- Department of Recreation and Conservation, B.C. Parks Branch. *The Stein Basin Moratorium Study*, 1976.
- Turner, Nancy, et al. *Thompson Ethnobotany*. Royal B.C. Museum, 1990.

Backcountry Travel, Ethics, and Safety

- Hampton, Bruce, and Cole, David. *Soft Paths*, Stackpole Books, 1988.
- Herrero, Stephen. *Bear Attacks: Their Causes and Avoidance*, Nick Lyon Books, 1985.
- Manning, Harvey. *Backpacking: One Step at a Time*, Vintage Books, 1980.
- Cox, Stephen, and Fulsaas, Kris, Eds. *Mountaineering: The Freedom of the Hills*, 7th Edition, The Mountaineers, 2003.

Natural History

- Ade, R. *The Trout and Salmon Handbook*. Facts on File, Inc., 1989.
- Bernd, Heinrich. *Winter World: The Ingenuity of Animal Survival*, Ecco, 2003
- Cowan, Ian McTaggart, and Guiguet, Charles J. *The Mammals of B.C.*, B.C. Provincial Museum, 1978.
- Duddington, C.L. *Beginner's Guide to The Fungi*. Pelham Books, 1972.
- Gadd, Ben. *Handbook of the Canadian Rockies*, Corax Press, 1986.
- Goward, Trevor, and Hickson, Cathie. *Nature Wells Gray*, Friends of Wells Gray Park, 1989.
- Hale, M.E. *How to Know the Lichens*. 2nd ed. Wm.C. Brown Co., 1979.
- Horst, Vicki. "The Pika," *Canadian Geographic*, Aug/Sept., 1986
- Klasson, Michael. "The Last Stand of the Cottonwoods," Canadian Nature Federation, Winter, 1990.
- Lynch, Wayne. " The Elusive Cougar," *Canadian Geographic*, Aug/Sept., 1989.
- Lyons, C.P. *Trees, Shrubs, and Flowers to Know in B.C.*, J.M. Dent and Sons, 1976.
- Maser, Chris. *Forest Primeval*. Sierra Club Books, 1989.
- Peterson, Roger T. *A Field Guide to Western Birds*. Houghton Mifflin Co., 1961.
- Pojar, Jim, and MacKinnon, Andy. *Plants of Coastal British Columbia*, Lone Pine Publishing, 1994.
- Scott, W.B. and Crossman, E.J. *Freshwater Fishes of Canada*, bulletin 184. Fisheries Research Board of Canada, 1973.
- Vitt, D.H., Marsh, J.E. and Bovey, R.B. *Mosses, Lichens & Ferns of Northwest America*. Lone Pine Publishing, 1988.
- Whitaker, John O. Jr. *The Audubon Society Field Guide to North American Mammals*, Alfred A. Knopf, Inc., 1980.
- Willoughby, L. *Freshwater Biology*. Hutchinson of London, 1976.
- Yalden, D.W. and P.A. Morris. *The Lives of Bats*, David Charles Ltd., 1975.

Alexandra Bridge 38
Alligator lizard 88
Alluvial fans 51, 52
Alpine Tundra zone 56
American dipper 107, 178
Anadramous fish 60
Anderson Lake 36
Andrew
  Fraser 181
  Leonard 181
Anemone Peak 176
Angel's Walk 156, 158
Ant lion 99
Arnica, heart-leaf 45
Arrowhead Lake 122, 176
Arrowhead Mountain 176
Aspen 54
Avalanche
  Creek 114–116
  lily 56, 152, 153
  slopes 41, 50
  tracks 50

Barkerville 38
Bats 68, 118
Bears 73, 80
  black 45, 46, 73, 177
  grizzly 45, 46, 73, 152, 177
Beaver 70
Beetle
  pine 146
Bellevista Ridge 176
Biogeoclimatic zones 52
Birds 45, 62
Black-capped chickadee 64, 65
Black fly 124
Black tree lichen 160
Bloomer, Jerry 112
Blowdown Creek 27, 173
  Logging Road 27
  Lake 19, 27, 150, 174
  Pass 17, 18, 27, 107, 145, 148, 151, 153, 155
Blue grouse 63
Blueberry Hollow 137, 142, 143
Bobcat 73
Botanie Valley 30
Bracket fungi 92

Brimful Lake 135, 140–142, 172, 181
British Columbia
  Forest Service 76, 100, 180
  Government of 180–183
  Mountaineering Club 180
  Wildlife Federation 180
Burnt Cabin Creek 107
Bushy-tailed woodrat 69

Crossing lower 55, 96, 101
Caltha Lake 122–126, 177
Canadian National Railway 37
Canadian Pacific Railway 37
Cariboo Road 36, 38
Cattle Valley 134, 137, 139, 140, 161, 172
Cedar
  groves 53, 100
  western red 100
Cherry Pip Pass 122, 123, 176
Chickadee 64, 65, 178
Chinook salmon 57, 60
Chipmunk 69, 71
Chochiwa Glacier 178
Christina Creek 97
Cirque 48, 141
  Lake 149, 150, 173
Clark's nutcracker 143
Cloudraker Mountain 176
Columnar jointing 48
Common nighthawk 67
Conglomerate 48
Cottonwood 55, 105
  Camp 107, 145, 162
  Creek 18, 46, 48, 105, 106, 108, 144, 148–163, 173
  Falls 107, 162
  Junction 155, 156
  North Fork 154
  Northern black 105
  South Fork 150, 155
Cougar 45, 73, 110
Cow parsnip 35
Coyote 72

Deer, mule 45, 74, 178
Deer mouse 44, 111
deGroot, Leo 113

Devil's club 113
Devil's Escalator 171
Devil's Staircase 97, 98, 171
Devils Lake 50, 137, 139
Dipper, American 107, 178
Dolly Varden char 34, 57, 59, 61
Douglas fir 42, 44, 53, 90
Dragonfly 106
Duffey Lake Road 22, 55, 27, 174
Dunstan, Ruby 181
Dusky Shrew 134

Eagle, golden 157
Earl, Fred 100
Earl, Thomas 37
Earl's Cabin 100
Earl Creek 53, 59
Earlobe Lake 137, 142, 143
Earlscourt Farm 37
Ecological zones 52
Ecology 40–46
Elton Creek 117, 130
Elton Lake 130
End moraines 50
Endangered Spaces Campaign 183

FMCBC 180
Fickle Creek 103
Fickle Creek West 103
Figure Eight Lake 124–126, 132
Fir
  subalpine 56, 134
  Douglas 52–56, 90, 104
Fireweed 159
Fish 57
Fisher 71
Five Thousand Foot Meadows 131
Fletcher Challenge 181, 182
Fraser Glaciation 48, 49
Fraser River 24, 30, 40, 46, 52, 57, 58
Fraser, Simon 35
Freeman, Roger 180
Forks, The 50
Fungi 92, 109

Giardiasis 83
Geology 47–51

Golden crowned kinglet 66
Golden eagle 157
Gold rush 36
Gott Peak 152, 173
Granitic rock 47
Grizzly
  bear 46, 71, 73, 152, 177
  Creek 113
Grouse 175
  Blue 63
  Ruffed 63, 175
Guardian Spirit 31

Harrison
  Lake 36
  Trail 36
Hawk, red-tailed 148
Heart Lake 122, 176
Heath 56
Heather vole 149
Hill, John 37
Hill-Tout, Charles 32
Hoary marmot 125
Horsefly 93

Indian hellebore 136
Indian paintbrush 115

Kamloops 36
Kayaking 170–171
Kent Creek 159
Kent Lake 50, 159
Kidney Lakes 148, 150
Kinglet 66
  golden crowned 66
  ruby crowned 66
Kinnikinnick 31
Klackarpun, Mt. 177, 178
Klein, Adam 101
Knapweed 52
Krummholz 56
Kumsheen 30, 36
Kwoiek Glacier 178
Kwoiek Peak 178

Lay, Ken 113
Lichen 53, 56, 160

Lillooet 26, 36
  Lake 28, 175, 177
  Tribal Council 181
Little Ice Age 50
Lizzie
  Cabin 120–122, 175, 176
  Creek 28, 175, 177
  Lake 17, 28, 120, 175, 176
Log Creek 177, 178
Logjam Camp 107, 110–112
Long Lake 176
Long-tail weasel 145
Lookout Camp 111, 113
Lower crossing 96–101
Lynx 45, 73
Lytton 22, 23, 38
  Ferry 23, 24
  Indian Band 38, 101, 112,
    181, 182

Mammals 68
Maps 16
Marmot 71, 125
Marmot Gardens 152, 154
Marten 45, 71
Mason, Roy 180
Mayfly nymph 131
Meadow Lake 143, 144
Meares Island 181
Merlin 62
Metamorphic rock 48
M'Gonigle, Michael 182
Mice 69
  deer 69, 111
  cascade deer 69
Mini-traverse 19
Mink 71
Moose 73, 74
Morris, Ken 180
Mountain chickadee 166
Mountain goat 74, 142
Mountain huckleberry 126
Mountain sheep 74
Mountain whitefish 57
Mount Currie 26
  Indian Band 112, 181, 182
Mule deer 45, 74, 178
Munro, Jack 104

Mushroom 35
  pine 35
  oyster 35
Muskrat 70

Nahatlatch Creek 178
Nesbitt Creek 34, 55, 59, 96, 110
Nlaka'pamux 30–38, 105, 109, 165
North Fork Scudamore Creek 149
North Shore Trail 88
North Stein 18, 116, 129, 164–167
  Ridge 116, 166, 167
North West Company 36
Northern chipmunk 71
Nuthatch 65

Oregon grape 53, 54
Otter, river 71
Owl
  barred 60, 62
  pygmy 63
  spotted 104, 105

Pemberton 26
Petluskwohap Mountain 48, 159
Pictographs 31–33, 78, 98
Pika 68, 155
Pileated woodpecker 42, 67
Pine
  beetle 146
  grosbeak 66
  lodgepole 53, 55
  Ponderosa 53, 102
  western 55
  whitebark 55, 56, 144
  siskin 64
Pit houses 33, 87
Pleistocene Epoch 48
Ponderosa
  Creek 106, 142, 145
  Shelter 104
Porcupine 70
Port Douglas 36
Ptarmigan, white-tailed 63
Public Advisory Ctte. 180
Puppet Lake 127–129
Pygmy owl 63

Rainbow Ridge 139
Rainbow trout 57

Raven
  Common 113
  Flats 110
Red crossbill finch 122
Red-tailed hawk 149
River otter 71
Rock glaciers 48, 51
Rodents 69
Rogers creek 123
Rowat Crossing 109
Ruffed grouse 63, 175
Rufous hummingbird 67, 130
Rutledge Creek 48, 55, 178
Rutledge Glacier 50, 178

Salmon 35, 57–61
  chinook 57, 60
  coho 57, 60
  pink 57–60
Saskatoon berries 52, 54, 97
Save the Stein Coalition 180
Schist 48
Scudamore Creek 46, 48, 59,
  108–110, 149–151, 167, 174
Sedimentary rock 48
Sheeting joints 47
Shelter Creek 103
Shrews 68
Silver Queen Mine 102,
  150–151, 156–158
Siwhe Creek 18, 25, 134,
  137–139, 172
Siwhe Mountain 51, 142
Skimath Creek 25
Ski-touring 172–178
Skook Jim, Mount 177
Skunk 71
Sky Pilot 156
Snow cranefly 173
Snowshoe hare 68, 178
Solifluction 51
South Moresby 181
Spencer, Colonel 37
Spotted owl 45, 104, 105
Springtail 175
Spring beauty 56, 164, 165

Squirrels 69
  red 69
  northern flying 69
Stein
  Festivals 87, 135, 181
  Lake 18, 20, 52, 96,
    116–118, 127–131
  Mountain 51, 142
  Public Liason Ctte 180
  Trailhead 18, 20, 96
Stonefly nymph 58
Stryen Creek 50, 53, 90–94, 97
  East Fork 92
  West Fork 93
Subalpine 55, 56, 134
  fir 55, 56
  parkland 56

Tabletop Mountain 123
Teaspoon Creek 53, 99, 100
Teit, James 30, 32, 33
Texas Creek 25, 134, 136, 172
  East Fork 25, 134, 136, 172
Thompson, David 180
Thompson River 23, 30
Three Summits 153
Thrush, varied 158
Topographical maps 16
Trans-Canada Highway 22, 38
Trout 57
  rainbow 57, 61
  steelhead 57, 59, 61
Tundra Lake 123–128, 131
Tundra Peak 123, 176
Turner, Nancy 35

Ultramafic 48
Ungulates 74
Unnecessary Knob 162
Upper cable crossing 115–116

Van Horlick Creek 174
Van Horlick Creek
  Logging Road 27, 164, 174
Van Horlick Pass 164–167, 174
Van Winkle Bar 38
Van Winkle Bar Hydraulic
  Company 38
Varied Thrush 158

Vegetation 52–56
Victoria Ridge 106, 145, 146
Vole, meadow 69, 148

Warbler 63, 64
Waterfall Creek 103
Weasels 71
  long-tailed 72, 145
  short-tailed 72
West Fickle Creek 103
West Side Road 22, 24, 86, 87
Western anemone 56, 135
Western Canada
Wilderness Committee 101, 112,
  181–183
Western hemlock 55, 101
Western red cedar 36, 54, 100
Western tanager 111
Whistler 26
White bark pine 144
White-tailed ptarmigan 63, 121
Wickwire, Wendy 182
Wilderness Advisory Ctte. 181
Winter recreation 172–178
Wolf
  grey 45, 72, 167, 176
  lichen 53, 98, 161
  spider 138
Wolverine 45, 72, 173, 178
World Wildlife Fund 183

Yarrow 112

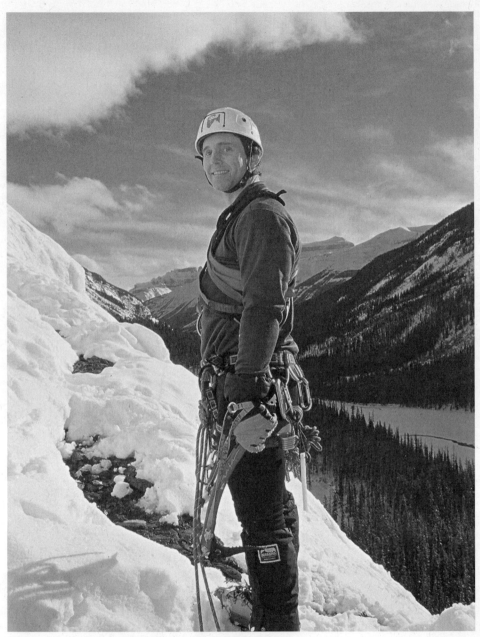

Definitely awake now: Climbing on the Weeping Wall.   IGNACIO VALENZUELA

The author developed his passion for nature and the outdoors exploring the parks and wilderness areas near his home town of Kamloops. A resident of North Vancouver, Gordon lives to explore wilderness through backpacking, mountain climbing, river and ocean kayaking, and ski-touring. He aspires to develop proper footwork some day so he can climb rock and ice with a semblance of style.